ANTONIN CYRIL

STOJAN

Apostle of Church Unity

Official portrait of Archbishop Antonin Cyril Stojan

ANTONIN CYRIL
STOJAN

Apostle of Church Unity

HUMAN AND SPIRITUAL PROFILE

BY

Ludvik Nemec

DON BOSCO PUBLICATIONS
New Rochelle, N.Y.

NIHIL OBSTAT:

Sidney C. Burgoyne
Censor Liborum

IMPRIMATUR:

✠ John Cardinal Krol
Archbishop of Philadelphia
April 8, 1983

Printed in the United States of America, 1983

DEDICATION

to

The Memory of my late Friend and Professor
PRELATE FRANCIS DVORNIK (1893-1975)
Scholar, Ecumenist and Historian of renown
for his guidance

and to

Rev. Sister Vincent Ferrer Clifford, S.S.J.
an English scholar and educator.
for her friendly inspiration in scholarly research,
in appreciation and gratitude

by the author

TABLE OF CONTENTS

LIST OF ILLUSTRATIONS

ABBREVIATIONS

AAS — *Acta Apostolicae Sedis*
ACV — *ACV Congressus* (Conventus) *Velehradensis*
Apoštolát - *Apoštolát sv. Cyrila a Metoda* - a journal
Apostolate - *Apostolate of Sts. Cyril and Methodius* - a principal organization of Velehrad
ASS — *Acta Sanctae Sedis*
AV — *Academia Velehradensis*
BCW — *Byzantine Catholic World*
BKV — *Bibliothek der Korchenvater*
CCH — Bohemian historical periodical - *Český časopis historický* (Prague)
CIC — *Codex juris canonici*
ČKD — *Časopis Katolického Duchovenstva* (since 1848)
CML — Archive of the SS. *Cyril and Methodius League*
ČMM — *Časopis Moravského Musea*
Coll. — *Collection of the laws and regulations of the Czechoslovak Republic*
DTC — *Dictionnaire de la theologie catholique*
ES — Denzinger-Bannwart-Umberg: *Enchiridion Symbolorum* (Friburgi Brisgoviaw: Herder and Co., 1931)
Jednota — *Jednota katolického duchovenstva* (Union of Czech clergy)
JES — *Journal of Ecumenical Studies* (Philadelphia)
KA — *Katolická Akce* (Catholic Action)
LA — *Leonis XIII acta.* Romae: Ex Tipographia Vaticana, 1881-1905, 23 vols.
LaDC — *La Documentation catholique*
NCFE — *National Committee for a Free Europe, New York*
NCWC — *NCWC News Service, Archives in Washington, DC.* (News service issued by the Press Department of the National Catholic Welfare Conference)
NŽ — *Nový Život* (New Life). Organ of the SS. Cyril and Methodius League, Rome
PA — *Pii IX Acta*, Rome, 1854-78
Unionism - *movement toward Church unity*

INTRODUCTION

This biographical account of a spiritual Moravian giant is a natural result of the author's familiar social and educational background which has included life-long involvement in Byzantine, Cyrilomethodian, Ecumenical studies and developments in Church history. Born a short distance from Velehrad in Moravia, he shared from childhood the affectionate sentiments of all Moravians for their beloved Antonín C. Stojan. The writer's father was a good friend as well as a political and social associate of Stojan who was constantly involved in the spiritual and material welfare of all people. Later as a student of Charles IV University in Prague, the author became affiliated with the professor, Msgr. Francis Dvornik, a protegé of Stojan, who had been sent to the Sorbonne in 1920 for advanced Byzantine studies. The latter became a renowned scholar, ecumenist and historian who not only promoted the idea of Stojan's Unionism but greatly advanced it to scholarly levels. He was also the first to indicate an urgent need for an English biography of Stojan.

The author continued research in Church Unity and became personally involved in the Unionistic Congresses held at St. Procopius Abbey in Lisle, Illinois, in the years 1956-59. Vatican II further stimulated a keen interest in Ecumenism. This in turn was reflected in scholarly concerns for such issues as the Greek Catholics (Uniates); Photian problems, Orthodox-Catholic encounters, plus the sad persecution of the Church of Silence behind the iron curtain and the difficulties of all Eastern Churches. These interests together with a deep sympathy for the suffering Church in his fatherland awakened a profound solicitude for the type of Church Unionism envisioned by Stojan as a possible solution of this sad national tragedy.

The constantly increasing accumulation of source materials for Church Unionism aroused considerable interest in the revival of the beatification process of Stojan. Eventually the writing, a book *"Our*

Lady of Hostyn" (1981) revealed other aspects of Stojan and further extended the significance of this Churchman. Thus final decision was made to utilize the extensive accumulated materials and to undertake a biographical account of Stojan in English. To facilitate the work, the author took part in a symposium called "Initial Unionistic Endeavors toward Church Unity" at the Spring Conference of the American Historical Association (ACHA) at St. Louis University, April 16-17, 1982. At the latter the author presented a scholarly paper, "Antonin Cyril Stojan (1851-1923) a Unionistic Zealot." He also presented a paper on Church Unity and chaired a similar symposium held at the eleventh "World Congress of the Czechoslovak Society of Arts and Sciences" convoked at the University of Pittsburgh October 28-30, 1982. All this helped to synthesize a biography of Stojan.

In a search for concrete information concerning the present status of Stojan's cause, the author turned to His Eminence František Cardinal Tomášek, S.T.D., Archbishop-Metropolitan of Prague and Primate of Bohemia. He kindly sent an outline of the preparations for the process of the beatification of God's servant, Archbishop Antonín Stojan, by way of an appropriate form for a forewood to a book. The author wishes to express profound gratitude to Cardinal Tomášek for his kindness in providing this much needed information. He also sincerely appreciates the kindly service of Dr. Francis Hradil of Denver who as a zealous unionistic specialist and admirer of Stojan supplied some material utilized in this book. Sincere gratitude for appropriate illustrations of Stojan's life details should go to the late Professor Francis Dvornik, who supplied most of them, to Cardinal Tomášek, Archbishop of Prague, for providing graphical illustrations of the Czech academic painter J. Bouda, to Mr. Eduard Fusek of Washington, DC, for lending from his collection three photographs pertaining to the funeral of Stojan, to Mr. Emil Petřík of Chicago for two photographs from Stojan's life, to Mr. Oldrich Holubar, Designer in New York City for photographs regarding Mount Hostyn as taken from my recent book, *Our Lady of Hostyn.* Some illustrations were taken from the publications: V. Juza's Kroměřiž (Prague, 1963) and from R. Šmahel's *Olomouc ve Fotografii* (Octrava, 1965), for which public acknowlegement is here given. Special thanks should go to Rev. Alois Vyoral, S.D.B., for his numerous suggestions. Thanks are also due to all the authors quoted in my notes and bibliography. The writing of the story of Stojan's life was not an easy task because access to reliable source materials was really difficult. However, this is a research account from all available sources and as such it is more than a synthetic profile of all Czech and other accounts, especially those written by Msgr. Francis Cinek and Professor Bohumil Zlámal combined with other fragmentary sources of reports noted in the bibliography. The author cannot forget the considerable help of Rev. Joseph Koláček, S.J., Director of the Czech section of Vatican Radio, for checking the status of stojan's cause in Rome and all the authors of any materials concerning the cause.

Appreciation is due to Rev. Sister Rita Patricia Shanley, SSJ, an English scholar at Chestnut Hill, for reading the manuscript and improving the style of the English phraseology, and to Rev. Sister Grace Catharine Herron, SSJ, for the typing. Last but by no means least, the author wishes to express heart-felt gratitude to Professor Thomas E. Bird of Queens College, Flushing, N.Y., scholar and specialist in Ecumenical slavic matters and Professor Josef Kalvoda, historian at St. Joseph College in West Hartford, for reading the original manuscript and giving invaluable suggestions.

Ludvik Nemec

Nativity of the Blessed Virgin Mary,
September 8, 1982

FOREWORD

The desired and much sought for concrete information about the present state of the "Stojan cause" is appropriately reflected in the outline of preparations for the process of beatification of God's Servant, Archbishop Antonin Cyril Stojan, as these were in process.

The external impulse for starting preparations for the beatification process of Archbishop Antonin Cyril was the 25th anniversary of his death in 1948. On Sunday, September 26, 1948 an impressive popular pilgrimage took place at Velehrad to celebrate this anniversary. On September 28 and 29 a pilgrimage of the clergy and episcopate from the entire Czechoslovak Republic, under the leadership of the archbishop of Prague and primate of Bohemia, Dr. Josef Beran and the archbishop of Olomouc and metropolitan of Moravia, Dr. Josef Karel Matocha, was held at Stojan's grave.

While in Rome, in February 1949, archbishop Dr. Josef Karel Matocha held personal negotiations with Clement Cardinal Micara, then prefect of the Sacred Congregation of Ceremonies who, in his capacity as nuncio of Prague, consecrated A.C. Stojan bishop on April 3, 1921. He was enthusiastic about this idea and promised his assistance.

The beatification process was undertaken by the religious association of the *Apostolate of Sts. Cyril and Methodius* which had been founded by Stojan himself. During a committee meeting on March 28, 1949, attended by Metropolitan of Moravia, Archbishop Dr. J.K. Matocha, the *Apostolate* acted as proponent (actor causae) and nominated Rev. Dr. Josef Olšr, S.J., professor at the Oriental Institute in Rome, as postulator. The very same year the latter nominated two vice-postulators to collect Stojan's writings and all documents pertaining to his activities to make sure that the procedure of collecting information would be initiated in the Olomouc diocese. Because of well-known circumstances no further activities could be undertaken.

Only after archbishop Matocha's death (November 2, 1961), Dr. František Cinek, Stojan's biographer, succeeded in obtaining permission to form a preparatory commission for the beatification of A.C. Stojan. Vice-postulators were then able to file an application with Josef Glogar, capitular vicar for the nomination of a judicial tribunal to start the examinations. Permission was granted, and on July 14, 1965 the first session of the tribunal took place. All members took the required oath, assumed their tasks, and began the examination of witnesses. All together 73 witnesses were heard, among them 4 bishops, 23 priests, 6 friars, 6 nuns, 25 lay men and 9 lay women. The tribunal also summoned ex officio a number of further witnesses. Their depositions referred to Stojan's saintly fame. Other witnesses were heard to prove that our Servant of God had already enjoyed some kind of veneration (processus de non cultu).

Great difficulties have arisen with the written material, which was preserved in large quantities in the State Archives of Olomouc and in Stojan's memorial hall at Velehrad. This material primarily contains letters received from supplicants for help or advice (approximately 90,000 pieces). It was arranged by way of a systematic record (regesta) and amounts to 27 typed volumes offering a unique insight into Stojan's workmanship, as well as his life as a whole. Some of the items may seem trivial or superfluous, but their enormous quantity, the amazing variety of all kinds of supplications, and Stojan's inexhaustible patience in carrying out his correspondence bear most eloquent testimony to his love for suffering people and for God as the moving force in service to one's neighbor to the point of exhaustion.

In addition to all the recorded material there are 31 volumes of copies of Stojan's own writings. They contain his diaries, letters, sermons, political speeches, magazine articles, etc. This remains, of course, only a small portion of what this Servant of God wrote. Much of it was lost, especially the letters, of which only some 2,000 were preserved, while in reality he wrote perhaps several hundred thousand.

All these volumes along with other written documents will be presented to the tribunal which will then send them to Rome for further action. We hope the diocesan procedure can be completed and the documentation sent to Rome in 1983, the year which will be the 60th anniversary of the death of God's Servant.

I trust this pertinent information will be a fitting Foreword to this needed and meritorious work in making this humble servant of God better known, by bringing such a spiritual giant into the international forum.

With God's blessings,

František kard. Tomášek

František Cardinal Tomášek,
Archbishop-Metropolitan of Prague
and Primate of Bohemia

Prague, April 25, 1982.

I
STOJAN'S BIOGRAPHICAL BACKGROUND IN PERSPECTIVE

Stojan's Youth

The youngest and sixth child of Francis Stojan and his wife, b. Josephine Kubičková, was born May 22, 1851 in Beňov, near Přerov, Moravia, at that time a part of the Austrian empire. He was baptized Antonín and confirmed Cyril. The Stojan family was noted for piety, orderliness, and zeal for work. Francis had a small farming household with several fields. He was also a skilled shoemaker, and sacristan at the church of Benov. His wife was an exemplary pious woman who reared her children for God. Each morning and evening the family prayed together. The children attended church from infancy. The oldest daughter, Filomena, died in childhood. A son Francis helped on the farm which he inherited. Others were Cecilia, Marie, Frances who married a certain Berger, and Antonín.

From infancy the latter had a predilection for music and songs. He attended the local grammar school, was always first in his class and had only one desire - to become a priest. In this he was supported by a somewhat wealthy Uncle Fabian who roomed with the family. Later it was decided that Antonín should go to the principal school in Stará Voda, supervised by the Piarist Fathers of Příbor, to learn German, a prerequisite for German secondary schools. He began a two-year term on October 1, 1862. His function as a singer in the monastery church earned him a scholarship which enabled him to stay in school. In 1864 he was accepted into the lower gymnasium (a secondary school) of the Piarist Fathers in the city of Příbor where he lived with the family of Raimund Buzek, a meat cutter. Here he excelled in all his studies and was noted for his piety.

From 1860, when the Austrian Constitution was promulgated, the idea of a national awakening[1] burgeoned in the city. A national pilgrimage to Hostyn in 1861, one in Radhost in 1862, followed by the Cyrilomethodian festivities of Velehrad in 1863 created veritable national excitement, especially among students of the Příbor gymnasium which had several patriotic Czech professors, despite its Austro-

Stojan's birthplace in Beňov at Přerov,

The baptistry in the church in Horní Mostěnice at Přerov,
where Anthony Stojan was baptized, May 23, 1851.

German orientation. In 1868 he was transferred to the higher gymnasium in Kroměříž where national feelings were more in evidence because the students were zealous promoters of Slovanic consciousness raising. Stojan graduated with distinction on July 18, 1872 and immediately applied for acceptance into the major seminary of Olomouc, contrary to the urging of his friends who were advising him to become a teacher.

Stojan the Seminarian

After finishing gymnasium, Anthony Stojan entered the theological seminary in Olomouc; there he completed his studies (1872-1876) at the school of theology, the only department of the University of Olomouc to survive the dissolution of that university.[2] This school of theology was historically unique, since it was the only remaining school of the University of Olomouc[3] founded originally as a college by Bishop Prusinovsky of Olomouc in 1556.

The major seminary in Olomouc was also affected by the spirit of national awakening and patriotism.[4] From 1839 there was the *association of Slovanic Seminarians* under the name of *Literatur-Verein* and since 1848 *Vlastenecká Jednota* (the Patriotic Union) promoted the cultivation of the Czech language. Unfortunately, both were banned during the *Bach era,* a period of repression, in 1860, despite the fact that Cardinal Someran-Beck, then archbishop of Olomouc, patronized them. In 1868 the seminarians of Olomouc, Brno and Prague established a new magazine called *Cyril a Metod* and in 1869 the *Velehrad Union* was established for the support of the shrine of Velehrad.[5] Most active, however, was *Odbor pro Zakládání knihoven na venkově* (Association for the foundation of rural libraries) which were instrumental in upgrading popular culture. All these organizations were stagnating in the 1870's; but when the young Stojan entered the seminary in 1872, he began to revitalize them. He initiated the seminarians' pilgrimages to Velehrad and gave that idea great support during his chairmanship of the *Velehrad Union.*

As a seminarian he also completed the required one year of military training. Since he was not certain whether he would be able to complete his theological studies because of the political situation at that time, and to realize his goal of ordination, he took the examinations and qualified as a public school teacher. As a seminarian, he was one of the leaders in a movement which promoted the founding of libraries in rural communities; he was also active in all then-existing cultural societies at the seminary.[6] None of these activities interfered with his theological studies[7] or his progress in the spiritual life.

Stojan - Priest

Cardinal Fürstenberg, Metropolitan of Moravia, ordained Stojan in the Cathedral of Olomouc July 5, 1876. The newly ordained had prepared himself well and was determined to keep his idealism alive.[8] The Moravian poet-priest František Sušil's well-known dictum, "Let my life be one praise of God, Christ be my joy, the Church be my spouse, the beauty of virtue be my desire and the people's salvation my reward,"[9] became his ideal. He celebrated his first mass on July 9 in the parish church of Beňov. Rev. Father Martilik, a dear friend, preached. The assistants were Rev. Harna, the Capuchin Father Ettl, his pastor Rev. Roubal, Rev. Pavlík, pastor of the neighboring church, and Rev. Martinak Vyplel. Nothing was left undone to make the occasion memorable. Attendance was overwhelming.

Rev. Martilík's sermon referring to SS. Cyril and Methodius and Velehrad seemed to foreshadow Stojan's future apostolate. The new priest with his relatives made a pilgrimage to the shrine of Our Lady of Hostyn on July 10. He had gone there frequently as a seminarian. He went to Velehrad to celebrate a votive Mass of Sts. Cyril and Methodius August 2 and 3, 1876. There he used the chalice donated by Father Sušil. On the same day he attended the Seminarians' Congress and spoke to them about how they could contribute to the much desired union of their Slavic brothers. This faithfully reflected his own spiritual longings and his life's program. From Velehrad he went on his first apostolate with the prayer: "SS. Cyril and Methodius, with you I have begun, help me now."

Father Antonin's first apostolate was to Šilperk (now called Štítný), beginning on August 5, 1876. On his arrival, he knelt and prayed his favorite slogan, that of St. John Bosco, *Da animas, cetera tolle!*"[10] (Give me souls; take the rest!). With great fervor he dedicated himself immediately to all parish activities.[11] His pastor said: "This priest is able to run half the world."[12] Unfortunately, his stay was only one month. He was transferred to Příbor, the town of his studies and of many friends, where Rev. František Holeček was the Pastor and Dean. There Stojan remained for eleven years, (1876-1887) be-

Šilperk, the city parish church, Stojan's first assignment.

Příbor, Stojan's second assignment.

Svébohov, third assignment for Stojan.

coming known as a zealous priest and a patient, popular and dedicated confessor. In fact the confessional became the most important part of his apostolate. For him the confessional was a therapeutic clinic which purified one's character and kept one's conscience alive. In this he was a faithful follower of Blessed John Sarkander[13] whom he greatly venerated.[14] He advocated frequent general confessions and spent much of his time hearing them. He assumed the spiritual and administrative direction of almost all the societies of his parish. He founded new societies, and even became a member of the city Fire Department. During his years in Příbor, he organized two important movements, one for the renovation of Our Lady's shrine in Hostyn, and the other for the restoration of Velehrad. He became the chairman of the *Družstvo Svatohostýnské* (Mount Hostyn Association), organized a pilgrimage of Slavs to Rome, and made the pilgrimage himself in 1881. In those early days of his priesthood, he showed he was a man of action.

In addition to all Stojan's activities, there is another aspect of his life to be clearly observed, namely his well developed national Czech consciousness and a sense of patriotism as integral parts of his personal charisma. He had an opportunity to prove this in the city of Příbor, with a Czech population of several thousand that had a German gymnasium, though only 342 German-speaking people lived in the city. In 1883 city representatives sent a petition to the Ministry in Vienna that the gymnasium be changed to a Czech one, but the request was not granted. In May 1886, the city was informed that the German gymnasium would be closed by the end of the school year 1886-87. The people strongly protested[15] this, because in their city there had been a gymnasium - first Latin, then German - for over 200 years. Since there was no legal objection to it, they decided to build a private Czech gymnasium in the city.

To insure support for this institution, a residential hall was established; i.e., a College where students would lodge while attending the Czech gymnasium. This was located in the house of Mrs. Blažková, once an inn called "At the Green Tree #247." It was called the Hall of John Sarkander, a city native, and had space for 40 students. The new Czech private gymnasium and college residence was solemnly opened September 19, 1886 with 108 students. The people with the blessing of the Archbishop were overjoyed. Meanwhile permission for the opening of a Czech gymnasium was requested from the Minister Gautsche. September 21, 1886, a telegram arrived from Vienna. It stated "permission is not given and everything has to be closed." The people of the city were surprised and chagrined. All students had to be transferred to neighboring institutions, despite the intervention of the city mayor and Father Stojan. This demonstrates the gravity of the situation and the difficulty of working with Czech organizations to which the Austrian government was hostile. One had to have great zeal to survive the odds but Stojan met the challenge. He succeeded because of his sensitive and patriotic national consciousness which enabled him to make any sacrafice. The German (Austrian) authorities resented him and suddenly he was appointed administrator of Veřovice.[16] This was apparently the result of the intervention[17] of the irritated Minister Gautsche who was displeased with Stojan's zealous stand in the matter of the Czech gymnasium and the residence hall in Příbor.[18] Father Stojan remained in Veřovice until June 6 when he returned for a brief time to help Dean Holeček whom he greatly loved. On August 12, 1887 he received a new decree as Exposita to Svébehov near the city of Zábřeh.[19] His departure saddened all the people and actually broke the heart of Dean Holeček who died.[20] The whole city of Příbor was so affected by all Stojan's apostolates that they unanimously named him an honorary citizen in appreciation on November 11, 1887. Dean Francis Holeček before his death had written a superlative testimonial about the exemplary zeal and pure idealism of his once beloved Chaplain.

Stojan - Exposita in Svébohov

The transfer of Stojan to Svébohov, where he worked from August 12, 1887, to November 30, 1888, puzzled many. There Protestant-Catholic tension and rivalry made the situation extremely difficult, but the arrival of this priest was actually beneficial for a territory that had a special missionary status. It was administered by Rev. Josef Weisner (1834-1889), a dedicated priest who completed 25 years of service before dying in 1889.[21] The zealous Fr. Stojan succeeded in receiving approbation for teaching in a German and Czech gymnasium on September 5, 1888 as well as permission to hold the first doctoral rigorosum exam at the Theological Faculty in Olomouc November 20, 1888. His brief stay at Svébohova created an atmosphere of calm and his ability to improve religious relations was deeply appreciated.

Pastor in Dražovice

On November 27, 1888, Cardinal Fürstenberg nominated Stojan pastor of Dražovice near Nový Rousinov in the Slavkov deanery. Although Dražovice belonged to the diocese of Brno, its pastor was provided by the Archbishop of Olomouc who was its patron. This parish had an ancient tradition going back to pastor Gracius in 1382. A follow-up of regular pastors or administrators continued from the second half of the 16th century. It had a filial church in the villages of Podbrežice and Letovice. There is no definite information about the parish for the 14th or 15th century, except that it had remained Catholic in spite of all Hussite and Protestant inroads elsewhere.

The main church dedicated to St. John the Baptist survived several devastating wars, but had greatly deteriorated. Cardinal Schrattenbach, its patron, built a new one, but that too had fallen into decay. Pastor Fuska was later entrusted with its renovation but was transferred to Frenštát before it could be completed. Fr. Stojan fell heir to this work. It can be assumed that Dr. J. Schneider, pastor in nearby Křižanovice, and Bishop Bauer of Brno had advised Stojan to apply for the parish. Cardinal Fürstenberg was happy to give the appointment as compensation for the suffering Stojan had to endure to achieve success in Czech national affairs under Minister Gautsche of Vienna. All Velehrad zealots applauded the appointment. Thanks to his boundless energy, Stojan was able not only to enlarge the church but to have it richly decorated. Solemn consecration of the new church occurred August 29, 1889. The whole region celebrated.[22] Bishop Bauer of Brno performed the rites of consecration. The faithful and clergy attended the festivities of national folklore in great numbers.[23]

Stojan was much more interested in the spiritual affairs of the parish than in the temporal. The parish was rather rich but the very generous pastor made it poor to take care of all the needy. One time his housekeeper niece said sadly: "Today we have nothing but bread for supperı" Stojan said: "This is enough." Suddenly a beggar asking for bread knocked at the door. The housekeeper said: "Forgive me, man; today we have nothing to give." This upset Stojan who said: "Why are you lying˄ Do you not have breadˮ He offered it to the beggar who gratefully departed with the last piece of bread.

"And what shall we eat" said the housekeeper. "We shall pray and go to sleep."[24] This was typical of Stojan's endless generosity.

Spiritual concern for the salvation of souls was Stojan's foremost priority. He used all possible means for educating and inspiring his parishioners to follow Christ. He organized pilgrimages to Marian places such as Němčany, Hostyn, Velehrad, Žarošice, and other places Impressed by Stojan's great zeal, Bishop Bauer of Brno nominated him Consultant[25] of the episcopal consistory January 3, 1892. His pastoral and spiritual responsibilities were conscientiously fulfilled, but the Cyrilomethodian Apostolate and the renovation of Holy Hostyn still remained special concerns, for both of these were basic components of Stojan's spiritual make-up.

The parish church in Dražovice, Stojan's first pastoral assignment.

NOTES

1. Ferd. Pokorný, *Vlastivěda moravská: Příborský okres* (Brno 1917), 145-146.
2. *Listář Olomoucké University* (Documents of the University of Olomouc 1566-1964. ed. Olga Uhrová-Vávrova (Olomouc, 1946) pp. 9-11. This is a summary of the history of the University of Olomouc, pp. 15-105, and publication of a selection of twenty-five significant documents. See Rudolf Smahel, *Olomouc ve Fotografii* (Ostrava, 1966) pp. 166-167.
3. Later legislation reinstating the University of Olomouc was enacted by the Czechoslovak Government on February 21, 1946, changing its name to the University of Palacky.
4. Oldřich Zlámal, *Providka mého života* (The Story of my life) (Chicago, 1953) passium, describes the patriotic atmosphere in this major seminary. He himself was caught in its national waves.
5. Ant. Daněk, "Dr. Ant. Cyr. Stojan, vzpomínka z let studentských" *Moravská Orlice* no. 223 of October 1, 1923.
6. Ant. Šuránek, "Drobty k životu Stojanovu" *Museum* 57 (1925-26), 16-25.
7. *Index lectionum* of October 29, 1872, p. 112 reveals that Stojan had eminenter in all subjects except in Old Testament, in which he received a mark of prima. F. Cinek, *Archbiskup Dr. Antonín Cyril Stojan* (Olomouc 1933), 46.
8. *Deník* (records from July 5, 1876 to October 25, 1877) was found after his death. It is a spiritual record in which the young priest-zealot expressed the soliloquia of a deep soul. It is the most valued autobiographical memory left to us. See F. Cinek, *op.cit.*, p. 47.
9. These words of Sušil were Stojan's favorite slogan through his whole life.
10. "Da mihi animas, et cetera tolle." Leonard von Matt and Henri Bosco, *Don Bosco* (New York: Universe Books, Inc., 1927) 111, 112; J.B. Lemoyne, S.C., *A Character Sketch of the Venerable Don Bosco, Founder of the Salesian Society and the Daughters of Our Lady Help of Christians* (New Rochelle, NY, 1927) Peter Lappin, *Give Me Souls* (Huntington, Ind., 1977), 141 and *Passim*. This saying is traced back to St. Francis de Sales, although originally it is biblical. Some others associate it with St. Francis Xavier, but this author had difficulty in locating it in his works. Furthermore, *Give Me Souls* was the title of a biography of Raphael Cardinal Merry del Val (Sr. M. Bunetta, OSF, Westminster, MD, 1958). This author revealed that the great prelate who served St. Pius X so effectively had a lifelong devotion to St. Francis Xavier. Phrases with a similar theme found in other works on St. Francis Xavier are the following: "More, O Lord, give me more souls," p. 167, and "da mihi fortes Belgas," p. 182 (Arthur R. McGratty, SJ., *The Fire of St. Francis Xavier, the Story of an Apostle* (Milwaukee, 1952). "Plus ultra," ever onwards, a phrase depicting Francis' determined drive to save ever more souls in distant lands, p. 228 (James J. Broderick, SJ, *St. Francis Xavier* (1506-1552) (New York, 1952). Most intriguing is the following sentence of Francis especially in view of the fact that upon his death, his right arm was severed from his body and brought to Rome where it is publicly

venerated: "If ever I forget thee, O Society of Jesus, may my own right hand be forgotten." The Society's major superiors ordered this. (D. Bartoli and J. Maffei, *The Life of St. Francis Xavier* with preface by the Very Rev. Fr. Faber, (New York, 1882). Cf. also for similar phrases, Theodore Maynard, *The Odyssey of Francis Xavier*, (London-New York, 1936). Jean-Marc Montguere, *St. Francis Xavier*, (Garden City, NY., 1963).

11. Ant. Šuránek, "Šilperský panáček", *Našinec* (Olomouc, Jan. 1, 1929).
12. Cinek, *op.cit.*, 61.
13. Bohumil Zlámal, *Blahoslavený Jan Sarkander* (Rome 1943 passim.
14. "Das gesetzliche Bestimmungen nicht erfullt, had as bei der Ersten Entscheidung zu verbleiben. Austallt sofort zuschlissen," see F. Cinek, *op.cit.*, p. 171.
15. *Hlas* no. 222 of Sept. 25, 1886, no. 227 of October 5, 1886.
16. *Olmützer Zeitung* of March 3, 1887 carried this news of appointment of Stojan to Veřovice, even before he received his decree for it.
17. This letter is written to archdiocesan chancery office in Olomouc in Latin. Quoted in Cinek, *op.cit.*, p. 184.
18. This place is well described in *Časpois katol.duchovenstva* vol. 24, no. 6 (1883), p. 354 and passim, and in *Pamětni Kniha* (The Memorial book) of this parish.
19. Created by the archdiocesan chancery office as statio *misionarii per modum cooperatoris expositi*, which was in pastoral care of volunteers rather than of regular appointees. It was adjacent to the parish in *Jedle*.
20. *Hlas* no. 165 of July 23, 1887, where there is a detailed description of this zealous priest, who consumed himself completely for the benefit of the area Catholics in their difficult struggles with the area Protestants.
21. Dr. Gregor Wolný, *Kirchliche Topographie von Mähren*, II Abteilung. Brünner Diozese III Band (Brunn, 1860) p. 485 and 508 and passim.
22. *Hlas* no. 200 of Sept. 1, 1889 described it in great detail. Even P. Václav Kosmák, *Kukátko* II (Brno, 1905) pp. 350-361 dedicated much space to it.
23. Cinek, *op.cit.*, pp. 214-222.
24. Cinek, *op.cit.*, p. 222. Housekeeper was his niece, Marie Hřiva, sister of Dean Hřiva, later pastor in Napajedla.
25. Latin text of this decree can be found in Cinek, *op.cit.*, 229 and it is signed by Most Rev. Francis Salesius Bauer, Bishop of Brno.

II
THE TWO BASIC COMPONENTS OF STOJAN'S SPIRITUALITY:
THE MARIAN DEVOTION AND
CYRILOMETHODIAN HERITAGE

Inspired by the Rev. Placid Mathon of the Benedictine Abbey at Rajhrad, Father Antonin C. Stojan, then chaplain at Příbor, took to heart the matter of Hostyn and was dedicated to this service until his death.[1] Owing to his efforts and his zeal, a new organization, the *Foundation of Hostyn,* was formed to gather donations both for building a monastery and for the support of religious priests.

Baron Loudon in the meantime had become owner of the dominion of Bystřice and, in 1883, had given permission to build a house for the religious on condition that they live there only in summer, while the regular administration of the Church of Hostyn would be in charge of the parish in Bystřice. The parish house was finished in 1885, and in 1887 the spiritual charge for the summer given to the Jesuit Fathers. On May 4, 1887 the first Jesuits came to the Hostyn, namely Fathers Jan Cibulka and Francis Zimmerhackel along with Brother Jan Houf.[2] Father Chibulka took up his duties after the painting of the church was finished in 1890. Paintings were executed by Jan Zapletal of Prague and Jesuit Brother Francis Obdržálek. This newly adorned and refurbished church was solemnly consecrated by Bishop Francis Bauer of Brno, August 15, 1891, in the presence of Frederick Cardinal Fürstenberg, then too ill to perform the rite himself.

The growing popularity of the mountain of Hostyn, site of the Marian Shrine, aroused the speculation of some local businessmen who planned to exploit the place for commercial and secular purposes. They drew up plans to buy the top of the Hostyn hill from the Lord of Bystřice that they might there introduce the project of a recreation area for the people. This, of course, spelled danger, a

Holy Hostyn, Church of the Assumption of the Blessed Virgin Mary,
with pilgrim house, the most frequented Marian Shrine in Moravia.

Interior of the Shrine of the Assumption
of the Blessed Virgin Mary at Holy Hostyn.

secularization of the pilgrimage site. To circumvent this, on the advice of Father Cibulka the *Foundation of the Holy Hostyn* was constituted, with the stated task to protect continuing development of the pilgrim site. Through the interest of this organization, the top of the Hostyn mountain was bought in 1895 from Baron Loudon for 55,000 guldens. Later the monastery was enlarged with a restaurant and dormitories provided for pilgrims. Furthermore Father Cibulka was successful in building the lookout tower atop the mountain for the pilgrims' enjoyment in 1899. In this manner, the whole of the mountain of Hostyn was preserved exclusively for religious purposes.

The idea of the Hostyn pilgrimage gradually became influenced by the events of the times. Religious aspects with historical overtones expanded to include the heroic antiquity of the nation. A natural process aided this, as did also the controversial parchment manuscripts: the *Rukopis Zelenohorský* (Green Mountain Manuscript - Grünberg Manuscript) and the *Rukopis Královédvorský*[3] (Queen's Court Manuscript - Königinhof Manuscript) allegedly found by Václav Hanka[4] and Rev. Borč in 1817. These two manuscripts gave the nation an idealized picture of Slavic antiquity. *Jaroslav,*[5] one of the poems of the *Queen's Court Manuscript,* deals at epic length with the Hostyn miracle of 1241.[6] Stojan himself believed and accepted this poem "Jaroslav." Leaving aside the question of the authenticity and/or controversy aroused by these manuscripts, especially the *Queen's Court Manuscript* in regard to Hostyn, we are interested mainly in the circumstance that Hostyn was its vital subject. Since these two manuscripts, allegedly forged, have been regarded by some as genuine Old Czech literary works, one can comprehend that the *Queen's Court Manuscript* was instrumental in the growth of a veneration of Mount Hostyn. Likewise instrumental, though later, was the influence of Father Josef Hrdina of Sazovice near Holešov, who had already written the first history of Hostyn[7] to be followed soon after by the poet, Vincenc Furch.[8] *The Hostyn idea* was incorporated by Father František Sušil (1804-1868)[9] in his program for the national and religious rebirth. For many years his vast following promoted the idea. Sušil's disciples, like Bílý Bečák, Kubíček, Obdržálek, Potěhník, Mathon, and many others, had celebrated Hostyn as a pilgrimage shrine. The Hostyn idea had been, therefore, promoted by the "Sušilites" even before they took up the Velehrad idea that did not fully develop until the 1850's. The Hostyn aspect of Sušil's program was propagated with no ulterior motive but based on authentic local tradition. His Hostyn program was twofold, religious and national. For its national dimension, Father Sušil borrowed the idea from the priests who preceded him in working toward a renascence of the Czech language. In that pre-Romantic era, he could himself be numbered as one of them with his first attempts at Czech Anacreontic poetry. For the religious dimension, Sušil promoted the Hostyn idea as nourishment for spiritual renewal. The times were with him.

Sušil's role was new and different: to adopt, to justify, and to sanctify nationalism in the Church. No role more difficult could have existed in any other country, since Austria, a composite of many nationalities, had gradually become, since the time of Maria Theresa (1740-80) and Joseph II (1780-1790), a centralized German state. One principal aim of this state had been to suppress any move toward nationalism, nor did it hesitate to use even the church as an effective means to this end.

European nationalism was, however, much too powerful for even a tight border guard to stop it[10] at the boundaries of the Austria of Metternich (1815-1848). Sušil is to be credited with giving to the clergy as well as to the laity their own national and religion-based program. The nation and the Church regenerate the healthy, unspoiled core of a people, devout peasants and rural inhabitants, in that they make use of the native wisdom of the people as expressed in their customs, their proverbs, sayings, songs and tales - in short, in the collective store of their culture and mores. That was Sušil's program. Therein was an echo of the activity of the Catholic priests who preceded him in the Baroque and post-Baroque eras, those who espoused the cause of the simple, morally unspoiled, subservient man against the nobility. The German, Johann G. Herder,[11] in his Philosophy and predictions of the future of nationalities experiencing an awakening of their national consciousness, quite naturally fell, as did the Romanticists, into imaginative vision. Sušil was more practical. By his extensive travels he was busy pursuing Moravian folk songs, by which he not only activated the national awareness of people but implemented it with his program of spiritual renewal.

Stojan was inspired and moved by Sušil's well-known slogan: "Církev a vlast" (Church and fatherland). In this way, he had come to be Sušil's pupil and follower, one who surely equaled his master in propagating the Hostyn idea. Stojan is better understood as a

Crowned statue of Our Lady of Hostyn, victorious protectress of Christians.

Hostyn pilgrim if we remember that, into the integration of Sušil's program with the pilgrimage Shrine - the most famous in Moravia - Stojan could integrate his own personal relationship to that same Shrine - his memories of boyhood days, the daily view from the Beňov fields and meadows, the sight of the white church whose windows seemed to gaze on Beňov, the yearly pilgrimages across Domaželice and Dřevohostice and beyond to Bystřice, to the foot of Hostyn hill, up the mountain, praying and singing accompanied by instruments that played Moravian music, wore native dress, followed native customs. Among the pilgrims, too, were his parents, for the parishioners of Most as of other parishes in the area, were wont to go, each year from 1845, on pilgrimage to Hostyn. Even earlier, in 1820, the people of Dřevohostice, led by their pastor, had begun the practice when the miraculous picture was yet in Bystřice. They venerated the Mother of God, in her shrine on Mount Hostyn, as the "holy guardian of Beňov." Stojan wished to extend her protection over all Moravia, over the entire nation. The Baroque Hostyn Hymn, though this is not certain, may have already been sung in Stojan's day. It was composed near his birthplace[13] according to Sušil's notes.

In Stojan's early priesthood, the *Hostyn idea,* for entirely understandable reasons, seems to have outweighed that of Velehrad. Other than the memories of his youth, the very closeness of his home to Hostyn and its great popularity were to influence him, though Velehrad was likewise at the time a place of pilgrimage. After ordination, he immediately went to Hostyn as a pilgrim. Stojan noted in his diary: "Here at Mount Hostyn, where I used to pray so devoutly as a student, I have invoked the Mother of God for the first time as a priest."[14] He was fortunate, moreover, to deliver his first sermon at Hostyn.

Stojan's activity in promoting the shrine was indirectly motivated by the second visit of Cardinal Fürstenberg to Hostyn on May 19, 1878. On that occasion the prelate gave permission for daily Mass to be celebrated at this shrine. By this action he would ensure its fame for all time. This was indeed an act of true devotion to Our Lady of Hostyn. On the Cardinal's first visit there in 1855, Hostyn, we must note, was really singled out as a Marian shrine. There the Cardinal publicly and officially announced the Dogma of the Immaculate Conception and, in remembrance of the occasion, left there a bell dedicated to Mary and named it Immaculate Conception. Due to the devout concern of the Cardinal for this place, anything Stojan did later to promote Hostyn was favorably received by Fürstenberg. Through the initiative of the assistant priests in Příbor, Antonin Cyril Stojan and Dr. Jan Schneider, their parish organized on May 31, 1881 the Sodality of Mount Hostyn or "Družstvo Svatohostýnské." The sodalists proposed to build a monastery for religious and a hospice for pilgrims at Hostyn. The archbishop approved the proposal.

Stojan was the soul of the project. He sent out 80,000 letters, most of them appeals for funds. He also arranged collections and loans. The booklet he wrote, *Památka ze Sv. Hostýna*[15] or *Souvenir from Mount Hostyn,* contained prayers for the success of the undertaking. His efforts for the shrine were considerably aided by the pilgrimage of Slavs to Rome, September 3-4, 1881.[16] On that occasion the Holy Father Leo XIII blessed a picture of St. Václav (Wenceslaus), which was solemnly conveyed to Hostyn. This was also Stojan's inspiration. The number of sodality members increased to ten thousand, the monastery completed, and in 1887 the Jesuits took up residence. Bishop Francis Bauer of Brno on August 2, 1891 consecrated the renovated church with Cardinal Fürstenberg present for the rite.[17] The seminarians renovated the chapel of Blessed John Sarkander.

The sodality of Mount Hostyn in 1895 became the *Matice Svatohostýnská*[18] or Mount Hostyn Foundation which purchased land including the summit of Mount Hostyn and obtained exemption of the Hostyn church from jurisdiction of the Bystřice pastor. Antonin Cyril Stojan, leader in these affairs, was then the pastor of Dražovice, 1892-1897, delegate from 1897, and provost of Kroměříž from 1908. He contacted the greatest number of benefactors, propagated the devotion, and provided for the solemnity of liturgical services. It was Stojan who invited royalty to Hostyn and arranged for the visit in 1897 of Emperor Franz Joseph I of Austria[19] and in 1904 for the visit of Granito Pignatelli di Belmonte, the papal nuncio. Stojan put into writing much about Hostyn, and he experienced the height of success when Francis Bauer of Olomouc, as Pope's delegate, crowned Our Lady of Hostyn on August 15-22, 1912.[20] Pope St. Pius X had blessed the precious crown for this occasion in Rome. Stojan is to be credited also with ornamenting Our Lady's statue at Mount Hostyn with precious stones, rendering it the most ornate of any shrine in

Czechoslovakia. The artistically wrought golden crown of the Mother of God glows with 27 diamonds, 546 pearls, 158 rubies, 138 emeralds, 113 sapphires, 21 topazes, 47 opals - a total of 1,040 precious stones. The crown of the Divine Infant is radiant with 30 rubies, 20 moonstones and 5 topazes - a glory of 55 precious stones. The crowns were the designs of Professor Josef Fanta.[21]

All his life Stojan worked tirelessly for Mary's shrine. For him Hostyn was a goal, not a passing fancy. Dying, he asked to be carried to a window that he might gaze at the massive cupola of the Hostyn Marian Shrine. During his final illness he had an image of Our Lady of Mount Hostyn placed before him. As he looked at it he prayed: "Help, help, dear Mother of God! Never has it been heard that you abandoned any one. Help me, too!"[22] All this certainly reflects the evidence that Marian devotion was not only the primary and vital component of Stojan's spirituality, but also the most effective way for his maturity to the heights of Christian perfection which he actually attained. His achievement was a successful and faithful following of the Ignatian dictum: Per Mariam ad Jesum.

Concomitantly the Cyrilomethodian heritage was another natural component of Stojan's personal make-up. And appropriately so, since it represented a most powerful force against the XIX century's liberalism[23] which had been the ideological cornerstone of the nation since its inception.[24] The Cyrilomethodian program was timely and relevant. The situation of the Church in Bohemia and Moravia toward the end of XIX and the beginning of the XX century was a path of great decline. Especially after the Vatican Council (1870), all apostasies to the "Old Catholic Church" were favored through the influence of the "Away from Rome"[25] movement of the Lutherans, the sympathies of many Czech liberals aimed at an Eastern Orthodox Church and the ideals of the Hussites. In reaction, Czech and Moravian Catholics sought to unify Slovanic Catholics from all Slavic nations. In Bohemia, Václav Štulic worked on this plan, and Bishop Jirsík lent his cooperation. In Moravia, the pre-eminently learned priest and patriot, Father Francis Sušil, labored strenuously along these lines.

At the twelfth Catholic Day celebration of German Catholics in Prague in 1860, Štulc, the honored guest, announced the establishment of the *Association of Saint Cyril and Saint Methodius* to work for the unity of all Slavic nations. This religious organization was behind the movement led by Father Francis Sušil to celebrate the thousandth anniversary of the arrival of these saints in Moravia. Later the idea was taken over and supported by Fathers Matěj Procházka and Karel Šmídek, and again by Antonin Cyril Stojan. All these priests were educated, generous and famous, but Father Antonín Stojan became particularly prominent.[26] He so aroused Moravia that Brno and Olomouc became centers of Catholic activities. Catholic political parties arose as a result of this movement. It was the scholarly Dr. J. Horský who led the Catholic National Party in Bohemia. The president-elect of the second party - the Christian Social Party - was Monsignor Jan Šrámek. These organizations achieved some measure of success in 1900 and again, but for the last time, in 1907.

Besides these political parties, an association of Czech Catholic intellectuals was established to educate the Czechs for participation in public life. Tomas G. Masaryk saw a substantial danger to progress in the Cyrilo-Methodian movement and in keeping with his revision of the political program, he fought it. He claimed that "Those who are in favor of the Cyril-Methodian idea are holding the line against progress and are advocating an idea that is not of Czech character."[27] Also, "The proclamation of the Cyril and Methodian idea by Young Czechs (at that time the leading Czech political party) who have no regard for its outlined characteristics, is a resignation and a retreat from our free thinking Czech program."[28] Furthermore, "As to the methodological point of view, this idea is a reference to the exaggerated history of the very distant past. . ."[29] He lamented: "The idea finds support among clerics; especially that man of such high education and devotion, Matěj Procházka. . ."[30] Masaryk was unhappy with the influence of this idea even among liberals. He wrote: "The idea of Cyril and Methodius is being proclaimed. The formulation of this concept by its authors, as is apparent to the reader of the newspaper *Národní* Listy (the Young Czech party newspaper) (of July 28, 1894), insists that only through the realization of the Cyril-Methodian idea will the Czech nation accomplish its revival. We would welcome it, even though we consider it wrong. But it is intolerable for us to write about religious problems with a liberal ink and to be zealous for religion and drink national lousy drink."[31] He added, however, that "the idea of Cyril and Methodius, as advanced by convinced Catholics, must be viewed in another light."[32]

Velehrad in Moravia, the center of the Cyrilo-Methodian cult
and of the Church Unity movement among the Slavs.

The magazine *Athenaeum*[33] carried these opinions of Masaryk, while the *Sborník Velehradský*, with its center in Brno, and various periodicals of Czech clerics published the Catholic point of view. Through this Cyrilo-Methodian idea, Catholics tried to win over the Czech liberals. Some of the latter favored the Orthodox Church, for the benefit of which propaganda was being spread in Bohemia, specifically through the publication of the Orthodox catechism,[34] and the introduction of the Orthodox liturgy into Bohemia by Mr. Valečka. Catholics successfully retaliated by introducing the Greek Catholic liturgy and advancing ideas of unionism. In this way they proved themselves staunch supporters of national Slavic solidarity. As a result the wave of apostasies retreated.

As one can see from a review of the Czech cultural developments, the Cyrilomethodian program proved to be very effective and timely in combatting all the hostile forces against the Church, which was then attacked from all directions and was vulnerable in several of them. Pope Leo XIII (1876-1903) himself sensed the importance of this program and issued his Cyrilomethodian Encylical *Grande Munus* on Sept. 30, 1881. This was also a signal to Stojan, so that he began to be intensely involved in this idea. All Catholic Slavs were pleasantly surprised by this papal move and to express their gratitude they prepared for a pilgrimage to Rome. Stojan characterized it this way: "This is indeed a remarkable move made by Pope Leo XIII to place our holy faith missionaries before all Christian nations as examples to be imitated. In some sense the Slavic nations were made equal with other western cultural nations. It is especially fitting for us, the Moravians and Czechs, to manifest our gratitude as much as possible."[36] Leading positions for the pilgrimage were filled: Provost of Velehrad, Msgr. Šulc, Canon Karlach and Father Kozeluha, chaplain in Polešovice were appointed. Stojan, who did most of the work, remained in the background. A great body of pilgrims assembled on June 26, 1881, first at Velehrad, thence to Polešovice and Vienna where pilgrims from Poland, Prussian Silesia and elsewhere also arrived. The Greek Catholic Ruthenians led by Archbishop Sembratorič should be mentioned. The pilgrimage continued to Lublan (Croatia) where they were cordially greeted by all the people. After solemn Mass at the cathedral, the pilgrimage reached Trieste where the pilgrims boarded ships for Ancona. They visited the famed Marian site in Loreto and traveled by train to Rome. The climax was an audience with the

Pope on July 5 in St. Peter's Hall. Cardinal Ledóchowski, Prelate Joenig, Graf Belcredi and Msgr. Schónbron agreed to ask the Pope to bless three pictures: Annunciation of the Virgin Mary and St. Wenceslaus for Hostyn; St. Agnes for Prague; Blessed John Sarkander for the mountain of Radhost. These were placed in the room near the hall, and when the Pope was about to enter, Father Stojan made a Latin petition asking for the blessing of the pictures. The Pope smiled graciously and blessed them. The principal spokesman of all the Slavs was the Croatian Bishop Joseph Strossmayer who made a magnificent speech[37] to which Pope Leo XIII replied: "Return, beloved sons, happily to your countries and narrate to your brothers and sisters what you have seen and heard in the city of Rome. Give testimony that we embrace with fatherly love all the noble and great Slavic nations, asking from them nothing except that they belong to the Catholic Church with the greatest zeal and unbroken faithfulness, so that no one may be lost from that holy ark about which St. Jerome says, 'He who is not in it, will perish in the flood.' "[38] This was an inspiration to all in attendance, for the Pope reminded all Slavs of the importance of the mission entrusted to them.

Subsequently, Father Stojan capitalized on the Pope's conception of the immportance of the principal Cyrilomethodian Slavic heritage not only for church unity but for mutual understanding when he organized a national pilgrimage to be held on Mt. Hostyn September 4, 1881 as an expression of gratitude for the Pope's graceful stand for the Slavs. About 100,000 pilgrims came to honor the Blessed Mother, and about 18,000 bricks[39] were carried by the pilgrims to the hill destined for the renovation of the Marian sanctuary. Stojan preached on that occasion and appraised the Roman pilgrimage as a most significant event for all Slavs. This created such a far-reaching impression that affairs for the advancement of Hostyn Marian Place as an independent parish and the construction of a religious house for the Jesuits who took charge of it in 1887 succeeded beyond all expectations.

Stojan was also preoccupied with the Velehrad development. After the successful Velehrad Lottery, he published a -proclamation[40] concerning the unique and important unionistic mission of Velehrad through the Cyrilomethodian heritage. He aimed to begin preparations immediately for the forthcoming millenium, planned for 1885.

The Velehrad Basilica

The Jubilee Year of 1885

This was a great Cyrilomethodian celebration for all Slavs, especially those of Moravia, because the millenium of the death of St. Methodius was to be solemnly commemorated. On the eve of the Jubilee, the Archbishop of Olomouc, Cardinal Fürstenberg, and the bishop of Brno, Francis Bauer, published pastoral letters announcing not only a decree of the Holy See about the special indulgences, but also outlining the order of all Jubilee devotions, which were divided into five octaves:

1) The octave of the death of St. Cyril (from the eve of 14 to 21 of February);
2) The octave of the death of St. Methodius (from the eve of the 6 to 13 of April);
3) The octave of the feast of SS. Cyril and Methodius (from the eve of 5 to 12 of July);
4) The octave of the Assumption of the Blessed Virgin (from the eve of 15 to 22 of August);
5) The octave of St. Clement (from the eve of 23 to 30 of November);

The Jubilee Committee was organized on July 16, 1884, at Brno under the chairmanship of the Lord of Belcredi, who entrusted the finances to the zealous organizer, Father Stojan. This Committee issued a proclamation inviting all peoples of Czech lands to participate in the Velehrad Jubilee. For this purpose special booklets: *About the Meaning of the Velehrad Jubilee,* and *About the Cultural Activities of SS. Cyril and Methodius, Apostles of the Slavs,* were published. Simultaneously came the pastoral letter of the Czech Episcopate and that of the famed bishop, J. Strossmayer of Diakov, in which he announced his coming to Velehrad and invited all Croatia to take part in a pilgrimage. Publicity, both informative and instructive, was generously provided by all Catholic journals, with Stojan in the leading role.[41]

It should be pointed out that the Viennese government did not favor these Cyrilomethodian festivities, but rather deeply resented their all-Slovanic undertone. Thus, Bishop Strossmayer was not allowed to bring the widely announced pilgrimage of the Croats. Instead he arrived privately in Velehrad on August 16, 1885. The same happened with the Polish pilgrimage. The idea of *Panslavism*[42] was simply abhorred in Vienna. The Velehrad festivities could take their course only because of the zealous interest and participation of Cardinal Friedrich Fürstenberg of Olomouc.

In view of all this, Stojan encountered great difficulties with his long-standing plan to create an organization aiming at the reunion of the Church, based on the Cyrilomethodian idea and heritage, namely, the *Apostolate of SS. Cyril and Methodius.* The idea was already in Stojan's mind in 1881, on the occasion of his pilgrimage to Rome, and matured in the Jubilee Year of 1885. Stojan was imitating in this the already prosperous *St. Bonifacius Verein* in Germany. He wanted a similar one for the Slavs. He submitted his first official petition to Cardinal Fürstenberg June 12, 1885 at Velehrad. This had been signed by the vicar general of Olomouc, Lord Emmanuel Pötting. The Cardinal approved it and in a subsequent conference held August 18, 1885, the *Apostolate of SS. Cyril and Methodius* was established at Velehrad. Present were: Rev. Josef Vykydal, dean of Velehrad, Dr. J. Schneider, pastor in Křižanovice, Bon. Kittrich, pastor in Domanín, Rev. J. Krejčiřík, professor in Kroměříž, Rev. J. Krátký, chaplain in Těšetice, Rev. F. Koželuha, professor in Prostějov, Rev. Fr. Snopek, chaplain in Velehrad, Rev. Jan Vychodil, chaplain in Velehrad, Rev. D. Ohnheister, pastor in Slavičín, Rev. Frank Vymazal, chaplain in Jalubí, Rev. P. Thun, pastor in Duzov, and Father Ant. Stojan, chaplain in Příbor.

The headquarters of this new organization were in Velehrad. The original statutes outlined by Rev. J. Krátký were formulated and made more precise. The presidium especially was made simpler to avoid beaurocratic complications. In this structure the prosperous *Association for the Spread of the Faith* in Lyon was imitated. In addition to these difficulties the *Apostolate of SS. Cyril and Methodius* was very much handicapped by its very nature and mission. It seemed to be a panslavic action rather than a religious organization and this created obstacles for government approval. The pressing Germanization of the land necessarily caused difficulties in the matter of public approval.

The formulation and approbation of the statutes were Stojan's prime concern. To avoid any suspicion of *Pan-Slavism* he was instructed to transfer half the contributions to the Holy See. An opportunity to promote the *apostolate* was offered by a Catholic

Congress held in Vienna in 1889 and Stojan hurried to put it on the agenda. This memorable conference was held on April 30, 1889. It was attended by 52 Czechs, 13 Poles, 5 Slovenes, 2 Croats and 1 Slovak. Stojan was elected secretary. Dr. J. Schneider was the principal resource person regarding Statutes. Lord Stanislav Tarnowski, professor of the Jagellonian University and secretary of the Art Academy in Cracow was elected chairman. After a full debate on the statutes, they were finally approved and Velehrad became the seat of the *apostolate*.[43] Subsequently the *Provisory Supreme Council of the Apostolate* was elected at a meeting held May 23, 1889. The officers chosen were: Rev. Jan Pospíšil, arch-priest in Bzenec as president, Dr. J. Schneider as vice-president, Rev. Antonin C. Stojan as secretary, Rev. Jan Vychodil as treasurer. The members of the Council were: Msgr. J. Vykydal, pastor in Cholina, Adam Lord Potulicke, provost in Kroměříž, Rev. Karel Wisnar, vice-superior of the seminary in Olomouc, Rev. Josef Pospíšil regent of the Seminary at Brno, Rev. Vladimir Stastny, professor in Brno. Substitutes were Rev. Jan Hruby, dean in Jalubí, Rev. Ignatius Zavřel, chaplain in Přerov, and Rev. Jan Hudeček, chaplain in Ivanov. Asked to mediate contacts with the Holy See in Apostolate matters were: Msgr. Lorencello and Rev. Zapletal, directors of the Czech College in Rome. All Slavic neighbors were asked to form national councils and to have one representative in the Supreme Council. This insured the international character of the *Apostolate*. The formation of a delegation to His Eminence, Cardinal Fürstenberg, with an urgent petition for the final approval of the newly formulated Apostolate Statutes was the first decision of the Council. As the Cardinal promised, the Ordinariate of Olomouc permitted the establishment of the *Apostolate*[44] under two conditions: the Apostolate be limited to the two dioceses of Moravia and the Council would request permissions from the Ordinariate as well as from government authorities. This way final approval of the Statutes was given on October 12, 1891, by Cardinal Fürstenberg and on November 20, 1891 from Bishop Bauer of Brno. Trouble came with the State authorities. The Ministry of the Interior in Vienna on February 20, 1892, rejected the petition and proclaimed the establishment of the *Apostolate* illegal. To counteract this, Bishop Bauer of Brno was asked to adjust the Statutes to the requirements of the Ministry. The Reich's deputy, Dr. Helgelet, was to intervene on behalf of the Apostolate. Stojan was impatient with these obstacles but went twice to Vienna with Dr. Schneider to negotiate all controversial points with the government. Finally they came to an understanding with the government officer, Dr. Saller, on point #12 about the meetings.

In the meeting of the Provisional Supreme Council of the Apostolate, held April 18-19, 1892, the Statutes were corrected and reformulated according to State requirements, and publicity for the press was prepared to inform the Catholic public. A *proclamation* was published in all Czech, Moravian, and Silesian newspapers and journals.[45] Simultaneously, 10,000 copies of the Statutes were sent to all Moravian parishes. A German proclamation was prepared by Francis Bauer, Bishop of Brno. Eventually government sanction was obtained. After the approval Stojan quickly published several notices[46] to show that great benefits would accrue to Slavs and, as soon as formalities related to the *Apostolate* were solved, he speeded activities.

December 28 and 29, 1892, he convoked a meeting of the Provisional Supreme Council to review activities and receive the consent of appointed revisors. Subsequently the reconstruction of the Council was completed, diocesan departments were established, a new Supreme Council was formed. It was composed of the same members of the previous Provisional Supreme Council plus two delegates from the Archdiocese of Olomouc, Rev. J. Kubánek and Rev. J. Kinstler, and two from the Brno diocese: Mr. Franz Tesařík and Mr. Aug. Kleveta. Rev. J. Pospíšil, the new president of the Supreme Council, directed all business of the meeting and gave directives for further activities. Stojan began to propagate the Apostolate in all parishes with considerable success.

In 1893 the first solemn general meeting of the *Apostolate* was planned and organized for July 31 and Aug. 1 in Velehrad. Invitations and programs were sent to all parish councils; pilgrimages of women and Slavic academicians were organized. The indefatigable Stojan provided lodging and meals gratis. The meeting was so successful that the *Apostolate of SS. Cyril and Methodius* was not only recognized as important but was accepted as a vital channel for the best utilization of Slavic heritage. It became the basis of everything the Slavs hoped and planned for their common good.

•

Stojan's Efforts to Spread the Apostolate among All Slavic Catholics

Following the approval of the *Apostolate* in Moravia, Stojan requested all Bohemian dioceses to initiate it in their areas. The Ordinariate of Prague answered positively on January 8, 1894. Breslau, headed by Cardinal Kapp instituted it in the arch-diocese on January 20, 1894. That same year the zealous leader sent letters to Polish and Ukrainian bishops, and with Dr. Schneider attended the Catholic Congress at Cracow where he personally presented the *Apostolate* to the bishops.

The Greek Catholic Metropolitan of Lwov, Cardinal Sembratowič approved the statutes of the *Apostolate* with certain changes on July 14, 1894 and the Vice-government endorsed it in November, 1894. Petitions for introduction of the *Apostolate* were sent to all Ordinaries of the Slovenes on July 1, 1894. Their answers were rather cautious. The Prussian Ordinariates, where there were Slavic Catholics, were approached on November 5, 1896 but their answers were somewhat negative. In memory of the three hundredth anniversary of the Church reunion, festivities were held in Lwov, October 10-12, 1896. Father Stojan presented his *Apostolate* there and Cardinal Sembratowič with other Uniate bishops promised their support. The indefatigable Stojan even repeated his petitions to those bishops who had previously refused, until he eventually got them on his side. He published an article[47] about the *Apostolate* for the general public on the feast of the Epiphany in 1894, and the issue was again raised at the first Congress of Czech Catholics held in Brno July 30-August 1, 1894. Interest was so stimulated that a special *resolution*[48] was voted on by the Supreme Council of the *Apostolate* to establish the first Catholic Czech Cyrilomethodian University in Moravia. Stojan tried to get leading personalities involved in this venture. Dr. Antonín Rezek, resource person at the Ministry of Education, was interested in the idea and was really enthusiastic that young priests should involve themselves in a study of literary and scholarly activity in this direction.

Stojan, Pioneer of Spiritual Retreats for Laymen

One of the most important activities of the *Apostolate of SS. Cyril and Methodius* was the initiation of spiritual retreats for laymen. In August, 1892, Stojan recommended retreats for Czech and Moravian teachers to be held from August 26-30 in the Velehrad

Our Lady of Union – Palladium at Velehrad

monastery. The significance of this providential act was felt later. One hundred nine teachers attended the first retreat conducted by Rev. Jan Cibulka, SJ, superior at Hostyn, and Stojan. After this favorable experience, retreats were extended to include professors, teachers and university students. When permission was requested from the Archbishop of Olomouc, Dr. Theodore Kohn suggested that they include Germans also. The Ordinariate of Olomouc approved plans by a special letter July 2, 1894, and requested a report after each retreat. A retreat for teachers, conducted by Rev. Alois Jemelka and Stojan, was held August 21-24, 1894. However, this spiritual activity was not without outside harassment provided by anti-clerical liberals who attacked the participation of teachers.

Some teachers were frightened so that only 25 women attended the retreat given August 25 to 29, 1894, and only 22 were present for the one held for university students September 3 to 7. Despite these difficulties 20 retreats were held every year and became a continuing important program for the *Apostolate*. Liberal teachers created an anti-Catholic atmosphere but Stojan was determined to recruit teachers to attend them. The Jesuit Father Tomechek, characterized his efforts this way: "By the help of spiritual exercises he wanted to build a firm foundation on which the whole structure of a spiritual religious, national, cultural and social life could safely exist."

In addition to these spiritual exercises, Stojan regulated pilgrimages with people's popular renewals, replete with folklore, band music and songs. To increase their effectiveness, he frequently invited well-known choirs like the *Cyril Jednota* from the city of Slavkov or the Cyril choir from Sborovice. He had a special predilection for the all-Slavic expression of these pilgrimages and always invited guests from Slovakia, Galicia, or elsewhere. Liturgy was always as solemn as possible. Pontifical celebration was assured by visiting prelates, invited guests, domestic ordinaries of Olomouc or Brno; less frequently from Prague or other episcopal sees. Last but not least, celebrated preachers or orators frequently occupied the pulpit so that spiritual inspiration was provided for all participants of Velehrad. Results of all these activities were especially visible in the increasing membership of the *Apostolate* which reached a peak of 60 to 70,000 in 1895-96. This included only Moravia, Bohemia and Breslau, although in other dioceses potential appeared later. Velehrad's activities produced a reservoir of good in all directions, and one must remember that Stojan's preoccupation with Velehrad was only a side but important issue in addition to his pastoral obligations in assigned parishes and numerous public activities in which he was involved.

In retrospect, it could and should be said that this Cyrilomethodian heritage was more than an ideological program for him. It was so natural a component in Stojan's personal make-up as any Moravian can feel about "the heritage of Fathers" to be kept and appreciated. More so since the Cyrilomethodian Velehrad was here not only to remind everyone of its glorious historical past but mainly to influence its lasting legacy of faith[49], and Stojan, having been always more practical than scholarly, decided himself to become a willing instrument and an effective vehicle to fulfill that legacy faithfully.

NOTES

1. Ludvik Nemec, *Our Lady of Hostyn, Queen of the Moravian Garden of the Czech, Moravian, Silesian and Slovak Madonnas* (New York, 1981) 10, 18 and passim; Frant. Cinek, *op.cit.*, 100-102.
2. Karel Eichler, *Poutní místa a milostivé obrazy na Moravě a v rak. Slezsku* (Places of pilgrimages and miraculous pictures in Moravia and in Austrian Silesia) 2 vols. (Brno 1887, 1888) II pp. 40-50.
3. Jan Vrzalík, *Svatý Hostýn ve Sví Slávě a ponížení* (unpublished manuscript, Prague, 1974), pp. 245, passim. A copy is preserved in the Ministry of Education in Prague and another in possession of Professor Sidney T.S. Rutar in New York.
4. Vladimír Kopecký, *Plno Záhad kolem Hanky* (Many mysteries around Hanka) (Prague, 1969). Here is an attempt to clear up some widespread misguided views about the celebrated Václav Hanka (d. 1861), the alleged forger of manuscripts.
5. Václav Flajšhans, "Drobné články, Dalimil Tatarech," *Český Časopis Historický* 40 (1934), pp. 219-225.
6. The entire translation can be found in Karel Eichler, *op.cit.* II, pp. 19-23; it is reproduced also in Frant. Palacký, *Dějiny národu českého* 2 vols. (Prague, 1897) I, pp. 312-313.
7. In my research I was unable to locate this first history of Hostyn.
8. Taken from *Písně Hostýnské* (1845), quoted by B. Zlámal, *op.cit.*, p. 40. The whole text is reproduced by Karel Eichler, *op.cit.* II, pp. 34-35.
9. Jan Drábek, *Z času nedlouho zašlých* (From times not long past) (Rome, 1967) pp. 77-78, 354; Václav Flajšhans, *Písemnictví České*, 2 vols. (Prague, 1900-01) II, p. 620.
10. Zlámal, *op.cit.*, p. 40; Eichler, *op.cit.* II, 38.
11. Eichler, *op.cit.* II, pp. 40-41.
12. Zlámal, *op.cit.* p. 41; Eichler, *op.cit.* II, 39.

13. Hans Kohn, *Pan-Slavism. Its History and Ideology* (Notre Dame University Press, Ind., 1953), pp. 11-99; see also Paul Vyšný, *Neo-Slavism and the Czechs* 1894-1914 (Cambridge University Press, 1977), pp. 1-17.

14. Thomas P. Neill and Raymond H. Schmandt, *History of the Catholic Church* (Milwaukee, 1937), pp. 484-499.

15. Johann G. Herder, *"Journal Meiner Reise im Jahr 769"* in *Herder's Werke in fünf Bänden*, Band 1 (Alban Verlag: Berlin and Weimar, 1969) I, pp. 135-137.

16. In *Cyril a Method* (Olomouc, 1849), *passim.*

17. František Cinek, *Arcibiskup Dr. Antonín Cyril Stojan, Život a dílo* (Olomouc, 1933), p. 33 and *passim.*

18. V. Flajšhans, *Písemnictví České II* (Prague, 1901), p. 820.

19. Cinek, *op.cit.*, p.53.

20. Cinek, *ibid.*

21. I was unable to procure this booklet that his biographers frequently mention. Cinek, *op.cit.*, pp. 115-128; A.C. Stojan, *"Pouť do Říma,"* Škola Bož. *Srdce Páně* (1881), p. 182 and *passim.* Herein is described the whole pilgrimage P. František Videňský, T.J., *SV. Hostýn ve svém původu a svých osudech* 1913), pp. 114-116. P.R. Rozkošný, *"Matice Svatohostýnská* (25 letá činnost její)" *Hlasy svatohostýnské* XIX, pp. 30-32 and *passim.* (F. Cinek, *op.cit.*, 273). Ant. Janda, ed. *Papežská korunovace Matky Boži svatohostýnské* (Papal coronation of the Mother of God of the Hostyn) (Brno, 1913), *passim,* especially pp. 66-68. Cinek, *"Korunovační slavnosti svatohostýnské* 1912," *op. cit.*, pp. 717-719.

22. Josef Olšr, *Služebník Boží, Antonín Cyril Stojan, Olomoucký archbiskup* (Rome, 1966), pp. 42-43.

23. Ludvik Nemec, *Church and State in Czechoslovakia* (New York, 1955), 117-118.

24. Francis Dvornik, *Byzantské misie u Slavanů* (Prague, 1970); idem, *Byzantine Mission among the Slavs* (Rutgers Univ. Press, 1970).

25. "Die Los-von-Rom Bewegung in Oesterreich," *Hist. Pol. Bl.* CXXVI,-CXXVII (1900-1901) in several articles; Franz Stauracz, *Los von Rom* (1900), 16-17; T.G. Masaryk, *Los von Rom* (Boston 1902).

26. Monsignor Stojan was a generous benefactor and worked arduously for social reforms that would benefit the people. The success of the Catholic center in Velehrad is one result of his work. Cf. *Nový Život* (The new life), III, No. 7, July 1951. "Muž modlitby a práce" (Radio broadcast by Cardinal Clement Micara on the 100th anniversary of Archbishop Antonín Cyril Stojan, on May 22, 1951). See a detailed study in articles, appearing weekly in *Katolík*, LXI (1954) by Monsignor Dr. Josef Bezdíček: "Antonin Cyril Stojan, God's faithful servant."

27. Tomáš G. Masaryk, *Jan Hus*, (Prague 1923) 10.

28. Tomáš G. Masaryk, *Česká Otázka* (Prague 1908), 200.

29. Tomáš G. Masaryk, *op.cit.*, 228

30. Tomáš G. Masaryk, *Jan Hus*, 89.

31. Tomáš G. Masaryk, *Česká Otázka*, 210-11.

32. Tomáš G. Masaryk, *ibid.*, 224.
33. T. Polívka, "O Kontroversích Cyrilomethodéjských," in the *Athenaeum*, Oct. 15, 1885.
34. Eduard Winter, *Tausend Jahre Geisteskampf in Sudetenraum* 2nd (Salsburg 1938), p. 389.
35. *Grande Munus* of Sept. 30, 1880, see *Acta Leonis*.
36. Ant. C. Stojan, "Pouť do Říma", *Škola Bož. Srdce Páně* (1881) p. 182-184.
37. It was published in *Sborník velehradský* II (1881), 7-9.
38. Humble speech of Pope Leo XIII was published in *Škola Bož Srdce Páně* XV (1881), 212-21.
39. Ant. C. Stojan, *Hlasy Svatohostýnské* (1923) p. 166, where he refers to this effect.
40. R. Rozkošný, T.J. "z činnosti Ant. C. Stojana, Kaplana Příborského" *Hlasy svatohostýnské* 21 (1925), *passim*.
41. Especially the journal *Hlas* (no. 1 of Jan. 2, 1885), (no. 16 of Jan. 20, 1885.
42. Hans Kohn, *Pan-Slavism: Its History and Ideology* (Notre Dame Univ., Ind., 1953) pp. 11-19; Paul Vyšný, *Neo-Slavism and the Czechs 1894-1914* (Cambridge Univ. Press, 1977), *passim*.
43. *Jednatelska Kniha*, pp. 26-27 (*Acta of the Apostolate of Sts. Cyril and Methodius*, Velehrad.)
44. F.J. "Křížová cesta apoštoláních stanov." (The Via Dolorosa of the Statutes of the Apostolate). *Apoštolát sv. Cyrila a Metoděje* no. 2 (1931), 42-43.
45. Cinek, *op.cit.*, pp. 245-246 mentions all these journals.
46. Three o them are published in Frant. Cinek, *op.cit.*, pp. 247-251.
47. *Hlas* no. 4 of Jan. 6, 1894.
48. *Resolution* 2B of August 1, 1894, quoted by F. Cinek, *op.cit.*, 303.
49. František Cinek, *Velehrad Víry* (Velehrad of Faith) (Olomouc 1937) *passim*.

III
STOJAN'S CHURCH UNITY
WORK AND VELEHRAD

When Stojan was first inspired with the idea of Slavonic ecumenism, the Holy See had already passed through certain experiences and had formulated hopes in the matter of bringing Christianity and the East closer together, especially its political representatives.

The time of Pius IX (1846-1878), pope in the midst of revolution, was not yet ripe for Church and state co-existence.[1] But his successor, Leo XIII (1878-1903), the pope of peace,[2] tried in every possible way to reach an understanding with governments and states — often, as appeared to many — to the detriment of the Church. How far he was willing to go in this direction is indicated by the termination of the cultural struggle in Bismark's Prussia.[3]

In this spirit of local retreats, Leo XIII hoped to arrive at a better understanding with the Russian rulers,[4] Alexander II (1881-1894) and Nicholas II (1894-1917), and in that way to ease conditions under which Catholics in Poland were laboring in Polish territories under Russian domination since the partition of Poland.[5] After many reversals in the negotiations, in which even the Moravian biographer, Beda Dudík, took part, Leo XIII became convinced that the great Russian state as the chief spokesman for the Slavic nations would not refuse to accept the extended hand and would perhaps eventually become amenable to the great idea of unity.

The first encyclical concerning the Slavs was a consequence of these considerations and caused Pope Leo XIII to be called "The Pope of the Slavs." This is the famous encyclical letter *Grande munus* of September 30, 1880, by which the Slav saints, Cyril and Methodius, were proclaimed as saints by means of an "equivalent canonization" (Canonizatio aequipollens) and their cult was extended to all the rest of the world and throughout the Church. They were to shine as examples for teachers, missionaries, bishops, and preachers of universal church unity. At the same time, the encyclical imposed on Catholic Slavs the duty of working for unity of faith among the Slavs.

It is no less important, that, due to Pope Leo XIII's decision, the Cyrilo-Methodian observances, which had been successfully held at Velehrad before that date, exerted their influence and served to propagate the Cyrilo-Methodian idea throughout Czech lands. At least that is how it was interpreted by the people at that time, and that is how it was expressed in the address of gratitude delivered during the pilgrimage to Rome in 1881: "Especially since the celebration of 1863, our nation has been preparing the way for the idea of unity of all Slavs in the Cyrilo-Methodian Faith. For that reason, the sons of our nation exult with joy that even the Vicar of Christ, with his supreme authority, now approves the efforts which they have exerted up to this time, and so warmly and earnestly recommends the matter to all Slav nations."[6]

Stojan was only four years ordained a priest when Leo XIII's missionary politics included the vast world of the Slavs in his gigantic program. Until that time the Slav world had been considered a kind of outlying territory. In Pope Leo XIII's action, Stojan saw a divine invitation especially for himself. The Cyrilo-Methodian idea developed in his mind and he began to comprehend it, not only as the most effective program for the internal renewal of the Czech nation, but also as a force of pan-Slavic solidarity. Later he wrote in the Apostolate journal of Sts. Cyril and Methodius: "As early as our student days at the Olomouc Seminary in the 1870's, the unity of Slav nations founded on Faith was our cherished idea."[7]

We know that already as a theology student, Stojan promoted Slomšek's Brotherhood of Sts. Cyril and Methodius among both Czech and German students. But his personal experience in Rome and his audience with Pope Leo XIII during the thanksgiving pilgrimage of Slavs in 1881 gave him a world-wide perspective and inspired his decision to raise the Moravian Velehrad to a pan-Slavic Velehrad, to make it a center of unionistic efforts among the Slavs.

Even a cursory study of Stojan's thought reveals a well defined theme underlying each of his works, namely, concern for the reunion of East and West. To uncover the source of the inspiration behind this recurring theme, one is led inevitably to Velehrad where the roots of its history and traditions were deeply implanted. While engaged in his Cyrilomethodian studies, Stojan could hardly fail to grasp the centuries-old tradition inherent in its original historic meaning: the reunion of East and West. A native Moravian, Stojan's personal interest was an added incentive to probe the relation between history and tradition. From his early years, Velehrad exerted an influence which became more meaningful to him as a student, and later as a seminarian in Olomouc[8], See of the Moravian Metropolitan, whose specific care for the Cyrilo-methodian heritage became both an institution and a privileged mission. Viewed in retrospect, these factors may be seen as exercising a dominant role in determining Stojan's course as a Catholic priest as well as a Churchman. They influenced his determination to bring Velehrad into focus from the standpoint of history and, from what Professor Cinek terms "the standpoint of faith,"[9] for the union of East and West, once a reality, still an unrealized desire. It is obvious that the orthodox-Catholic dialogue which was set in motion against Velehrad's historic background should be given a more prominent place in the writings on ecumenism[10] than some have been willing to accord it, for the Unionistic Congresses at Velehrad represent not merely a movement, but a determined action directed to the realization of Christian unity. Dvorník rightly stated: "they represent an important contribution to the solution of problems concerning the reunion of Churches."[11] Their importance may be seen more clearly when one realizes that they arose of necessity as a challenge to the aims of *pan-Slavism,*[12] which implicitly favored the Orthodox.

Catholics were thus alerted to the danger from the Russian Slavophiles, who propagated the idea that Catholic Slavs should abandon their faith to become Orthodox. The Slavic Catholic hierarchy, perceiving the danger, took steps to avert it. The Croat Bishop of Diakov, Joseph George Strossmayer (1815-1905), reactivated[13] the Cult of Sts. Cyril and Methodius, Apostles to all the Slavic nations, stressing the fact that although of Greek origin both worked among the Slavs under Rome's jurisdiction; were canonized by Rome; and were accepted by the Eastern Church. Initial archeological activities which began in *Staré Město-Velehrad*[14] were accelerated, thus inspiring an enthusiastic search for the burial place of St. Methodius.[15] This was a challenge to substantiate related historical facts that would elicit an appreciation for the merits of the Catholic Slavs and their traditional claims for reunion. The Panslavists and the Orthodox, uneasy in their opposition to the movement because of their inability to support their own claims, were forced to moderate their assertions in view of this historic Catholic preponderance. Catholics made good use of their historic claim to the Cyrilomethodian heritage by public commemorations in Velehrad marking the anniversaries of those events closely associated with Sts. Cyril and Methodius — the millenium of their arrival in 1863, the death of St. Cyril in 1869, the death of St. Methodius in 1885.

Rome was well aware of the issues at stake, and gave every encouragement to unionistic efforts. As was mentioned, Leo XIII, recognizing the importance of this movement, published the Bull *Grande Munus,* ordering the observance of the feast of Sts. Cyril and Methodius in Roman Catholic churches throughout the world. This gave renewed impetus to the Cyrilomethodian cult, and the union of all Orthodox Slavs became the dominant theme in numerous meetings held by the Moravian clergy and the intellectuals of Velehrad. The *Apostolate of Sts. Cyril and Methodius,* an organization founded in 1891 by the young Moravian priest, Antonin Cyril Stojan under difficult circumstances, aimed to promote the idea of reunion, and to pray for its realization.[16]

The *Apostolate* was to realize a domestic role, to preserve the purity and unity of Faith in its own nation (like the Skt. Bonifatius-Verein in Germany), to provide for the Catholic diaspora, to care for the Czech emigrants, and to support the Holy See in missionary activities among Eastern Slavs. According to the wish of Pope Leo XIII it was also to have a church-wide and world-wide role: to work for unity of Faith among the Slavs. Stojan beautifully adds "This idea is close to our heart."

The great work also had many enemies. The most dangerous of these was "Catholic" Austria. Stojan was conscious of this: "Even though the idea is so noble, nevertheless, from the experience we have gained, we have realized that it will be denounced as pan-Slavism." For this reason Stojan was zealous to search for protectors in Rome, where especially Cardinal Domenico Bartolini gave the *Apostolate* a hearty welcome and said: "Eminent in the midst of a large group of willing and enthusiastic fellow-workers, A.C. Stojan was the real founder of this providential work, the many-faceted benefits of which are maturing in our own days. Stojan's heart overflowed with joy as he initiated this work. "Is it utopian to hope for the unification of Slavs? Will the world ever see unity in the Church?" He immediately answered his own questions: "It is not for us to know the times or dates which the Father has fixed by his own authority (Acts 1:7), "We know that the present pope, Leo XIII, has dedicated himself to that hope and arouses it in us."[17]

In the Slavic world, there was no lack of men who were similarly interested in the Cyrilo-Methodian idea — concerned about the great role of the Slavs in the universal Church — men who perhaps were even better spokesmen for this idea than Stojan. One such man, already mentioned, was Bishop Joseph G. Strossmayer. There were others among Stojan's older fellow-workers, like Dr. Jan Schneider, the two Velehrad priests Josef Vykydal and Jan Vychodil, and others too numerous to mention. All these could be called co-founders of the Apostolate of Sts. Cyril and Methodius.

Stojan himself used to recall Rev. Ambrose Kaese of Würzburg with gratitude. The latter repeatedly assured Stojan in 1880 that the Czechs and Moravians particularly were chosen by Divine Providence to "initiate union, work for it, and with the help of God, bring it to realization." Of all this, the soul and the moving spirit was A.C. Stojan.

It would be vain to expect from him some theoretical work, a speculation, for example, concerning what the *Apostolate* is, what direction it would take, what means it would use to attain its goal, or similar questions theoretically discussed, that would be natural for an organization arousing such widespread interest. Stojan was a practical ideologist without a written ideology. He preferred to leave this to his co-workers, whom he allowed to put him to work bearing the burden and the heat of the day.

Stojan's doctoral dissertation, *Concerning the Union of the Slav Nations with the Roman Catholic Church According to the Intentions of the Holy Father Leo XIII,* as well as his addresses dealing with the Cyrilo-Methodian idea, are manifestations of his soul and heart, indicating his yearning for action rather than an inclination toward systemic intellectual speculation. But love, a concern of the heart, is something more eloquent than words. Stojan's main thoughts, which were his guiding principles in this work, will be quoted later.

As if compensating for this inadequacy in the program, there was extensive publicity in the printed media, generally in Moravian and Czech periodicals and newspapers. Ten thousand copies of the statutes of the *Apostolate of Sts. Cyril and Methodius* were distributed in the parishes of Bohemia and Moravia.

The encyclical *Grande munus* was published by the Benedictines of Rajhrad Abbey in a polyglot edition (seven languages). The *Apos-*

tolate was promoted everywhere, in print, sermons and lectures. *The Dědictví sv. Cyrila a Metoděje* (Heritage of Sts. Cyril and Methodius), a publishing firm in Brno, greatly assisted in this outlet. Stojan's personal contribution to this publicity is evident in the fact that he tried to interest the whole Catholic world in this idea, as he did when he again addressed invitations to all the Catholic nations of Europe to participate in the Velehrad celebrations of 1885. This was the most splendid event in the jubilee year commemorating the millenium of St. Methodius's death.

A world-wide outlook never left Stojan after this occasion. Words were followed by great deeds. This was, above all, an effort to attract Rome and its representatives toward the goal of the Moravian Apostolate, to further develop its goal, and to further implement the *Velehrad Academy*[18] as an institution for training Cyrilo-Methodian unionistic experts, and finally to convoke the first three unionistic congresses and two unionistic conferences at Velehrad, certainly the place of not only historical witness to its glorious past,[19] but also an embodiment of a legacy of Church unity[20] waiting to be fulfilled.

NOTES

1. E.E.Y. Hales, *Pio Nono* (New York, 1954) 1 G.F.H. Berkeley, *Italy in the Making* (Cambridge, 1936) passim; Cathbert Butler, *The Vatican Council* (London, 1930).
2. Thomas P. Neill and Raymond H. Schmandt, *History of the Catholic Church* (Milwaukee, 1937), 540-529, and passim.
3. James Corrigan, *The Church and the Nineteenth Century* (Milwaukee, 1938) passim; James MacCaffrey, *The History of the Church in the Nineteenth Century*, 2 vols. (Dublin, 1909) I, passim; Eduardo Soderini, *The Pontificate of Leo XIII* (London, 1934).
4. Francis Dvornik, *The Slavs in European History and Civilization* (New Brunswick, N.J., 1961), 549-536.
5. R.H. Lord, *The Second Partition of Poland: A Study in Diplomatic History* (Cambridge, Mass., 1915); idem, "The Third Partition of Poland," *Slavonic Review* 3 (1925).
6. Quoted previously.
7. Quoted previously.
8. *Cath. Enc.* XI cols. 247-48 of L. Tittel, *Historia archidioecesis Olomucensis ejusque Praesulum* (Olomouc, 1889).
9. František Cinek, *Velehrad Víry* (Velehrad of Faith) (Olomouc, 1936).
10. Edward F. Hanahoe, *Catholic Ecumenism* (Washington, DC, 1953) cf Hans Küng, *The Council, Reform and Reunion* (New York, Sheed and Ward, 1961) cf Thomas Pater's review, *The Catholic Historical Review* 48 (1962) 278-80.

11. Francis Dvornik, "The History of the Velehrad Unionistic Congresses," *Proceedings of the First Unionistic Congress September 28-30, 1956.* (Lisle, St. Procopius Abbey, 1956) 37-39. cf. Felix Mikula, "Unionistické kongresy: (Unionistic Congresses) *Nový Svět* (New World) (Cleveland, Oct. 25, 1956) 3.
12. N. Riasonowski, *Russia and the West in the Teaching of the Slavophiles.* (Cambridge, Mass., 1953) passim.
13. Smiciklas, *Strossmayer* (Agram, 1906) cf. Granderath-Kirch, *Geschichte des vatikanischen konzils* (Freiburg, 1903-6) II. III. passim. Under his direction Augustin Theiner edited *Vetera Monumenta Slavorum Meridionalium* (1863). He sought to win the Orthodox Serbs for Rome by the use of the Old Slavonic liturgy.
14. Josef Poulík, *Staroslovanská Morava* (Prague, 1948) cf. Vilém Hrubý, *Staré Město-Veligrad.* (Gottwaldov, 1955) cf. A.V. Isacenko, *Začiatky vzdelanosti vo Velkomoravskej ríši* (Turčiansky Sv. Martin, 1948) cf. V. Hrubý, v. Hochmannová and J. Pavelčík, "Kostel a pohřebiště doby velkomoravské na Modré u Velehradu," *Časopis Moravského Musea* 40 (1955) 42-126; cf. Josef Poulík, *Jižní Morava, Zemé DAVNÝCH Slovanů* (Brno, 1948-52); cf., Josef Cibulka, *Velkomoravský kostel v modré u Velehradu a začátdy křesťanství na Moravě.* (Prague, 1958), Outlines the controversy concerning the origin and age of these churches; cf. Josef Pekař, O poloze Starého Velehradu," *Velehradský Sborník* 9 (1038) 5-9; considers various views concerning the position of ancient Velehrad; cf. Jacobus Hudeček, "Archeologicae excavationes in regionibus Velehradensis prope Vetus Uh. Hradiště," *Acta Acad. Velehr.* XII, 42-52; cf. L. Niederle and A. Zelnitius, "Slovanské pohřebiště v Starém Městě u Uh. Hradiště," *Zprávy státního ústavu archeologichého I* (1929) 1-35; cf. A. Zelnitius, "Slovanské pohřebiště ve Starém Městě u Uh. Hradiště," *Sborník Velehradský* 2 (1931) 12-25; 3 (1932) 45-53.
15. The enthusiasm which the search for the body of St. Methodius engendered led archeologists to seek it in various places which up to the present are not clearly identified. The interesting news that the body was located in Staré Město was revealed by *Frankfurter Allegemeine* on January 17, 1961, but that has not yet been officially confirmed by the archeologists' reports.
16. Frantisek Cinek, *Arcibiskup Dr. Antonín Cyril Stojan: život a dílo* (Olomouc, 1933) wherein profuse material concerning unity and related problems is to be found; cf., "Muž modlitby a práce," (The man of prayer and work), *Nový Život* (The New Life) 3 (1951) 3-5; Radio broadcast by Cardinal Clement Micara on the one hundredth anniversary of Archbishop Stojan, on May 22, 1951; cf. Josef Bezdíček, "Antonin Cyril Stojan, God's faithful servant," *Katolík* 61 (1954) in many articles comprising a detailed study of Stojan. Archbishop Stojan was also a prolific writer of Cyrilomethodian booklets, each serving a practical purpose; cf. Josef Olšr, "Dr. Antonin Cyril Stojan, Olomoucký Arcibiskup: 1. Stojan Lidumil," (Dr. Ant. Cyril Stojan, Archbishop of Olomouc: 1. Stojan a philanthropist) *Nový Život* 12 (Rome, 1960) 189-90 cf. *idem.* "Stojan Kněz," (Stojan, the priest),

ibid., 12 (1960) 253-2; *idem*, "Stojan Světec," (Stojan, the Saint), *ibid.*, 13 (1961) 8-9; idem., Muže býti arcibiskup Stojan kanonizován" (Can Archbishop Stojan be canonized?) *ibid.*, 13 (1961) 104-6.

17. Quoted previously.
18. See Satzungen der *Academia Velehradensis* in Adolf Jašek, *Was ist die CyrilloMethodeische Idee* (Velehrad, 1911), 75-80.
19. See especially Bohumil Zlámal's historical and ideological introduction to Rudolf Šmahel's *Velehrad in photography* (Prague, 1969).
20. Ludvik Nemec, "The Recent Reinvestigation of Cyrilomethodian Sources and Their Basic Problems" in *Czechoslovakia Past and Present* ed. by Miloslav Rechcigl, Jr., 2 vols. (Hague: Monton 1972), II pp. 1151-1174. See also Josef Macůrek, *Magna Moravia*. Sborník k. 1100 Výročí Příchodu Byzanské mise na Maravu (Prague 1965), 17-70 and passim; Josef Cibulka, "Velkomoravský kostel v Modré u Velehradu a začátky Křesťanství na Moravě" *Monumenta Archeologica* VII, (Prague 1958), 290-291. Josef Poulík, *Staří Moravané budují Svůj Stát* (Ancient Moravians build their State.) (Gottwaldov 1960), 193-206.

Before World War I the Neo-Slavic movement reflected the prevailing mood among the Czechs and most of the other Slavic nationalities in Austria-Hungary. Its founder, Dr. Karel Kramář, the leader of the Czech politics in the Vienna parliament, was the author of the Neo-Slavic program that he presented to the Slavic deputies in the parliament on November 27, 1907. Later Neo-Slavism emphasizing all-Slavic unity, spread also outside the Danubian monarchy. Kramář rejected Pan-Slavism with its Uvarov trinity—absolutism, orthodoxy and nationalism; instead, he built a new Neo-Slavic trinity: freedom, equality and brotherhood. The Cyrilomethodian idea, attacked by Masaryk, was reflected in the Neo-Slavic movement.

The Neo-Slavic agitation in the Austro-Hungarian monarchy, as well as outside of it, prepared the ground for the independence movement during World War I and the attainment of Czechoslovak independence in 1918. See Vladimir Sis, "Slovanství a zahraniční politika dra K. Kramáře" (Slavdom and the Foreign Politics of Dr. K. Kramar) in Vladimir Sis, ed., Dr. Karel Kramář *Život-Dílo-Práce, vůdce národa* [Dr. Karel Kramar. Life-Works-Labor, the Leader of the Nation](Prague 1936), pp. 153-190.

IV
STOJAN AND THE UNIONISTIC CONGRESSES
AT VELEHRAD

The Moravian Cyrilomethodian movement, led by Stojan, grew from provincial limits into magnificent Catholic Action. Holy Velehrad, cradle of Slavic faith and culture, in historical aspect developed into the spiritual foundation of the great and important idea of Slavic unity. Envisioning the reunion of churches and its practical attempt, Velehrad stepped into the international forum and doubtlessly revived a concern for unity in a wide circle of Slavs.

From previous events it is evident that a practical attempt toward Church unity was in Stojan's mind for a long time until its point of maturity. There was the uninterrupted build-up of Velehrad as a center of spiritual retreats for people of all walks of life, of regular congresses of Seminarians and theologians, as headquarters of the *Apostolate of SS. Cyril and Methodius* to be used as a tool toward the promotion of the idea of the Cyrilomethodian heritage in place of the historical Velehrad, as the background of its beginning and its glorious past.

The idea of the Unionistic Congresses was crystalizing in Stojan's mind from about 1900. The Secretary's book of the *Apostolate* records that definite preparations for the *First Unionistic Congress* were made in 1906 at a meeting attended by Father Stojan, Father Špaldák, S.J., and the Canon Antonín Podlaha. The distinguished zealots for Church reunion from Russia, Ukrainia, Bulgaria, Macedonia, France and Italy were invited. The program was well prepared and lodgings for foreign guests provided. The *First Unionistic Congress*[1] was held July 24-26, 1907 – under the protectorate of the then Metropolitan of Moravia, F.S. Bauer, Archbishop of Olomouc. It was attended by the Metropolitan Andrew Szeptycki, Archbishop of Lwov; Msgr. Mennini, Archbishop of Sophia; Rev. Aurelio Palmieri, O.S.B. of Rome, outstanding scholar for the Oriental Church, especially the Russian one; Father Jan Urban, S.J. of

Cracow; Univ. Professor Frant. Grivec of Lublana; director J. Njarady; Professor of Zagreb; Professor Česlav Sokolowski; Professor Svetozar Rittig of Diakov; Professor D. Doroziwskij of Lwov; Leonida Fjedorov; several substitutes of bishops; Professor Fr. Reyl of Hradec Králové; Archivist Frant. Snopek: Jesuit Father Špaldák and various clergy of all ranks and nationalities: Czechs, Slovaks, Russians, Ruthenians, Croats, Slovenes, Italians, Germans, diocesan or secular — together about 76.[2]

Stojan was fortunate to have among others a collaborator of great caliber. The true servant of God, Andrew Szeptyckyi (Czeptycki) (1865-1944) has such a distinct place in the history of the Ukraine[3] that he stands out as a history maker before men and God as well. One of the greatest metropolitans of the Ukrainian Church in Western Ukraine 1900-1944, he excelled as a great defender of the Ukrainian nation under the Polish rule in 1921-1939, as a defender of the Orthodox Church during the Polish persecution in 1938-39, and such a staunch defender of the Jews during the Nazi occupation in 1941-1944 that Rabbi Kahane said of him: "I do not believe in Saints, but if there were any Saints I am sure the greatest of them all is the Ukrainian Metropolitan Andrew Szeptycki."[4] He was right because the cause for his beatification is in process in Rome.[5] This in itself capsulizes his saintly profile in heroic performances in all the roles of his life, namely those of scholar, states man, Churchman and Ecumenist, and above all, of an apostle in and for a modern world.[6] Many of his ideas about a reunion of the Churches[7] and ecumenism and relations with the Orthodox East[8] have been forerunners of several movements that have been fulfilled by the Second Vatican Council. All this calls for our attention and reflection on one[9] who speaks meaningfully to our modern times.

The Metropolitan Szeptycki was elected President of the Congress, while Dr. Stojan, Rev. Špaldák and Rev. Černý were secretaries. Father Jan Urban, S.J. gave the first lecture: *"What can the Catholic Seminarians do for the Oriental Church?"* The discussion following was shared by Fr. Špaldák, Fr. Werner, P. Fjedorov and Metropolitan Szeptyckyi. The Second lecture: *About Catholic trends in Russian Theology* was presented by P.A. Palmieri, O.S.A. All present took part in the discussion. In the afternoon Professor Francis Grivec offered a third lecture: *Concerning the attempts toward Church Reunion.* The fourth lecture: *Concerning the epiclesis in the East-*

ern Liturgy was the contribution of Basilian Father Em. Haluscinskij, with follow-up discussion by Professor Sokolowski, p. Urban, p. Palmieri, prof. Rittig and Fjederov.

The second day, July 26th, the Congress began with a Pontifical Mass celebrated by Archbishop F.S. Bauer of Olomouc. Congress proceedings continued with greetings, speeches and resolutions. The principal speaker was the Archbishop of Sophia, Msgr. Mennini, who expressed satisfaction with the Congress. After him Metropolitan Szeptycki spoke about the dogmatic differences between the Catholic Church and the Oriental ones. Father Špaldák, S.J. offered a lecture *"How the Russians should act in regard to the Catholic Church."* In the discussion following Dr. Rittig recommended that the idea of Church reunion should be spread in the press among the intelligentia and the people.

In the afternoon, Archivist Dr. Francis Snopek of Kroměříž lectured *on the relation of SS. Cyril and Methodius to Rome,* to show their complete Roman Catholic orthodoxy. After that, discussion gravitated toward the practical accomodation of a mutual relationship between the Latins and the Orthodox. Among others, Father Škárek S.J. accepted a recommendation apropos the establishment of a Slovanic library in Velehrad. It was to hold all books and studies related to the reunion of the Church. Furthermore, it was agreed to recommend a study of Russian in all theological institutions. The Holy Father would be requested to elevate Velehrad's Church into a basilica.[10] The next Congress would take place in 1909. The Congress was truly informative and full of promise, as one can sense from its decisions:

1) All controversial questions were to be developed in great detail in articles published in the periodical, *Slavorum Litterae Theoogicae.*
2) Oriental theologians would be requested to explain their teaching in this journal.
3) Among western nations, writings about the need of Church reunion and its suitability for contemporary times would be spread.
4) Works of Easterners concerning their Church history and Oriental affairs should be translated into Slavic languages and Latin so that they would become better known and more appreciated.
5) New interpretations, made by others, should be published in Slavic languages so that the idea of Church unity could spread.

6) Works of the Western Church should be translated into Russian to prepare minds toward mutual understanding and respect.
7) Teachers of Eastern and Western Churches should discuss theological matters and further mutual correspondence.
8) Professors of Theological Western faculties should attend Russian faculties and vice versa.
9) The Eastern Church should be requested to establish an organization to support attempts toward Church reunion.
10) An organization to support Church unity must be established by each Slavic nation.
11) Works from the Slavic library at Velehrad should be sent to all zealots for Church unity gratis.
12) Institutions and benefactors in East and West should be requested to initiate rewards and distribute articles and works dealing with Church unity.
13) Chairs in western universities, especially Slavic ones, should be established to deal with the problems and critique of the Greek-Russian confession.
14) Learned Religious Orders and Congregations, especially the Jesuits and Benedictines, should be urged to dedicate themselves to the study of controversial theological problems.
15) Publishing houses and writers should give their works to the Velehrad library, and the western writers should donate their works to eastern theologians.
16) Old works dealing with Church unity should be republished.
17) In the forthcoming year minor congresses of the individual nations should be held in support of unionistic attempts.
18) Each second year a principal congress dealing with the problems of the Eastern Church could be held.[11]

These resolutions reveal how the search for Church unity through Unionistic Congresses was real, serious, and practical with a full anticipated knowledge of all difficulties along the way.[12] Behind all this idealistic planning there was, however, realism in expectations of Unionistic results.

On the occasion of the First Unionistic Congress, the annual meeting of the *Apostolate* was held. All Slavs were present: Russians from Petersburg, several Poles from Cracow, Ruthenians from Lwov, Slovaks, Serbians, Croates, Slovenes, Bulgarians and Rome were represented. At the same time a Congress of Seminarians was held July 29-30. To increase the effectiveness of all unionistic actions and ideas, Dr. Stojan established a new organization called *Cyrilometho-dian Press Organization*[13] in 1907 with headquarters in Velehrad. The statutes that were formulated by Stojan and his associates were later approved and authorized.

Despite the complete involvement of Stojan in these unionistic endeavors, he continued his efforts to gain young people's interest in spiritual renewal. The majority were recruited from farming families. On September 8, 1906, the first congress was held at Velehrad. A delegation led by the teacher, J.M. Kadičák, and by the deputy in the Vienna parliament Josef Šamalík, visited Stojan for his approval of the idea and requested his patronage, both of which he granted. Then the Council was established as a new organization, called *Omla-dina*[14] (Youth). It prospered under Stojan's sponsorship and became the avant garde of young people's involvement in Catholic causes in times dominated by liberals.

The Second Unionistic Congress - 1909

After two years of preparation by Stojan, professor Grivec of Lub-lana and Rev. Špaldák, S.J., of Velehrad, a Congress was held from July 31 to August 3, 1909 with marked success.[5] The need and importance of this Congress were commented on in *Církevní věstník,* of the Theological Academy in Petersburg, as overdue because of past negligence of East-West contacts, especially in theological aspects. The Metropolitan of the Uniates in Lwov, Archbishop Andrew Szeptycki, was again elected president; Stojan was secretary, and the Archbishop of Olomouc, Frant. S. Bauer, was the protector. The program was divided into four sections, namely (I) The Western Section (Palmieri, Gratieux, Franco) dealing with attempts supporting Church reunion; (II) The Eastern Section (Malcev, Goeken) dealing with a modification of the old controversial problem; (III) The General Theoretical Section (Palmieri, Goeken, Jugie) dealing with the support of the study of doctrines of both Churches; and (IV) The General Practical Section dealing with the resolution of all difficulties. For an introduction, there were two Latin lectures about Velehrad, with Rev. Vychodil lecturing on the origin and importance of Vele-hrad, and professor Nevěřil on Velehrad's antiquity.

Several guests from abroad took part in the Congress: Josef Bakšys of Innsbruck, Dr. Josef Bocian of Busk, Dr. Nic. Brinzeu of Petrohrad, Professor Bukowski of Widnau, Ing. Cehelskij of Innsbruck, Th. Czerwinski of Sosnovice, Basilian Father Davidiak of Lwov, Paul Denuzuk from Rome, Dr. Kam. Dočkal of Zagreb, Dr. Jan Dujmusic of Sarajevo, Dr. Julius Florian of Vienna, Professor A. Gratieux of Châlon sur Marne, France, Professor Frnt. Grivec of Lublana, Dr. Julius Hadžega of Užhorod, Dr. M. Jugie of Constantinople, Anast. Kalyš of Žolkiev, P. Kandiuk of Lawriv, Mat. Končar of Sarajevo, Lisovski Adam of Munich, Rev. Alesij Malcev, Orthodox Protereus of the Russian Embassy in Berlin, Josafat Malkevič of Innsbruck, Dr. Josef Marušič of Senj, Dr. Basil Masčui of Przemysl, Arn. Matzel of Chyrov, Basil Merenkov of Stanislav, Dr. Titus Myskovski of Lwov, Dr. Dionysius Njaradi of Zagreb, Aurelius Palmieri, O.S.A. of Cracow, P. Patrylo of Tarnopolis, Dr. Josef Pazman of Zagreb, Alf, Pirngruber of Munich, Dr. Svetozar Ritig of Diakov, S. Salaville of Istanbul, Dr. Ant. Straub of Innsbruck, Dr. Jiří Šuba of Užhorod, Dr. Basil Suciu of Balazov, Dr. Dan. Šajatovič of Holy Cross, and several others.

The Congress began July 31, 1909 in Slovanic Hall of Velehrad at 4 o'clock in the afternoon. The Protector, Archbishop of Olomouc, Dr. Francis Salesius Bauer, delivered the welcoming speech. The Congress was to continue the next day. At 6:00 p.m. of the same day the annual Conference of the *Apostolate* to act on organizational business was held. The President of the *Apostolate,* Canon Josef Pospíšíl, welcomed guests from abroad to make appropriate addresses. Then August 1, 1909 at 3:00 p.m., the President of the Congress, Metropolitan Szeptycki, explained the meaning and purpose of the Congress, emphasizing that the event was not political or missionary but rather a determined effort in a search of Church unity. He rejected also the suspicion that it was motivated by pan-Slavism, although the Slavs may have been conditioned to it. Then the Orthodox protoreus; Alexsij Malcev, who came to the Congress with the blessings of the Metropolitan Anthony of Petersburg, gave a lecture on the *Epiclesis after Consecration*[16] comparing the Catholic and Orthodox interpretations. In follow-up, Rev. Aurelio Palmieri, O.S.A., lectured on the *Doctrine Concerning the Immaculate Conception of the Virgin Mary* according to the theologians of Kiev, revealing that the Russians, especially those of Kiev, simultaneously with the Latins defended the Immaculate Conception in the first half of the XVIIIth century. Besides those of Kiev, Bishop Dimitrij of Rostov (+1709), a canonized Russian saint, taught this doctrine and steadfastly adhered to it despite the fact that he was reprimanded for it by the Moscow Patriarch Joachim. After him the Assumptionist Father M. Jugie, a native of France but working then in Istanbul, presented a dissertation: *About the Defense of the Immaculate Conception by the Byzantine Theologians after the Schism.*

After these lectures, the Theoretical Section, composed of theologians and professors, was convoked and Professor Grivec introduced a discussion about the establishment of the Cyrilomethodian Academy. This was to be a scientific institution with three sections: 1) section in support of theological studies in Catholic Slavic countries; 2) an international section for Oriental affairs; and 3) the historic-Slavic section dealing with historical affairs of Slavic nations. Headquarters would be in Velehrad, with adjacent centers in places like Prague, Lwov, etc. The academy would begin with the year 1910, in memory of 1025 years since the death of St. Methodius. There was unanimous agreement on this. A Provisional Council was established, and the following were elected its members: Dr. Francis Grivec, Rev. V. Špaldák, S.J., and Rev. Aurelius Palmieri, O.S.A., with the cooperation of others, to prepare the Statutes. This institution proved later to be a very effective vehicle for the promotion of Church unity.

On August 2 the following lectures were given: Dr. Antonin Straub, Professor of Kalksburg, *On Church Unity and Its Principles;* Abbé Gratieux, Professor of Châlon sur Marne, France, spoke on *The Development of the Liturgical Studies;* Francis Snopek, *About the Disciples of St. Methodius and Their Relations to Rome*; and Professor Al. Bukowski of Widnau, on *The Penitential Practices in Eastern and Western Churches.* In the afternoon of the same day Dr. Svetozar Ritig, Professor of Diakov, lectured about *The Relationship of Vladimir Solojev to Croatians*; Professor Zdziechowski of the Jaggelonian University of Cracow on *What the Literate Russia Can Offer in Matters of Faith to Western Nations*; and Professor Al. Jacimirsky of the University of Petersburg on *Which Individual Problems and Which Proposals Should Be Deliberated.*

On August 3 the Congress continued with the following lectures: Dr. Mat. Končar, S.J. Professor of Sarajevo, *Concerning the Difficulties Involved in the Reunion of the Oriental and Western Churches and How These Progressed*; in the afternoon the Assumptionist Father Severin Salaville of Istanbul discoursed on *The Doctrine of the Studites apropos the Primacy of the Roman Pontiff.* After these presentations, proposals and delegates were accepted at the closing of the Congress. Members for the constituting Council of the Velehrad Academy were elected and the decision was made that *Litterae Slavorum Theologicae* would be published and subsidized by it.

The President of the Congress, Archbishop Szeptycky concluded the Congress with an address, and Stojan expressed gratitude to him for his splendid conduct of the Congress.[17] Great interest was aroused in Rome, Petersburg, Moscow, Istanbul, Sophia and elsewhere. Simultaneously in political circles in Vienna, doubts about the Panslavic tendencies of the Congress were expressed. Stojan, as delegate of the Parliament, was requested to give an explanation of this to the Ministry of Foreign Affairs, and he did so. The fact was that the Slavs felt at home with the Cyrilomethodian idea with its center in Velehrad, as can be evidenced by the visit of the Bulgarian King Ferdinand with his son Boris on June 9, 1909, just on the eve of the Congress. The King expressed appropriate sentiments: "We come to the tomb of St. Methodius and to the see of our common Slavic Apostles, in order that a renovated Bulgarian Kingdom might restore its contact with the Cyrilomethodian Velehrad, as is the wish of all Bulgarian people."[18] This certainly reflects the glorious past of the followers of St. Methodius, who once found their refuge in Bulgaria. Needless to say, the King was not only an admirer of the great Bishop Strossmayer, but greatly appreciated the wisdom of Pope Leo XIII for taking a special interest in the Slavs.

Besides the mostly positive acceptance of the importance of Velehrad and its unionistic efforts, there were hostile voices of liberals who undermined unionism as a politically explosive game of the abuse of religion for Church politics.[19] In this regard one should not forget liberalism had the upper hand in human thought by the end of the XIX and the beginning of the XX centuries. Stojan was well prepared and knew how to counteract it. In this, he and all unionistic zealots had to proceed carefully and prudently to avoid sharp criticism from liberal circles with great influence in government.

These increasing tensions of conflicting parties and ideologies of the times caused the establishment of a new journal, called the *Apostolate of Sts. Cyril and Methodius* under the Protection of the

Blessed Virgin Mary. Rev. Adolf Jašek, catechist in Kroměříž was initiator of this idea, which was actualized at the meeting of the Supreme Council of the *Apostolate* on Jan. 17, 1910. Father Stojan and Rev. Ad, Jašek became the editors. The main purpose was to publish popular articles for the information of the faithful. The placement of this journal under Marian patronage was utilizing the traditional popular Marian devotion.[20] In this it succeeded. Such a defense of the faith and the importance of religion in the life of a nation was apparent when the official organization of the liberal and socialistic teachers in their assemblies in Kroměříž and Uherské Hradiště published in 1910 its *manifesto* for the banning of religion from all schools. A direct confrontation with these liberal teachers occurred at the meeting of the Conference of the *Apostolate*[21] held July 30-31, 1910 at Velehrad, where a systematic defense of Catholics was formulated.

To insure the effectiveness of this Catholic defense, a decision from the Second Unionistic Congress (1909) to establish a scholarly journal was made at the meeting of the *Apostolate* held on August 1, 1910. The idea was to establish a supporting institution called *Academia Velehradensis*. The constitution[22] of the academia was finally formulated and approved under the Administrative Council composed of Dr. Antonin C. Stojan, Professor Frantisek Grivec of Lublana, Jesuit Father Adolf Špaldák of Prague, Dr. Josef Bocian of Lwov, and Father Adolf Jašek, catechist in Kroměříž. The by-laws of this institution had to be greatly modified before they were finally approved by the Ministry of the Interior in its decree #18-178 of May 18, 1910. Thus Stojan's systematic challenge to all opposition against unionism is a visible confirmation of his realistic evaluation of the times with problems with which he was well acquainted.

The Third Unionistic Congress – 1911

Interest in the reunion of Churches was greatly aroused thanks to the two previous Congresses. Consequently a *Third Unionistic Congress*[23] was called for July 26-29, 1911. In the East, even the liberal Russian critic of religious affairs, Menšikov, wrote a study about the need of Church reunion in the journal, *Novoje Vremia*. The Orthodox Metropolitan of Bayruth, Gersasimos, in agreement with the Metropolitan of Antioch, wrote a pastoral letter to all Orthodox communities making an urgent call for the restoration of ancient unity, based on the healthy and permanent foundations of Apostolic doctrine and tradition. In the west, the pastoral care of Pope St. Pius X (1903-1914)[24] continued faithfully in the steps of Leo XIII, stressing the urgency of Church reunion. The new journals like *Slavorum Litterae Theologicae* (from 1911), *Rome et l'Oriente,* published by the Basilian monk of Grotto Ferrata near Rome, the *Unions-Stimmen* in Germany, and others, considerably advanced the unionistic interest, as journals like *Bessarione, Echos d'orient* and others did in the East.

Among new participants were: the Uniate Bishop and Apostolic Vicar of Soluň, the Bulgarian Bishop Epifan Šanov, Arsenius Pellerini, Abbot of the celebrated monastery Grotta Ferrata near Rome, Pl. de Meester of Rome, Benedictine of the Belgian Congregation, a celebrated scholar on the Greek rites and a professor of Biblical studies. These joined old participants like Aurelio Palmieri, Dr. Francis Grivec, Dr. Josef Bocian, P.M. Jugie, Federov and others. After the experiences of the previous Congresses, which proved that long scholarly lectures were tiresome and weakened interest, organizers of this third Congress decided on short lectures with more sessions in the individual sections to capture interest. First, the Congress of the seminarians and university students was held before the Unionistic Congress to foster the idea of unionism in young people. The Jesuit Father A. Jemelka had an inspirational talk about *Priestly Activity in the Organizations* and seminarian Francis Cinek spoke on *The Seminarian and the Blessed Eucharist.* The seminarians surprised Stojan on the occasion of his 60th birthday by naming him an honorary member of the *Literary Union of the Seminarians of Olomouc.* They gave him an appropriate certificate. The occasion was solemnized by the arrival of Archbishop Frantisek Sal. Bauer of Olomouc, who was enthusiastically welcomed by the seminarians. Greatly missed was the Uniate Metropolitan of Lwov, Andrew Szeptyckyi, who was then very ill in a London hospital. He sent a telegram to the Congress. Also missing was the Russian Orthodox, for neither Malcev nor Goeken was able to come, but a lecture was delivered by Fedorov.

The theological faculties of Olomouc and of Prague and of all seminaries in Bohemia and Moravia were present; from non-Slavic nations, mainly Italians, Germans and Frenchmen attended, and from Slavic nations mostly Bulgarians and Ruthenians were represented The number of participants exceeded several hundred. The Congress be-

gan at 3 o'clock in the afternoon of July 26 at the Slovanic Hall
with an address by Stojan, who in his introduction stressed that any
kind of political Panslavism or any form of Modernism was to be
excluded from all proceedings. Subsequently Archbishop Bauer of
Olomouc was elected protector of the Congress, with two honorary
presidents, namely Bishop Šanov of Soluň and the Metropolitan
Szeptycky of Lwov, while Stojan was elected as the actual president,
and Špaldák, Fedorov and Jašek as secretaries. Then a decision was
proposed and approved that only two sections would be held,
(a) the *Theoretical One* presided over by Palmieri, and (b) the
Practical One presided over by Stojan.

In the *theoretical Section* Palmieri introduced discussion concerning use of Protestant polemics at certain times by the Orthodox
against the Catholics. Fedorov insisted that Latin be used in Russian
seminaries, but this idea was abandoned after the Petersburg Synod.
Afterwards Protestant influence increased, especially in polemics
against Catholics. The Orthodox should be made aware that they
were misled by this. A very interesting discussion was carried on by
Palmieri, Fedorov, Jugie and Herbigny. The latter especially affirmed
that the Greek theologians were more Protestant than the Russians.
In the evening of the same day, in honor of the Protector of the
Congress, Archbishop Bauer and Bishop Šanov of Soluň, a serenade
was prepared, accompanied by the solemn illumination of Velehrad
decorated with the flags of national, ecclesiastical and Slavic colors.
Near the chapel "Cyrilka" was the inscription: "Welcome, Protectors
and all Guests of the Third Unionistic Congress."

The next day, July 28th, the number of participants increased. In
the early morning at 6 o'clock there was a Pontifical Mass by Archbishop Bauer and the Congress reconvened at 9 a.m. Rev. P. Jugie
of Istanbul spoke on "Prayer for Church Union;" Dr. Šimrák of
Zagreb lectured on "The Difficulties in the Reunion of Churches in
the Croatian-Slovene Kingdom." There was a lively follow-up discussion. After these lectures, social affairs like the reading of telegrams and presentation of greeting to celebrated guests were in order.
In the afternoon Stojan addressed the Protector of the Congress for
his kindness in chairing it and expressed gratitude at the departure
of Bishop Bauer.

The *Practical Section* under Stojan's sponsorship initiated much
discussion. Dr. Dorožinskij observed that the Russian Orthodox were

not present. If the Russians did not take part in these Congresses, he averred that other autocephalous Oriental Churches should be invited, thus giving a larger basis to the Congresses. For this purpose all conditions for the possible reunion of Churches should be detailed and information sent to all Oriental Churches. Stojan solicited answers as a basis for the program of the Congress. After much discussion the participants accepted the proposals. The next day, July 29, Iguman Hristov lectured on the theme: "The Bulgarian Monk Panteleimon and a Relation between Frequent Holy Communion and the Reunion of Churches." Dr. Hadžega of Uzhorod spoke on "The Thought of Orthodox Theologians and That of St. John Hieronymous Concerning the Primacy of Peter." Dr. Fedorov discussed the question of Russian saints with a lively follow-up session carried on by Rev. Křikava, Jugie, Palmieri, Kmit, Schneider, Herbigny, Dostál and other scholars. The Congress President, Stojan, introduced a preposal that preparations be initiated for another Congress to be held in 1913, with well prepared questions on controversial subjects to be sent to all interested parties, and their advice for solutions encouraged. The following resolutions of the Third Unionistic Congress were made:

1) Results of unionistic efforts were to be collected together with views of how the reunion of Churches could be carried out. This material should be sent to individual Eastern Churches, and their views solicited in return.

2) The order should be established in which proposals would be dealt with in the Congress — earlier or later.

3) Publications about Unionistic Congresses would be translated into Russian. Books which described the views and resolutions of the Congresses would be published and distributed.

4) The Sacred Heart devotion was to be spread as much as possible with the expressed recommendation that all be one.

5) Priests favoring the reunion of Churches should offer Holy Mass at least once a month for that intention, and the faithful should offer Holy Communion for the same intention.

6) Not only Latin Catholics but also Westerners would be requested to pray for the reunion of both Churches.

7) The Eastern seminarians would be encouraged to study with Catholic theological faculties.

The Congress ended[25] after these resolutions were approved.

Simultaneously the convention of the *Apostolate* and of the *Velehrad Academy* were held. The festive convention of the *Apostolate*[26] was held Saturday, July 29, 1911, the closing day of the Congress, with a procession of members and of the organization of Catholic Youth, *Omladina.* The welcome address was given by Jesuit Father Stryhal. Stojan was the spirit of the event. The convention continued the next day, Sunday, when the official greetings of foreign guests and speeches of all functionaries of the *Apostolate* were made. The basic tone of this convention was its emphasis on the importance of the *Apostolate* for a successful realization of the reunion of the Churches.

Stojan did not miss any opportunity to stress the vital issue of Church unity. Thus he spoke at the Fourth Catholic Convention in Olomouc in 1911 on the topic: "Czechs and Unionistic Efforts." He also held a convention of the *Apostolate* at Velehrad on July 26-27, 1912, presided over by the famous Professor Francis Kordač of Charles IV University in Prague, who spoke on the *Goals of Theology in Modern Society,* while Professor Richard Spaček stressed the *Harmony of Faith and Science.* The convention closed with a service devoted to the great Apostles of the Slavs, Sts. Cyril and Methodius.

Stojan as a practical man also made every effort to make sure that facilities of Velehrad were provided and adequate for all activities. He constituted an organization, called the *Velehrad Association* to serve this purpose. Already established in 1902 on the initiative of Stojan and Jesuit Father Cibulka, this Association had as its goal the material welfare of Velehrad. Stojan was spiritually oriented but he was practical as well, for he knew that by applying the theological dictum: *Gratia supponit naturam,* a spiritual success is greatly conditioned by the material one. In other words, if the spiritual Velehrad was to prosper, the material Velehrad, i.e., the Church, buildings, pilgrim houses, etc. must be in order. Stojan made sure that both fully coincided. Several projects materialized through this *Velehrad Association,* making Velehrad an adequate and fitting center for the Cyrilomethodian Apostolates, the most important of which were:

1)   The idea of a pilgrim house was maturing every year.
2)   Spiritual retreats would be extended to all segments of the faithful, namely: workers, farmers, youth, women, married and

single, while those for teachers, students, professors and other intelligentia were well taken care of.

3) Bus transportation from Uherské Hradiště to Velehrad would be provided.

4) The Velehrad Museum was to hold all memorabilia.

5) The excavations in testimony of Velehrad's glorious past were to be encouraged and continued, as they were initiated by Professor A. Nevěřil of Uherské Hradiště.

6) The idea of a new Catholic gymnasium to insure a future generation of promoters of the Cyrilomethodian heritage should materialize.

Every year all these and other concerns of urgent interest were placed on the program and reviewed at the annual convention of the *Velehrad Association* under the zealous leadership of Stojan. Mr. Švec was a spiritual agent who succeeded in keeping membership at a high level, reaching over 13,100 in 1913. In time, all projects mentioned were fully or partially realized, according to the pace of financial support which was with great effort adequately provided by the *Velehrad Association,* whose Council members were elected. Others were asked to help according to the urgency of pertinent projects. The importance and vitality of this supporting organization can be seen in the constantly increasing material and spiritual welfare of Velehrad through the years.

The Cyrilomethodian Jubilee Year of 1913

To increase the significance of Velehrad, Stojan took advantage of every pertinent jubilee to promote it. Thus in 1913 he felt that the 1050th anniversary of the arrival of the Apostles of the Slavs, together with that of the 50th one of the Cyrilomethodian memorable year of 1863, should be celebrated adequately. *The Apostolate of Sts. Cyril and Methodius* held four meetings under Stojan's leadership, simultaneously with the *Velehrad Association* and the *Velehrad Academy,* to coordinate preparations for the jubilee. An added boon to Velehrad was provided by new electrical illumination of the Church, Slovanic Square, monastery, castle and all adjacent compounds. A special sculpture entitled: "A Tribute of Slavs to Pope Leo XIII" with a representation of him seated on the Papal throne, handing his encyclical to representatives of Slavs, was projected by

Stojan at a cost of 40,000 crowns, to be built in the Slovanic Square. Unfortunately this project never materialized, but its model is preserved in the Stojan museum in the major seminary of Olomouc. It definitely reveals the magnanimity of Stojan's soul and his feeling for Slavic solidarity, which was so distinctly expressed in his proclamation to all Cyrilomethodian devotees.[27]

The jubilee festivities were divided into several parts, with three memorial dates: 1) the anniversary of the death of St. Cyril, February 14; 2) the memorial of the death of St. Methodius, commemorated on April 6, and 3) the feast of Sts. Cyril and Methodius on July 5th, with many additional pilgrimages organized by certain districts of the land. Each of these solemnities drew great crowds of People, even some from abroad.

Stojan, in an attempt to popularize these Velehrad festivities, organized a special pilgrimage of Catholic farmers, July 6, 1913. On this occasion, not only a convention but a huge procession was held from the chapel of *Cyrilka* to the main Church. At the same time, the Convention of the Cyrilomethodian *Velehrad Association* was held at Velehrad. After the review of all activities and the program of this organization, Stojan singled out the need for a retreat house as urgent. As the organization then had about 13,000 members, Stojan recommended that each member should give a donation of one crown to insure materialization of the overdue and long-awaited project. During the debate, several distinguished visitors expressed support and delivered greetings.

Although originally planned for 1913, the Fourth Unionistic Congress could not be held because of the political situation in the Balkan region. Relationships with the Austrian Government in Vienna had greatly deteriorated. In spite of this, the Unionistic Conferences continued to be held to make the Unionistic efforts more effective and more acceptable among all Slavic nations. All festivities held in this and subsequent years tended to promote this cause, so sacred to Stojan — that is, Church unity.

NOTES

1. *Acta I. Conventus Velehradensis* Theologorum commercil studiorum inter occidentem et orientem cupidorum. (Prague, 1908); cf. reviews by J. Tumpach, *ČKD* (1908) 264.

2. Frantisek Cinek, *Arcibiskup Dr. Antonín Cyril Stojan* (Olomouc, 1933) 553-554.

3. Michael Hrushevsky, *A History of Ukraine* (Yale Univ. Press, New Haven, 1941) pp. 96-122 and *passim;* cf. D. Doroshenko, *History of the Ukraine* (Edmonton, 1939); cf. S. Konenenko, *Ukraine and Russia* (Milwaukee, 1958); B. Krupnyckyj. *Geschichte der Ukraine* (Leipzig, 1939); W. Allen, *The Ukraine: A History* (Cambridge, 1940); cf. *Ukraine,* A Concise Encyclopedia, 2 vols. (Toronto, 1963)' cf. *La Chiesa del Silenzio Guarda a Roma* (Rome, 1955); cf. J. Madey, *Kirche zwischen Ost und West* (Múnich, 1969); cf. idem. *Le Patriarchat Ukrainien* (Rome, 1971); cf. J. Mirchuk, *Ukraine and Its People* (Munich, 1949); cf. *Monumenta Ukrainae Historica,* 10 vols. (Rome, 1964-70); cf. I. Nahayewsky, *History of the Modern Ukrainian State,* 1917-1923 (Munich, 1966); cf. G. Prokoptschuk, *Der Metropolit* (Munich, 1967); cf. A. Welykyj, *Documenta Romana Historiam ecclesiae in terris Ukrainae et Biolorussiae spectantia,* 35 vols. (Rome, 1953-1972); cf. idem, *From the Annals of Christian Ukraine,* 3 vols. (Rome, 1968); cf. *White Book on the Religious Persecution in Ukraine* (Rome,1953); cf. Edward Winter, *Byzanz und Rome in Kampf um die Ukraine* (1955-1959) (Prague, 1944); cf. Dennis J. Dunn, *"Stalinism and the Catholic Church during the Era of World War II." The Catholic Historical Review* LIX (1973) pp. 404-428.

4. *Ukraine–A Christian Nation* (Melbourne, Australia Prosvita, 1973) p. 6

5. *The Voice of the Church* (Chicago II St. Procopius III no. 3) (June, 1959).

6. Josef Drozd "Andreas Szeptycky metropolita Leopoliensis, praeses Academiae Velehradensis 1910-1939" *Acta Academiae Velehradensis* XVIII (Olomouc 1947) pp. 92-102.

7. Ludvik Nemec, "The Ruthenian Uniate Church in its historical perspective," *Church History* 37 no. 4 (1968) pp. 1-25.

8. B. Paneyko, "Galicia and the Polish-Ukranian Problem," *Slavonic Review* IX (1931) pp. 567-587; cf. John S. Reshetar, *The Ukrainian Revolution, 1917-1920. A Study in Nationalism* (Princeton Univ. 1952); cf. idem, "Ukrainian Nationalism and the Orthodox Church" *The American Slavic and East European Review,* X (1951) 38-49. cf. Eduard Winter, *"Der Kampf der ecclesia ruthena* gegen den Rituswechsel," *Festschrift Eichman* (Paderborn, 1940), *passim.*

9. Cyrille Korolevsky, *Métropolite André Szeptyckji,* 1885-1944 (Rome, 1964) is a detailed biography. The collected works of a metropolitan Andreas Szeptycky are being published by the Redemptorist Fathers in Redeemer's *Voice Press* in Yorkton Sask., Canada. See *Bibliotheca Logos* vol. XXX in 1969 or vol. XV of *Opera Theologicae Societatis Scientificae Ucrainorum* (Toronto 1965).

10. *Hlas* no. 173 of July 28, 1907.
11. This is taken from *Hlas* no. 173 of July 28, 1907.
12. *Rozkvět* no. 4 of August 25, 1907.
13. Cinek, *op.cit.*, 562-563.
14. "Zakladatel a protektor Omladiny" (Founder and Protector of Youth) in Cinek, *op.cit.*, 564-570; see also "Deset let Práce a činnosti," *Ročenka Sdružení venkovské omladiny na Moravě, ve Slezsku a Dolních Rakousích* (Brno, 1917), 49 ff.
15. *Acta II. Conventus Velehradensis* (Prague, 1910).
16. *Cerkovnyj Věstník* (1909) of August 1, 1090 characterized this lecture as too much propaganda and didn't need polemics − Cinek, *op.cit.*, 658.
17. *Hlas* nos. 175 and 176 of August 3 and 4, 1909.
18. Cinek, *op.cit.*, 670.
19. *Lidové noviny* no. 216 of August 8, 1909.
20. Ludvik Nemec, *Our Lady of Hostyn, Queen in the Marian Garden of the Czech, Moravian, Silesian and Slovak Madonnas* (New York, 1981), *passim.*
21. *Našinec* no. 197 of August 30, 1910.
22. By-laws of the *Academia Velehradensis* (Academy of Velehrad) are in F. Cinek, *op.cit.*, pp. 680-682.
23. *Acta III, Conventus Velehradensis* Prague: 1912. See Adolf Jašek, "Třetí unionistický sjezd na Velehradě" (The Third Unionistic Congress at Velehrad), *Apoštolát sv. Cyrila a Metoda* no. 7 of 1911.
24. Raffaelo Merry del Val, *Memoirs of Pope Pius X* (London, 1939); Igino Giordani, *Pius X, A Country Priest* (Milwaukee, 1954); Katherine Burton, *The Great Mantle*, (New York, 1950).
25. *Acta III, Conventus Velehradensis* (Prague, 1912), *passim.*
26. *Apoštolát sv. Cyrila a Metoda* nos. 8-9 of 1911.
27. This was published in the *Apoštolát sv. Cyrila a Metoda* no. 1 of 1913.

V

STOJAN, THE THEOLOGIAN, THE CHURCHMAN
AND THE PUBLIC SERVANT

Stojan, the Theologian

Amazingly, Stojan with all his activities continued to study theology for spiritual motivation to increase the apostolic effectiveness of his priesthood rather than for the career's potential. He was too much a priest and too modest to proceed with ambitions to increase his personal prestige or position. This was totally alien to him. To acquire the doctoral degree of theology was not an easy task then. After graduation from the school of theology, the candidate had to complete four examinations called rigorosa: 1) the first *rigorosum* was from Moral and Pastoral Theology which Stojan fulfilled November 20, 1888; 2) the second from Fundamental and Dogmatic Theology which he made April 23, 1889; 3) the third was Church History and Canon Law which he completed November 14, 1889; 4) the fourth was Biblical Studies with Oriental Languages which were accomplished March 12, 1896. After these oral examinations, the candidate had to present and defend a doctoral dissertation. Stojan's thesis was: "Concerning the unity of the Slavic nations and Church reunion with the Catholic Church according to the intentions of the Holy Father, Leo XIII."[1] This was a rather practical topic close to the heart of Stojan who was a unionistic zealot. The dissertation was accepted June 27, 1896 and the doctoral graduation was set by the dean of the faculty for July 9, 1896 at 12 o'clock in the Hall of the School of Theology. Attendance of people from all walks of life was so huge that there was not enough space. It was really a graduation "sub auspiciis populi."[2] The great joy evinced over Stojan's scholarly achievement was an indication of his popularity among the people. The Dean of the Faculty, Dr. Francis Janiš, presided; pro-dean, Dr. Karel Wisnar and Dr. Jan Kubíček, with all professors acted as promoters on this solemn occasion. Seminarians sang in solemn choir. A testimonial dinner was served in the rooms of *Česká Beseda*

in the National House in Olomouc. During dinner about 200 telegrams arrived from all parts of the land – another sign of Stojan's
great popularity. From all came a message so appropriately expressed
by Dr. Wisnar, Superior of the Seminary, who toasted the graduate
with these words: "Let the new Doctor Stojan remain the same
Father Stojan he has always been to us!" If one wonders why Stojan
wanted to obtain a doctoral degree, the story goes that Stojan decided to study for it after his humiliating experience as a member of
Příbor's delegation in the matter of the Czech gymnasium with the
matter of the Czech gymnasium with the Minister Gautsch in Vienna.[3]
The latter turned his back to him, letting him know that he was a
nobody when Stojan presented himself as a mere chaplain, while
others boasted of their prestigious titles. Whatever it was, it doesn't
matter because Stojan was as humble after his doctorate as before
and never changed his ways with the people. For him humility was
the foremost natural virtue.

While Stojan was always more a practical man than a scholar, he
did not neglect to advance himself professionally. Due to his humility he never claimed to be a professional scholar and theologian, but
proved himself always very efficient as a working theologian in several
areas of his ministry – in fact he excelled in applying theology and
all social sciences to all his priestly services so skillfully that they were
not only greatly appreciated but accepted as truly professional ones.
Contrary to some misconceptions about Stojan's intellectual abilities,
it should be said furthermore that he distinguished himself as an expert in pastoral and sacramental theology; well versed in historical
and political theology; a great Mariologist, and excelled as a champion
in ecumenical theology, by which he became a zealot of Church unity
long before ecumenism became a fashionable issue of modern times.

Especially as a champion of Church unity did Stojan bring his best
to this cause so that his prominence was felt in all high academic circles and his methods and ways were accepted as those of high scientific value for any intellectual. It was a fact that Stojan was among
the first initiators of unionistic endeavors, in behalf of which he knew
not only how to assemble the best minds concerned about this problem, but to create and use the best organizational media to promote
them. This is perhaps the most telling evidence for Stojan's high level
scientific grasp in ecumenical theology. However, Stojan did not try
to propose original ideas in everything. Rather, he took every good

idea, no matter where it came from; and to transform the idea into fact, he gave it the form of an organization, association or society, and in a Cyrilo-Methodian manner he gave it life. An example of this is a significant Cyrilo-Methodian project, the *Velehrad Academy* (Academia Velehradensis). The idea of this Academy was conceived by Professor Frank Grivec, A Slovenian and a compatriot of Bishop Slomšek. The Academy was founded October 1, 1910. Its by-laws were compiled by Frank Grivec, Špaldák, a Czech Jesuit, and Aurelius Palmieri, a Roman Augustinian. Jan Šrámek contributed practical suggestions for the by-laws. But next to Grivec, the chief architect of this learned society was A.C. Stojan, not only as chairman of the preparatory committee of the *Academia Velehradensis,* but also as the moving, coordinating and appeasing force, although he did leave the scientific questions to experts. The organizational structure of the Velehrad Academy was also implemented by Stojan. He delivered the key-note address at the inaugural convocation of the Velehrad Academy.

The idea of the Academy harmonized with Stojan's goal of engaging all of the Czech and Slovak intellectuals in unionistic activity. This idea struck a sympathetic chord, not only on the "scientific" strings in his personality, but also on the strings of his interest in the heritage of Constantine (St. Cyril), leading philosopher of his time and a teacher of the Slavs.[4] The outstanding quality of St. Cyril's work in Great Moravia was an argument in favor of the Slavonic language in the liturgy.

This, incidentally, was in Stojan's mind as he indicated the purposes of the newly founded Academy; its very name and location was to highlight the significance of its Cyrilo-Methodian role in the world of learning, and to gain the reconciliation and cooperation of the separated (and at that time very hostile) Slav brethen.

The apostolate of the pen also came into its own, an apostolate which Stojan liked to stress, and which he again extolled at the inaugural convocation: "The first Christians spread the faith in two ways. by a holy life and by written defense – apologetics... The Academy is to work for union by means of the written word. I compare a schism to quarreling or divorced people... And we must begin a dialogue with them in our writings. Perhaps this will mean controversies, but soon enough there will be hope that we shall begin conversations and further negotiations."[5]

The relationship between the *Apostolate of Sts. Cyril and Methodius* and the *Velehrad Academy* was to be very close, friendly collaboration toward a single goal; achieving unity of faith, which Stojan had in mind constantly: "All of us have an ardent desire that unity be realized, for the beneficial results of union in every regard are constantly in our mind."[6]

The *Apostolate* was a society which was to influence the separated brethren "by means of a good life and especially by means of effective love." The *Academy* was an institution, the purpose of which was to centralize the means, aids, but above all, experts. It was to be an institution of learning, which was inspired by the success of the first two unionistic congresses of 1907 and 1909.

An excellent literary predecessor of the Academy was the supplement to the *Časopis Katolického Duchovenstva*[7] (Catholic Clergy Review), a Czech theological journal. The supplement carried the title *Slavica* but in 1905 the title was changed to *Slavorum Litterae Theologicae*. After the *Velehrad Academy* was founded, this supplement became the *Acta Academiae Velehradensis* (1911). About the same time, a popular magazine began publication, the *Apoštolát Sv. Cyrila a Metoděje pod Ochranou Blah. Panny Marie* (The Apostolate of Sts. Cyril and Methodius under the patronage of the Blessed Virgin Mary). This publication began in the year 1910, first in Kroměříž, then in Olomouc. The purposes of the *Apostolate* were also served by the *Velehradský Věstník* (The Velehrad Journal) published in Prague in 1909.

The Velehrad Academy developed, and the prospects were truly promising; it served as a clearinghouse for scholars interested in church unity, prepared the agenda for the unionistic congresses and helped organize them, undertook research and published works concerning Cyrilo-Methodian questions. A particularly eminent co-worker on the plans and in the activities of the Academy from its very beginnings was Canon Antonín Podlaha (later Auxiliary Bishop of Prague), who was a kind of "scientific" counterpart to the "popular" Stojan.

Just as the *Apostolate of Sts. Cyril and Methodius* became the leading Slav missionary society, so also the *Velehrad Academy* gradually worked its way to the position of being the foremost vehicle for the unity movement among the Slavs in the world of learning. How well the *Velehrad Academy* realized its purpose, which it defined in the by-laws – to foster and support scholarly studies of the Eastern Church (i.e., the Greek-Slavonic) – is evident in the 19 volumes of the *Acta Academiae Velehradensis*. In addition, it produced 7 volumes of the *Acta Conventus Velehradensis,* which was published under the sponsorship of the Archbishop of Olomouc. The collection called *Opera Academiae Velehradensis* contains a monumental work, a photographic facsimile of the *Olomouc Bible* of 1417, Tom. I.

Three sections were formed in the Velehrad Academy: (1) The Cyrilo-Methodian section, concerned with the life and work of Sts. Cyril and Methodius as well as the history of Velehrad, (2) The Eastern section in the proper sense of the term, and (3) The Western Section, which had as its purpose the fostering and publishing of theological studies for the benefit of Slav Catholics of the Roman Rite.[9]

After the *Apostolate,* the *Velehrad Academy* was Stojan's great pride and joy. As Archbishop of Olomouc, he was its vice-chairman. The chairmanship was left to Prince Andrew Szeptyckyi, the scholarly uniate Metropolitan of Lwov. The success of the *Velehrad Academy* made up for Stojan's two projects which failed to materialize, that is, the proposed Cyrilo-Methodian library at Velehrad, and the proposed Cyrilo-Methodian university in Moravia. This university was Stojan's idea. He spoke about it as early as 1892, during the seminarians' pilgrimage to Velehrad. He proposed it publicly in 1894 and received full approval for it from the new metropolitan, Theodor Kohn. Stojan offered the services of his *Apostolate of Sts. Cyril and Methodius,* which was to take upon itself the entire project. The plan was presented to the Ministry of Education, and even a considerable amount was received by way of contributions in support of the project. "The project is big," Stojan wrote enthusiastically in the book issued by the *Apostolate* as a subscription premium, "Fill your hands and make an offering to the Lord. O God, preserve and arouse good will! Holy Virgin Mary, Sts. Cyril and Methodius, intercede for us!"[10]

It is evident that, in this case, Stojan was influenced by events in other countries, where the idea of Catholic universities was being put into practice,[11] but Austria, suffering from a chronic internal crisis, was not ripe for such a thing. The Czech "referent" in the Ministry of Education in Vienna, Antonín Rezek, gave Stojan advice (which was to be an explanation, but really was an excuse): the university ought to be founded at a later time, if there proves to be a sufficient number of priests competent to serve as faculty members, who could then make sure that the university retains a Catholic character. Therefore, younger clergy ought to be encouraged to go into higher studies and scientific activity.[12]

The influence of Stojan's Cyrilo-Methodianism on Catholic intellectuals, constantly growing in numbers, became so strong that within a short time the following proposition was made: To reconstitute the scientific section of the prospering *Akademie Křesťanská* (Christian Academy) in Prague, founded in 1880, as a center of all Catholic cultural work under the name of *Společnost Sv. Cyrila a Metoděje* (Sts. Cyril and Methodius Association). In April, 1917, *the Skupina Společnosti Sv. Cyrila a Metoděje* (Chapter of the Sts. Cyril and Methodius Association) was organized in Olomouc. This Chapter published the *Věstník Společnosti Sv. Cyrila a Metoděje* (Journal of the Sts. Cyril and Methodius Association) but it never undertook any other project. However, the research on Cyrilo-Methodian questions was continued after 1918 by the Velehrad Academy.

One of Stojan's schoolmates, František Snopek, became an authority on Sts. Cyril and Methodius.[13] He refuted the biased opinions published by Alexander Brückner,[14] a Slavicist of Berlin, and defended the orthodoxy and honesty of the two Salonika brothers successfully, though not without difficulties due to the inadequacy of Cyrilo-Methodian research up to that date.

Frank Grivec contributed books and articles on the conditions of the contemporary Eastern Orthodox Church and on the Byzantine concepts of ecclesiastical primacy.[15] Grivec also defended the orthodoxy of St. Cyril from a theological viewpoint. Next to this Cyrilo-Methodian theologian, stands Josef Vajs,[16] a professor from Prague, an Old Slavonic philologist, a liturgist and biblicist. In his steps followed Professor Josef Vašica[17] with his prolific writings. Bonifac Segeťa[18] worked on translations from the Greek to show the differences between the Eastern and Western Churches, to name but a few.

Perhaps the most visible, Stojan revealed his scientific concerns by personally helping in 1920 the then young priest Francis Dvorník (1893-1975) to advance his historical studies in Prague and at the Sorbonne in Paris, to become a prominent scholar, *historian* of renown and an Ecumenist[19] who later cleared up a difficult way toward Church unity by his *vindication*[20] of Cyrilo-Methodian sources and by rehabilitation of the Patriarch *Photius.*[21] This further contributed greatly to the Vth and VIth Unionistic Congress, (1929-1933) at Velehrad. He also took part in the Unionistic Congresses held in St. Procopius Abbey in *Lisle*[22] (1956, 1957, and 1959), thus fully repaying his gratitude to his protector, whose unionistic legacy he transferred into an international forum. All this certainly points out the greatness of Stojan's theological and ecumenical comprehension of the issues at stake, well handled through his concern as a diligent Churchman.

Stojan, the Churchman

Stojan's all inclusive involvement in the apostolate of Church unity and in public services enhanced considerably his reputation as a zealous Churchmen. Church and public recognitions began to appear as a natural outgrowth of his constantly increasing popularity. Stojan's zealous work as pastor of Dražovice and as delegate to the parliament of Vienna was recognized by Church authorities. Bishop Paul of Brno nominated him October 31, 1904, a papal chamberlain with the title of Monsignor.[23] The same year he was appointed the Ordinariate's Commissary for the Czech Comenius School in Vienna. Secular authorities were not less generous in recognition of his tremendous merits for the people of towns and cities by nominating him honorary citizen or honorary mayor. All these honors did not change his totally humble personality.

Stojan, a Canon of Olomouc and a Provost in Kroměříž

Stojan was for over twenty years pastor in Dražovice, a country parish without a single good road, about 8 miles from the railroad station. He never requested a transfer, in spite of all the difficulties he had to overcome while frequently using the railroad to Vienna. Finally under great pressure from other Catholic delegates and public authorities, he applied for a canonicate in Olomouc. He was persuaded that this was necessary in the religious and national interest. Earlier in 1899, he did apply for a city parish in Moravská Ostrava, where he wanted to be socially active, but did not get it. He was motivated by increased pastoral interest rather than a better place. In 1910 he was responsible for building a second parish in this rapidly growing city to alleviate the difficulties of the *Apostolate* among workers. In 1908 Stojan submitted to great pressure and finally applied for a canonicate, especially when Bishop Pavel Huyn of Brno, his ordinary, warmly recommended his application.[24] He was appointed[25] to this post on May 16, 1908. The news of his appointment came on the feastday of St. John Nepomucene, a day on which Stojan had made his great oration in defense of this Saint before the whole Parliament. His nomination for Canon generated great joy and satisfaction everywhere. By the decree of the President of the Moravian Viceregency of May 20, 1908, the Archbishop of Olomouc was officially informed that Stojan was named non-resident canon of the Metropolitan's chapter. On May 25 Archbishop Bauer related the nomination to the chapter. On June 13, 1908, Stojan was installed in the Cathedral as its new Canon. Auxiliary Bishop V. Blažek conducted installation rites in a crowded Cathedral. When the new Canon left the Cathedral, the people gave him a spontaneous and sincere ovation.

On June 29, 1908, Archbishop Bauer nominated the new Canon as provost of the Collegiate Church of St. Maurice in Kroměříž,[26] where he was installed August 11, 1908 with great solemnity and an extraordinary attendance. Here again Stojan's nomination was warmly accepted. His transfer to Kroměříž made everything much easier and more convenient for his activities. Stojan appreciated this very much. The new dignity did not change anything of his previous simplicity of life. As provost he had four vicars charged with all pastoral aspects. Thanks to this arrangement he had more free time for his apostolates and more time for his duties as deputy in Vienna. Notwithstanding, Stojan always fulfilled his pastoral obligations whenever he was at home. He liked to take part in canonical hours, to preach, to hear confessions at every opportunity. St. Maurice Collegiate Church became a center for missions, triduums and spiritual conferences to which he invited celebrated orators and preachers. The famous Abbot Methoděj Zavoral of the Strahov Monastery became a frequent guest-preacher. His relations with other canons and vicars were very warm. He invited them frequently as guests for dinners, brought to them always some memorabilia from his official trips to Vienna, and was successful in providing for canons and vicars the special stipend of the *congrua*[27] to accomodate their annual income. Naturally they all loved their provost. Not long after, Stojan was nominated archiepiscopal commissary, or inspector of religion in the Czech Teachers Institute in the State German gymnasium and the German

Lands real gymnasium. He carefully supervised these institutions, making sure that religious instruction was provided.[28] On December 2, 1909 he was named a real archiepiscopal Councillor and assessor of the consistory of Olomouc. After the death of Msgr. J. Drobena, he was also appointed superior of the Convent of the Sisters of St. Ursula in Přestavlky. He extended paternal care to them in all their affairs.

Stojan during World War I (1914-1918)

With the announcement of general mobilization on July 26, 1914, the charitable and apostolic work of Provost Stojan increased in unprecedented dimensions. His Church of St. Maurice, in the city of Kroměříž, became a spiritual refuge for all soldiers. He not only extended his pastoral services: worship, devotions, confessions or visits to the sick, but he also collected and distributed good books to the soldiers. Father Adolf Jašek mentioned that under Stojan's care about 26,000 books, brochures or pamphlets were distributed from St. Maurice Church alone.[29] In fact, war affairs so affected Stojan that the planned and already well-prepared Fourth Unionistic Congress, scheduled to be held in 1914, had to be postponed, although invitations had already been sent. The Metropolitan of Lwov, Andrew Szeptyckyi, and Archbishop Doprečic, the Primate of Serbia, were to be at the Congress. Instead, in 1914 Stojan organized prayerful pilgrimages to Holy Hostyn and Velehrad to seek Divine protection and help in the troubled times of war. A pilgrimage to Hostyn was held the weekend of September 12 and 13, with special devotions for the soldiers killed or wounded. Public prayers were said and a special rogation procession with the Blessed Sacrament was held. A similar rogation pilgrimage was held the weekend of September 26 and 27 for the same intention. Both were huge manifestations. In Hostyn attendance was about 20,000 while that at Velehrad was even larger. Both filled with rich devotional programs and sermons were preached by well known orators. Stojan was the soul of all devotions and his zeal was present and felt by all.

The Central Theological Greek Catholic Seminary at Kroměříž, 1915

As in every war, so also during World War I, a great migration of peoples occurred. In the province of Galicia until the war there were three seminaries: Lwov, Przemysl and Stanislavov. Since fighting took place there, the seminarians were scattered over the whole Austriam Empire. Some remained at home, others joined the Red Cross or fled the province freely or involuntarily, not knowing where to go. Those who reached Vienna or Prague registered themselves at the Theological Faculties, while others were almost lost. The Vicar General of the Uniates of Galicia met Stojan in Vienna and complained to him about the sad fate of Greek Catholic seminarians. As always, Stojan was ready to help. First he tried in Velehrad, but the Jesuit gymnasium had already moved there. Then he thought of Hostyn, but this met with great difficulties. Finally he succeeded in finding some convenient rooms for a seminary in the city of Kroměříž. The Christian social organization gladly offered its social and theatre rooms, which were used for dormitories with 60 beds. The gymnastic organization (Catholic) *Orel* lent its huge hall for a study. A kitchen was established in the abandoned quarters of the building of the Piarists, and a dining room was located in the social hall of the Marian Sodality. Nearby St. John Church served as a place for worship. Archiepiscopal officials, at the request of Stojan, permitted all rooms of the Pavilion in the Archiepiscopal Park to be adapted conveniently for the purposes of a seminary. The faculty was composed of a director of studies, Provost Dr. Stojan, who also taught Canon Law; Vicar P. Josef Olšina became professor of Matrimony and of Hebrew; Canon Dr. Jan Grobelskyj of Stanislavov was professor of Pastoral Theology and Catechetics; Canon Dr. F. Ščepkovyc of Stanislavov became professor of Church History; Chaplain Dr. Alois Richter, professor of Moral Theology; Karel Fadrus, professor of New Testament; Dr. Augustin Štancl, professor of Dogmatics; Dr. Antonin Kubíček, professor of Christian Philosophy and Fundamental Theology; Msgr. Francis Snopek taught Hermeneutics and Catechist; Rev. Adolf Jašek lectured on Old Testament. Father Nazar Čeban, O.S.B., explained Liturgy and was simultaneously a spiritual director of the seminary. Dr. Josafat Kocylovskij was appointed by the Vicar General V. Filas as Director of the Seminary. "Venia docendi" for all was obtained from the Archepiscopal Consistory of Olomouc by its rescript (no. 8590) of July 21, 1915. Stojan succeeded in getting governmental approval of this newly established seminary, and examinations were recognized by the State. All professors were teaching *gratis*, with no demand for any kind of reward. The *Apostolate of Sts. Cyril and Methodius* was sponsor of all this, while the Ministry of Education promised some contribution for the maintenance of the seminary. Rev. Adolf Jašek acted as an econome for the institution. In the beginning, the seminary had 40 students, later 60, and finally 75, so that the seminary was full.

Seminarians arrived April 22, 1915, and the school year began April 24, 1915, with a solemn liturgy at St. Maurice Church. It was attended by the whole Collegiate Chapter, Faculty, public authorities, and a crowd of the faithful. Although most of the disciplines were taught in Latin, the Czech language was used for conversation and practical subjects. Professor Vocel of the State real gymnasium and Professor Fadrus were very helpful in teaching the Czech language to all who were interested. Stojan was again the soul of this establishment. The seminarians in gratitude, on the occasion of his feast, June 13, 1915, prepared an excellent program in his honor. Seminarian Michael Kravčuk lectured on the Cyrilomethodian Idea in Ukrainian, and Vladimir Koropeckyj had it in Czech.[30] Public gratitude was expressed to Stojan.

Seminarians utilized well their habitat in Moravia, for they made pilgrimages to Velehrad and Hostyn at the end of the school year, on July 30, 1915. The rector of the seminary expressed gratitude to the city, to all Catholic organizations and to Archepiscopal officers for their hospitality, before their departure to Galicia, to which they were permitted to return. This provisional establishment of the seminary of the city of Kroměříž[31] for the Greek Catholic theologians is perhaps the best illustration of how generous Stojan was in his selfless willingness to give help where it was needed.

Appeal of Stojan to the Czech Catholics of U.S.A.

During the year 1915 Stojan reorganized the rogation pilgrimages to Velehrad and to Hostyn with devotional services for all victims of the war and for the protection of soldiers. He also sent a petition to the Czech Catholics in America as follows:

> "A prayerful petition to the Czech Catholics in America! Beloved countrymen: From your old Fatherland, where the war is furious, this prayerful petition is sent to ask you to manifest your charity in these times to your countrymen. It concerns the support of families of killed and wounded soldiers. The laws guarantee partial support but this is not sufficient to abolish the present misery and poverty. There is need for effective love and generosity. All, for whom it will

be at all possible, please come to our help. *The Apostolate of Sts. Cyril and Methodius,* under the protection of the Blessed Virgin Mary, the purpose of which is to take care of the propagation of the Faith, is called to this important role of support in order that in lands affected by the war and deprived of their churches, services will be held and religious life continued. This role is very important and yet the means are scarce. One needs to keep in mind especially the holy places like Hostyn and Velehrad. We beg donations for these mentioned intentions and efforts. As in Hostyn, so at Velehrad prayers continue to be offered that the all-powerful Lord, through the intercession of the Mother of God and Sts. Cyril and Methodius, will reward each donor abundantly here and in eternity."

Dr. Ant. Cyr. Stojan, Reichs deputy in Kroměříž.[32]

This appeal indicates not only how Stojan did not lose any opportunity to solicit support for various causes of need or crises, but points out his close relationship with the emigrants abroad in any corner of the globe.

Stojan's Care for Emigrants and Refugees:

Stojan had a particular solicitude for all political refugees, emigrants or immigrants. During the war the expansion of the Austrian monarchy was decreased in size in the North and South through the victorious advances of Russian and Italian armies. Subsequently thousands of people from Eastern and Central Galicia, and from Goricia and Istria in the South, were forced to leave their homes and seek refuge in Moravia and elsewhere. In order to minimize the threat of the national strength of Slavs, the Slavic population was moved to the German parts of the country, while the Italian population was moved to Moravia. Stojan had great understanding of all emigrants, especially Slavic, and helped them when he could. He united and gathered the Polish and Slovenian priests to seek their advice on how to protect their youth. He established schools in the city of Kroměříž and elsewhere for their children. With the support of the *Apostolate of Sts. Cyril and Methodius,* Stojan negotiated the establishment of Slovenian and Croatian schools in Kroměříž and the transfer of the Teachers Institute from Galicia. The Austrian Government first sent the Italian students and then granted permission for Slovenian and Croatian schools. Archbishop Mikulas Doprečic of Montenegro wanted to have young priests and asked Stojan to help him. Stojan accepted four at the beginning and later more boys into the Croatian school where they were prepared for advanced study in the gymnasium of Kroměříž. Later P. Adolph Jašek accompanied these students when they returned to their native Montenegro.

In 1915 Stojan made an effort to send a Czech missionary into the industrial area on the Rhine. As a result of his negotiations, Rev. Jesuit Father Vídeňský was sent on a Czech mission into the dioceses of Münster and Osnabrück. In 1916 Stojan decided to go himself as a Czech missionary, but the German Government would not grant permission. Only Rev. Prachař succeeded in becoming a spiritual administrator of emigrants in Hamburg; others were not allowed to leave the country.

During the war, the *Apostolate of Sts. Cyril and Methodius* financially supported the Slovanic Seminary, later transferred to Plovdiv; further, the Slavic missions in Macedonia, Bulgaria, Turkey, Montenegro, Ukraine helped hungry children and orphans in Bosnia; took care of the Russian emigrants and maintained the mission institution at Velehrad — all this was due to the special efforts of Stojan. Thus Stojan's activities on behalf of all Slovanic nationalities during the war are clear evidence of his special concern for the Slavs. He had a special understanding of the suffering of all people during the war. He used to say, "The greatest sacrifices, the most generous alms and the greatest acts of mercy do not have any worth or reward before God unless they are done only from the pure love of God."[33]

Due to Stojan's care, the *Apostolate* sponsored spiritual retreats for drafted young men. These retreats met with great success and benefit. Stojan introduced into his rectory of St. Maurice at Kroměříž also a correspondence station for the soldiers to alleviate their sad stay at the front. Thousands of letters from the soldiers there went to Stojan, who in turn communicated them to their families. Multitudes visited Stojan to seek his intervention in various problems. In addition to all this, he established in his rectory a station for feeding the poor, beggars and children.

Special care was given by Stojan in efforts to help young men in farmer-family homes to remain home to keep their households alive. His slogan, "to preserve our families," became a cornerstone for these policies. He frequently visited Governmental offices in Vienna for this purpose and in many cases succeeded in keeping the young men at home. Stojan also helped young men who held indispensable jobs or positions.[34] His secretary, Rev. Adolf Jašek, says that Stojan's activities and acts of mercy on behalf of soldiers and other men involved in military service belong to the most illustrious chapters of his life.[35]

Stojan attempted not only to help everybody during the war, but to protect whatever he could, especially the Church bells, which were taken by military authorities often very recklessly and with no regard for the Church or community's need. It was very difficult to deal with an absolutist government, relying only on the military tribunal, especially after the dismissal of parliament. Yet, Stojan was successful in preserving the bells at Velehrad; Mount Hostyn, and those in St. Maurice Church in Kroměříž because he offered the government some metal substitutes, which he collected from good people all over the country. He published a special *proclamation* in this regard and people gladly collected all small metal things in their homes to save the bells at Velehrad, Hostyn and Kroměříž. On December 15, 1916, Stojan sent an application to the Ministry of Defense asking that the bells of the above mentioned places be left, for metal substitutes. His request was not answered positively until February 16, 1918.[36] Stojan likewise helped to preserve the 4,700 kg. metal cover of the Baroque tower of St. Michael's Church in Olomouc. This was almost a hopeless case because no one at Olomouc was brave enough to intervene with the Austrian authorities until Stojan did.

Stojan's Devotion to Blessed John Sarkander

Stojan's action for the celebration in 1920 of the three hundredth anniversary of the death of Blessed John Sarkander was another aspect of his apostolate to revive the cult of this Moravian martyr. Since his student days in Příbor, then as seminarian at Olomouc, and as a priest, Stojan had a special interest in this devotion and suffered a lot when he saw it on the decline. On April 10, 1917, Stojan gathered several priests in the Catholic House in Olomouc for consultation on the forthcoming jubilee of the death of Blessed John Sarkander, planned for 1920. Altogether Stojan convoked fifteen meetings of the working council during the years 1917, 1918, 1919, in different places, but mainly Přerov. The *Acta* of all these meetings were diligently written by the secretary, Rev. Antonín Dokoupil, while Stojan was again the soul of all activities. He assembled several distinguished scholars, among them the expert historian, Dr. Breitenbacher, who helped with good advice. The Council of professionals proceeded to preserve all memorabilia of Blessed John Sarkander and to awaken an effective interest in this subject. As a result, the great historical work, *Bl. John Sarkander jeho doba, život a blahoslavení* (Blessed John Sarkander, His Times, Life and Beatification) was written by J. Tenora and J. Foltynovský.[37] In addition, a popular biography of Blessed John Sarkander was provided for the people. Stojan's action on behalf of Blessed John Sarkander has not yet been fully appraised. We know that it was from these meetings under Stojan's care that all difficulties about Blessed John Sarkander were resolved.

Stojan, a Metropolitan Canon in Olomouc

Stojan went to Kroměříž as provost, as the last, i.e., 17th, non-resident metropolitan canon of Olomouc. While he was in Kroměříž three canons died: Auxiliary Bishop Blažek (1912), Baron Linde (1913) and Prince Hohenlohe-Langenberg, but Stojan did not want to move to Olomouc. Auxiliary Bishop Karel Wisnar wrote a letter May 19, 1917, to Stojan asking him to send a petition to Olomouc. Stojan followed the advice of his dear friend and sent the petition for the 14th residential canonicate. His request was granted. Stojan departed from Kroměříž, where he had been for ten years, at the beginning of April 1918, heartbroken but without any official farewell party. He moved out quickly and quietly. He packed all his materials into boxes, called his niece-housekeeper and told her: "I am moving to Olomouc. Pack everything and follow me." He moved into the old canonical residence on the Franz Joseph Avenue, now Štefaník Avenue. This massive but not very impressive house, occupied by the late Prelate Melchior Mlčoch, was rapidly changed with the arrival of the new canon. It became a huge, public paternal office of the deputy who was daily helping crowds of people. Stojan lived here simply and without any comforts. He observed a strict daily schedule: rising early, about 5 A.M., and going early to sleep at about 9 P.M. Hospitality was offered to everybody in his house. In this new canonical residence at Olomouc, Stojan, as a distinguished Churchman, continued the same apostolates concerning Hostýn, Velehrad, Church Unity and his charitable activities as before, even in an increased tempo, conditioned by the change of the political scene and atmosphere with the arrival of Czechoslovak National independence in 1918.

Stojan as a Public Servant

The term of public servant is used here in an attempt to rightly single out Stojan the politician, to avoid the bad connotation usually attached to politics in general. While there is no doubt that Stojan was deeply involved in politics, his involvement was only a selfless availability to do good and to serve people more effectively. There was no calculation or greedy ambition behind Stojan's decision to take part in the political arena except his desire and determination to become spokesman for distributive justice and to be an advocate for the needy and poor.

Stojan – Deputy in the Parliament in Vienna

The year 1897 began a new epoch in Stojan's activity in public life. The pastor of Dražovice entered the political arena as a representative of the Catholic National Party. For a long time Czech Catholic circles did not want to split the National Front, because of Vienna's Germanizing absolutism,[38] but the time came when the Catholics had to take a stand on their beliefs. In contrast to Germany, where Kelleher and Windhorst began their Catholic emancipation, Catholic circles in Czech lands were involved in the national Palacký – Rieger's party.[39] With the increasing anti-Catholic movement, necessity for Catholic defense was evident. Thus the awakening generation of Catholic clergy, grown up under Sušil's influence began after 1898 to organize defense in Catholic trade unions and to work in a Christian-Social direction in defense of their rights. Among those in this movement from the beginning was Stojan. An independent Catholic National Party[40] was established in Přerov, under the chairmanship of Dr. Mořic Hruban who formulated a program to challenge growing liberalism.[41] Stojan emerged in the political arena by a coincidence of circumstances. The well respected Catholic spokesman, Dr. Helcelet who was a candidate, died. The other candidate in the district of Vyškov, a certain radical Pokorný, was not popular. The temperate part of the Catholic National Party preferred the moderate Stojan, who for the first time became a candidate with a definite political involvement.

The Vienna Parliament (Reichsrat) was dissolved in 1897 and a new election was called for January 22, 1897. Stojan became a candidate for the fourth elect which included Vyškov, Kyjov, Kroměříž, Uh. Hradiště and Uh. Brod. The campaign was very tough because the

Social Democrats claimed Moravia as a region reserved mostly to workers.[42] Stojan, who campaigned hard but always nobly, won with a small majority, i.e., with 11 votes prevailing over all competitors. The final count was 342 to 331. All the Catholics who knew him well were greatly pleased. Stojan never resorted to political tricks or deals, yet he was always successful. His famous characteristic statement was: "The love of Jesus Christ is the best politics." The all-inclusive motto for his program was to help all, as he really did for more than a quarter of a century. He used the celebrated maxim: "Fortiter in re suaviter in modo" – i.e., bravely and uncompromisingly, with great concern for problems, while he always found ways to handle them mildly and kindly. It is heart-warming to read the laudatory comments of the contemporary press[43] about the selfless and zealous Stojan's political activity which aimed always and exclusively toward the common good. In attempting this he never compromised moral or ethical principles, although he was always the pragmatist whenever help for the people was at stake. He knew well how to do whatever was necessary without involving personal expediency. All Stojan's political activity was really an extension of his apostolate to the people he was elected to serve. Despite his all-inclusive kindness, he was a decisive fighter for the causes of social justice and morality.

Stojan was a selfless politician in that he used his mandate as a delegate in the Land Diet and a deputy in the *Reichsrat* in Vienna for the full benefit of the people. The press called him "a good spirit of the Parliament."[44] It was generally known that Stojan was the most efficient and helpful representative of the people. His biographer, František Cinek, laments that "It is a pity we don't have all the records of Stojan's activities as a deputy, for this was one of the most fruitful periods of his life, where he revealed the entire goodness of his heart."[45] He was a deputy truly beloved by all people; a helper even to those who were not worthy. His goodness of heart did not know political favoritism; he took care equally of anyone in need.

Stojan as supporter of Czech minorities in Vienna was well known and evident through all the years of his activities as deputy to the Viennese Reichsrat. Especially memorable was his active part in the *23rd Eucharistic Congress* held in September, 1912, when he took care of lodging the numerous participants from Bohemia and Moravia, in number some 20,000. Three Churches in Vienna were reserved for them, namely Maria Stiegen, one of the oldest Churches in downtown Vienna; a second one called the Czech Church on the Rennweg, in charge of the Conventual Fathers, and another Church. All were fully attended, with pontifical services held by all Czech bishops, with the Cardinals of Prague and of Olomouc.

It was characteristic of Stojan that he was also the principal organizer for providing financial help to the Czech Church in Rennweg, which had a debt of more than 200,000 crowns. *The Union of St. Methodius in Vienna* failed to provide an adequate sum. Interest in Czech minorities in Vienna was really minimal, because even Stojan's appeal was not strong enough to elicit sufficient generosity among wealthy people. Only one generous and kind patron, Jan Lord Harrach, appreciated the importance and need of Czech Liturgical Services in Vienna and offered to help the Union to preserve them. The Czechs in Vienna were mostly poor people, either workers or servants of all kinds. They had little or no voice in governmental circles. Stojan was their understanding supporter and successful advocate in need, especially in his role as Parliamentary representative, which he used exclusively for the benefit of the people.

A tense situation in Parliament was due to constant conflicts of Slavic minorities with the Viennese Government. Stojan was re-elected as deputy in the new elections held from June 19 to July 6, 1911. Because the results of these elections favored the Slavs, who outnumbered the Germans (295 Slavic deputies to 285 German), the Prime Minister Bienerth dismissed his government. His successor, Prime Minister Gautch, later did the same [46] because of the prevailing influence of the Slavs. A certain stability was achieved by the cabinet of the Prime Minister Sturgh, mainly because the Club of Czech deputies decided to vote for him if he would guarantee their economic demands. This was changed when war erupted in the Balkans on July 28, 1914, following the assassination of Prince Franz Ferdinand in Sarajevo. Subsequently a stern absolutism, supported by a military court, was imposed and political activities of parties and individuals were slowed down.

Stojan, however, was busy in the Reichsrat and the Moravian Land Diet even in these unfavorable times. He constantly intervened for his constituents and helped whenever he could. Dr. Mořic Hruban, a zealous politician himself, attests "that Stojan used his mandate and influence toward the establishment of parishes and the building of new churches. He always bravely defended the interests of the clergy. Many interventions were successful due mainly to Stojan's wide sympathy and popularity, for he was indeed an unusual man."[47]

Stojan had a special interest and concern for the Czechs of Vienna and he really fought for their religious, national and economic rights, especially when in 1909 the Austrian parliament voted against the Czechs and decided that the proposal of the infamous anti-Czech *Axman law* be presented to the Emperor for approval. Stojan's concern for the Czechs of Vienna was recognized by the fact that they always turned to him whenever their public affairs needed defense or improvements. In turn, Stojan was very popular with the Czech minority of Vienna.[48] His concern for them in a German atmosphere was natural because he had to cope frequently with Czech-German animosity in his previous priestly assignments, especially as chaplain in the city of Příbor and elsewhere. This reveals how Stojan was always patriotic and faithful to his national feelings but never became chauvinistic in a sense of national hatred. The fact that he frequently intervened for the Germans in their needs supports his balanced nationalism. He had a lively concern for the Slovaks in Hungary, for whom he frequently intervened with the papal Nuncio in Vienna. Furthermore, through the *Apostolate of Sts. Cyril and Methodius,* of which he had been general secretary since 1909, he was in frequent contact with the Slovenes, Croats, Bulgarians, and all other nationals of the Balkan area, in whom Stojan not only kept a spirit of Slavic solidarity, but cultivated in them the spirit of unionistic understanding regarding Church unity.

Dr. Stojan Investigated for Treason

With the prolongation of the war, mobilization into military service was extended for men to age 42. This recruiting was executed with no regard for their absolute need in homes and families, and without any concern for the state of their health. Czech and Moravian lands were especially affected. The inhabitants suffered greatly because German or Hungarian troops were located in Czech cities, while the so-called Fatherland's defense, called *Domobrana,* was sent far away. The situation worsened when the economy became critical and Hungary prohibited the export of grain to Austria. Subsequently Austria was dependent on the grain cultivated in Bohemia and Moravia.[49] Thus the Czech nation was oppressed and actually starved. Stojan helped as he could; he visited the ill and wounded soldiers in hospitals; comforted and inspired them to have confidence in God. Once he said to one soldier gravely wounded in the hospital: "Have hope in God; everything will be well again. Perhaps you may not yet go to the front."[50] For this he was indicted by the military authorities. He was forbidden to visit military hospitals and he was investigated for treason. Details of this episode are not known. However, it is a fact that this criminal process was cancelled by the rescript of the highest military authority in Vienna on February 22, 1915, which said that "Criminal process against the Reich Deputy and Land's deputy, Mr. Cyril Stojan, Provost in Kroměříž, has been cancelled, and he is again permitted to visit the wounded and ill in hospitals."[51] This document was delivered to Stojan through the magistrate of the city of Kroměříž, signed by Dr. Barták as the mayor. This episode is itself very characteristic of the tense times, and indicative of the malice of some Austrian authorities, always suspicious of Stojan for his Czech patriotism. Even such a benefactor and patriot as Stojan was not exempt from Austrian malice.

From this perspective, though brief, one can strongly feel full justification for Stojan to be called a public servant when so much good resulted from his actions in politics.

NOTES

1. This thesis was presented at the Cyrilomethodian Faculty in Olomouc and is registered as Dis. #19. Stojan was given this thesis by the rescript of Dean of the Theological Faculty in Olomouc on April 1, 1896 no. 518, with instruction by Professor Janiš that a thesis should be worked out in view of Pastoral Theology. It is interesting to note that dissertations from Pastoral Theology could be in the Czech or German language, while all others were in Latin.
2. *Našinec* no. 80 (Olomouc, July 12, 1896).
3. Cinek, *op.cit.,* 352.
4. Francis Dvornik, "The Significance of the missions of Cyril and Methodius," *Slavic Review* XXIII no. 2 (July, 1964) 195-238; Michael Lacko, *Sts. Cyril and Methodius* (Rome, 1963), 29-39.
5. Cinek, *op.cit.,* ibid.
6. *Ibid.*
7. The outstanding journal, founded in 1848 by Bishop Kirsik, to combat the anti-Catholic trends.
8. Bohumil Zlámal, *Antonín Cyril Stojan* (Rome, 1973), 73-78, especially p. 76.
9. *Ibid.*
10. *Ibid.*
11. According to J.H. Newman's theories—Louvain, 1835, and Dublin, 1851, several universities like Georgetown or The Catholic University in America, the French Catholic Institute in Paris, Lille, Lyon, Angers and Toulouse, 1875-1877, and Freiburg in Switzerland.
12. This is well described by Cinek, *op.cit.*
13. F. Snopek, *Die Slavenapostel, Kritische Studien* (Kroměříž, 1918); idem, *Konstantin-Cyril a Methoděj: Slovanští apoštolové* (Prague, 1913).
14. A Bruckner, "Thesen zur Cyrillo-Methodianischen Frage", *Archiv für slavische Philologie,* 28 (1906) 186 ff.; *cf. idem., Die Wahrheit uber die Slavenapostel* (Tübingen, 1913); he attacked Dvornik in his "Cyrillo-Methodiana", *Kwartalnik Historyczny,* 47 (Lwov, 1933); Zdeněk R. Dittrich, *Christianity in Great-Moravia* (Groningen, 1962), *passim.*
15. As he lectured on these topics at the Unionistic Congresses, as mentioned previously; see *idem., Konstantin und Method Lehrer der Slaven* (Wisbaden, 1962), *passim.*
16. J. Vajs, "Mešní řád charvatsko-hlaholského vatikanského misálu illi. 4. . ." *Acta Academiae Velehradensis,* 15 (1939), 89-141; *cf. Slovanské studie,* ed. J. Kurz (Prague, 1948), pp. 17-35, concerning the comprehensive view of Vajs' other pertinent studies.

17. J. Vašica, "Slovanská liturgie sv. Petra," *Byzantinoslavica,* 8 (1939-40) pp. 1-59.

18. He was professor and later canon at Kroměříž.

19. Ludvik Nemec, "The Festive Profile of Francis Dvornik, the Scholar, the Historian, and the Ecumenist," The *Catholic Historical Review* LIX no. 2 (July, 1973), 185-224.

20. Through his monumental work titled *Les Légendes de Constantin et de Méthode vues de Byzance* (Prague, 1933) *(Byzantinoslavica, Supplementa)* vol. 1.

21. Through his definitive work: *The Photian Schism: History and Legend* (Cambridge, 1948); see Ludvik Nemec, "The Success of Professor Dvornik's Research in the Vindication of the Patriarch Photius" in *The Czechoslovak Contribution to World Culture,* ed. M. Rechcigl, Jr. (The Hague, 1964), pp. 262-264.

22. Ludvik Nemec, "American Velehrad," *The Byzantine Catholic World* 7 nos. 14-15 (1962) 8-14.

23. The decree of October 31, 1904 says "Praeclara merita respicientes, quae Dominatio tua plurimum Reverenda tum qua *parochus* tum praeprinus qua ad comitia provinciae Moravicae atque ad comitia imperii *deputatus...*" The whole text is quoted in Frant. Cinek, *op.cit.,* 541.

24. Letter of recommendation of Feb. 1, 1908 is in Cinek, *op.cit.,* 634-635.

25. Latin decree of this appointment is in Cinek, *op.cit.,* 638.

26. Vilém Jůza and others, *Kroměříž* (Prague, 1963) 76-77, and passim.

27. *Congrua* was a stipend given by the State to the clergy to accomodate their usual income to compensate them for keeping records of baptisms, weddings or funerals for the purposes of public statistics.

28. Ad. Jašek, *Msgr. Dr. A.C. Stojan,* p. 19.

29. *Apoštolát* no. 1 of 1920, p. 4.

30. These lectures were published in *Apoštolát* of 1915, pp. 138-139.

31. P. Adolf Jašek, "Ústřední rusinský bohoslovecký seminář v Kroměříž" (The Central Ruthenian Theological Seminary in Kroměříž), *Apoštolát* (1915), 104-134 and *passim.*

32. The Czech text of this proclamation is in Cinek, *op.cit.,* pp. 813-814. The English translation is by the author.

33. *Apoštolát* nos. 2-3 of 1915, p. 18.

34. See Cinek, *op.cit.,* 820-829 with many reports based on journals of Stojan's efforts to keep many young men excused from the military obligation.

35. *Pozorovatel* no. 34 of May 2, 1921, mentioned that there are several boxes with correspondence during the War, preserved in testimonial of Stojan's activities. Cinek says that most of these boxes disappeared at times.

36. Rescript is published by Frant. Cinek, *op.cit.,* 836.

37. Ant. Cyril Stojan, "Jak uctíván byl bl. Jan Sarkander," *Škola Božského Srdce páně* (1876) no. 12, published in Olomouc (1920) by the Cyrilo-methodian Foundation on the 300th anniversary of his death.

38. Ludvik Nemec, *Church and State in Czechoslovakia* (New York, 1955) p. 104; Emil Ludwig, *Bismarck* (Story of a Fighter) (transl. by Eden and Cedar Paul, New York, 1926), p. 417.

39. Dr. Josef Doležal, *Český kněz* (Olomouc, 1931), 84-86.
40. Jan Drábek, *Z časů nedlouho zašlých* (From the not distant times) (Rome, 1967), 135 and passim.
41. Leo XIII—Encyclical, "Libertas praestantissimum," attacked liberalism as anti-christian and irrational.
42. Adolf Srb, *Politické dějiny národa českého od počátku doby konstituční*, Prague, 1962) II, pp. 162-164.
43. This is well described in *Hlas* no. 57 of March 1, 1897, no. 58 and of March 12, 1897, or no. 60 of March 14, 1897.
44. *Neues Wiener Tagblatt* of Jan. 25, 1907.
45. Cinek, *op.cit.*, 601-632 where there was praise in the press about Stojan.
46. Adolf Srb, *Politické dějiny národa českého od počátku doby konstituční* (Prague, 1926) II, pp. 354-356 and passim.
47. This from the interview of Dr. Hruban, quoted by F. Cinek, *op.cit.*, p. 773.
48. *Pravda* (the first Czech Catholic Weekly in Vienna) no. 18 of April 27, 1933. See also F. Cinek, *op.cit.*, 791-792 where he brings to the attention "Picture of Stojan's activities among the Czechs of Vienna."
49. Ad. Srb, *Politické dějiny*, p. 364 ff.
50. This is affirmed by Professor Ant. Janda, who shared this information with Cinek, *op.cit.*, 830.
51. This rescript in German was found among his personal documents and is fully quoted by Cinek, *op.cit.*, 830.

VI
STOJAN FOR CZECHOSLOVAK
NATIONAL INDEPENDENCE

This patriot of such grand and pure style relived dynamically in his tender heart the historical change which brought the Czech and Slovak nations a long overdue and much desired liberty and independence. His always active love for the nation and fatherland had become even more forceful after this political change. Right from the beginning, one can see Stojan among the distinguished representatives of the District National Council, with its role of taking over leadership in the name of the National Government and its care for the consolidation of the political scene. The *Proclamation*[1] to the Nation, issued by the District National Council, was signed by Stojan, with others, on October 29, 1918 at Olomouc.

When the Czechoslovak National Assembly was constituted, Stojan was among the first in November, 1918, to be nominated a deputy and took part in its first session on November 14, 1918. Stojan began this new phase of his activity with a Solemn Mass at the Church of Our Lady Tyn at 9:30 A.M. in Prague for the blessing of the Parliament and the new Czechoslovak State. Many members of the National Assembly and crowds of people participated. All sang St. Wenceslaus' and St. Adalbert's hymns. On November 19, 1918 he was elected by the People's party, founded by Msgr. Jan Šrámek, as a member of the Council of Schools and Petitions of the National Assembly.[2] The first meeting of the Council of Schools was held November 28, 1918, under Stojan's chairmanship. He was confronted from the very beginning with anti-Catholic pressure regarding the religious nature of schools. In that first session a proposal was made by Dr. F.V. Krejčí for the immediate change of the law concerning the University and the religious instruction in secondary and grade schools. On December 15, 1918, he was strongly opposed on the issue of religious instruction by the great majority in the Council of Schools which approved, against the votes of deputies Stojan and Professor Mareš, the following law concerning religious instruction:

Art. 1. Instruction in religion in all secondary schools, and in those equal to these, in grade and city schools, is not obligatory. It is up to parents, legal representatives, or their delegates to decide whether their children should participate in such instruction.

Art. 2. The Government will adapt accordingly the position of the catechists on their faculties; likewise it is the same with teachers of other non-obligatory subjects.

Art. 3. Religious actions, greetings, prayers, songs, etc. belong exclusively to religious instruction. Participation of students at liturgies and religious exercises does not belong in the teaching program.

Art. 4. Regulations in laws and directives which are contrary to this law are abolished.

Art. 5. It is up to the Ministry to express the regulations through special ordinances.[1]

Art. 6. The law becomes valid on the day of its declaration.[3]

Stojan was busy about other matters. On January 8, 1919, he proposed that a second Czech University be established in Olomouc, but the Council decided that it (Masaryk University) should be in Brno and would have four faculties: Law, medicine, natural sciences and philosophy. On January 21, 1919, Stojan proposed in the National Assembly that: 1) The Theological faculty in Olomouc be named the Cyrilomethodian one; 2) that chairs be created for theology of Southern and Eastern Slavs, for the comparative science of religion, and for sociology; 3) that this faculty be equal in privileges and salaries of professors to the faculty of Theology in Prague. He added a proposal for the establishment of sociology in episcopal theological seminaries. Due to his efforts, It was announced in the press that the library would remain in Olomouc.

On January 28, 1919, Stojan proposed that Masaryk University at Brno should have five faculties, including a theological one. Emphatically he requested that this university should reflect the character of Moravia and that it should be connected with a theological faculty. This was not accepted by the National Assembly because Professor F.V. Krejčí forced the view that a theological faculty is not scientific and does not deserve to be in the University at all. Stojan deserves

great credit for his defense of the status of the Cyrilomethodian
Theological Faculty at Olomouc despite the strong opposition of
liberals led by F.V. Krejčí, who was challenged by Professor Francis
Kordač[4] on behalf of the Catholics. Stojan's proposals were voted on
and approved by the Ministerial Council on April 28, 1919. This
meant that the status of this faculty was legally assured with subsequent establishment of chairs, namely that of Comparative Science
of Religion, for which Dr. Gustav Klameth was named; for the chair
of Old Slavonic Language and Literature was chosen Professor Josef
Vašica; and the chair of Sociology was occupied by Professor Bedřich
Vašek. Stojan's proposal of July 17, 1919, for the creation of the
Theological Faculty at Bratislava also won approval from the National
Assembly. Stojan was involved in the parliamentary debates concerning the controversial issue of State-Church separation,[5] which eventually was resolved in favor of Catholics. There was practically no issue[6]
in which Stojan would not take an active part and make a brave defense of the rights of Catholics and other religious denominations.

Due to his activities in parliament, Stojan came to be recognized as
a leader and gained such great popularity that on April 25, 1920, he
was elected senator, representing the People's party. (The Czechoslovak parliament consisted of two houses—National Assembly and
Senate). He was equally active, and on July 15, 1920 he was elected
secretary of the Senate. He should be given all credit as the defender
of the rights of the clergy, especially in matters of the so-called
congrua,[7] thus insuring a minimal existential care for clergy. Stojan's
popularity is manifested by this episode—When he became ill and was
hospitalized for several weeks, the Prime Minister, Antonín Švehla,
and Dr. Stránský visited him. Švehla sat on Stojan's bed, touched his
face and with a tenderly emotional voice told him, "Dear Stojan, you
must not die; it is sad to be without you."[8]

Stojan in the Lead of the Clergy in Tense Times of National Czechoslovak Independence

As is well known, the beginnings of Czechoslovak Independence in
1918 were troubled with religious disturbances connected with an
anti-Catholic cultural struggle. In its defense Stojan was "a man in
the right time and place."[9] *The Away-from-Rome movement*[10]
deeply affected all phases of national life, especially State-Church relationships. It greatly influenced the life of the clergy and orientation toward life in a new State.

It is understandable that Stojan as a priest shared the feelings of other Czech and Moravian priests who looked intensively for a new accommodation of the Catholic Church in the framework of the new Czechoslovak Republic. Inspired by the national awakening and Cyrilomethodian unionism, motivated by the *Catholic Moderna*[11] and the appeal of social movements, yet disturbed and frightened by the *Away-from-Rome movement,* the Catholic priests organized themselves into the *Union of the Catholic Clergy* called *Jednota,* which originally never intended to compromise its loyalty to the Church. Rather, it attempted to sustain its tried-and-true ideals and to project much desired and long overdue views especially suited to the new atmosphere created by the establishment of the Czechoslovak Republic in 1918.

The similarity between ideals promoted today, especially in the name of ecumenism, and those once sought by the Czech clergy, makes the efforts of the *Jednota* an avant-garde movement of modern clerical progressivism.[12] Present attempts on the part of Catholic clergy to form unions as a means to secure those rights frequently sacrificed in favor of legitimate but unchecked episcopal authority are also similar. The Czech *Jednota* represents a pioneering effort. Stojan appeared suddenly without any speculation, calculation, or ambitions, in front of the majority of the Diocesan clergy, who reacted to a newly emerging situation with some reservation and became a center around which the whole process crystallized over two years, eventually evolving into a total religious-ecclesiastical situation. He was elected chairman of the new diocesan *Jednota,* November 8, 1918, and was acting as moderator, counsellor, helper and spiritual director of most of the lower clergy in a most critical period. It was providential that the clergy had *Stojan* then and spontaneously put him in the lead. With the weight of his moral authority, his example, the strength of his pure priestly spirit, and his great, dedicated love, he brought into the world situation much positive and healthy thought. If all his previous activities could be characterized as *"guarere et salvum facere, quod perierat."* it is especially so in his care for priests. The gravity of the situation lay heavily on his heart. His word had weight even when a sense of canonical obedience disappeared. Stojan does not hide the fact that there is need to protect the Moravian clergy from the danger of radical currents in Bohemia. In a short time, from November 7, 1918 to February 17, 1919, 997 priests[13] became members of the *Jednota*. In all deaneries representatives were selected and an organization was formed. The *Jednota* of Olomouc proceeded harmoniously with the *Jednota* of Brno, which under the leadership of its excellent chairman, Rev. Ladislav Zavadil, had existed before. It was repeatedly proclaimed that the *Jednota* in all its efforts stood firmly on the side of the Catholic Church and condemned anything that could lead to uncertainty, schism or deterioration. Both diocesan Moravian *Jednotas* kept a firm line in harmonious proceedings. In the convention held August 19, 1919, the clergy expressed their desire for close cooperation with the People's party to get protection in national, political and ecclestical affairs. It was recommended that all extremism be avoided and that the clergy protect the Catholic Church against those individuals who attempted to spread confusion and disunity.

When in September 1919 Professor Msgr. Francis Kordač (1852-1924) was named Archbishop of Prague, a split in the Czech *Jednota* occurred as a radical wing formed the *Club of the Reformist Clergy*,[14] with determined efforts to reform and protest against Kordač. It is interesting that Kordač's appointment was praised in Moravia but greatly resented in Bohemia. The radical wing of the Czech *Jednota* eventually followed a complete course of schism when some of its members voted on January 9, 1920, for a schismatic *Czechoslovak National Church*.[15] This was prevented in Moravia due mainly to the zealous efforts of Stojan who, in spite of his authority, could not prevent some apostasies, especially that of Matthew Pavlík, who became a member of the Czechoslovak Church, and later the Orthodox Bishop Gorazd,[16] and a few others. It is worthy of note that even *Osservatore Romano*[17] of July 1920 had a statement by Stojan who expressed the firm stand of the *Jednota* of Olomouc with that of the Catholic Church. He was always the one who admonished priests to obey the voices of their bishops and the Pope. After deep reflection on Stojan's activities in the *Jednota* from the end of 1918 to the end of 1920, one is compelled to acknowledge that this represents extremely meritorious work for the Church. It is generally known and accepted that Stojan had a lion's share in saving most of the Catholic Church in the very turbulent years of its existence in the new Czechoslovak Republic which he also helped to form.

No wonder that Stojan's activities were also greatly appreciated in Rome. On September 29, 1920, the Apostolic Nuncio Micara brought a personal letter from Secretary of State Cardinal Gasparri to Lev Cardinal Skrbenský, Archbishop of Olomouc, accepting his resignation. Cardinal Skrbenský informed the Metropolitan Chapter of this; they in turn unanimously elected Canon Antonin Cyril Stojan as Capitular Vicar. This was well received by the whole archdiocese,[18] and it was a long overdue public recognition of Stojan's outstanding leadership. His first trip as Capitular Vicar of the Archdiocese was to Velehrad, where he fervently prayed that he would succeed in administering the see of St. Methodius and help to bring about the fulfillment of the legacy of Cyrilomethodian heritage.

Olomouc, the city of churches, since 1603 the see of the bishop of Moravia,
and since 1777 the see of the metropolitan of Moravia.

Our Lady of the Snows at the old university in Olomouc.
of St. Michael at the archdiocesan theological seminary.
The gothic dome of St. Wenceslaus and the archepiscopal residence.
The pilgrimage shrine of Our Lady on Holy Hill (in the background).

NOTES

1. This is published by Cinek, *op.cit.*, 879 and is directed to the Czechoslovak people.
2. *Našinec* no. 290 of December 17, 1918.
3. *Sborník zákonů a nařízení* (collection) no. 231, 1919, with subsequent legislation.
4. Josef Hronek, *Přehled katolické Theologie české* (Prague, 1935) 9-10; Eduard Winter, *Tausend Jahre Geisteskamph im Sudetenraums* (2nd ed. Salzburg-Leipzig, 1938), 386 and passim; RS, "Prázdninová vzpomínka na arcibiskupa Kordače," *Nový Život* 21 (Rome, 1969) pp. 101-111.
5. This was expressed in the *Declaration of Washington* of October 18, 1918, which was signed by T.G. Masaryk, R.F. Štefanik and Edward Beneš. The Declaration had twelve principal chapters, the third of which was titled: "The Church will be separated from the State." Later Beneš, as minister of foreign affairs, changed his mind and made every effort to avoid any possible conflict with Rome, because he preferred to maintain a good relationship with that city.
6. Cinek, *op.cit.*, 880-887 and 890-897 singles out several of these issues, in which Stojan was vitally involved.
7. Alois Kudrnovský, "Congrua katolického duchovenstva" (Congrua of Catholic Clergy), *Časopis Katolického duchovenstva* (CKD) 80, 105 (1940), pp. 161-191, 233-270, 313-361 and 393-400.
8. Cinek, *op.cit.*, 880.
9. Dr. J. Durych, "Stojanovská legenda," *Našinec* of Nov. 7, 1923.
10. Ludvik Nemec, *The Church and State in Czechoslovakia* (New York, 1955), 96-145; C. David, *Werdegang der los von Rom Bewegung bis 1899* (Wien 1906) *passim*.
11. Alexander Heidler, "Katolická Literatura v Novém Státě" (Catholic Literature in a new State), *Studie* V (Rome, 1978) 331-340; Anastaz Opasek, "Úvaha o katolické moderně a jejím poslání" (Meditation about a Catholic Moderna and its mission), *Studie* V (Rome, 1978) 323-330.
12. Ludvik Nemec, "The Czech Jednota, the avant-garde of modern clerical progressivism and unionism." *Proceedings of the American Philosophical Society*, vol. 112, no. 1 (Jan. 1, 1968), 76-100.
13. Out of a total number of 1200 priests.
14. Josef Doležal, *Český kněz* (Prague, 1931) 67-69; Rudolf Urban, *Die Slavisch-nationalkirchlichen Bestrebungen in Tschechoslovakei* (Leipzig 1938) 30-35.

15. Ludvik Nemec, "The Czechoslovak heresy and schism. The emergence of a National Church," *Transactions of the American Philosophical Society*, vol. 65, par. 1 (Philadelphia, 1975), 1-79.
16. Jaroslav Šuvarský, *Biskup Gorazd* (Prague, 1978), passim.
17. Of July 5, 1920.
18. *Lidové Listy* of October 2, 1923. Here Dr. J. Řehulka describes the first welcome of Archbishop Stojan, when he was appointed.

VII
STOJAN – ARCHBISHOP OF OLOMOUC

Stojan, as Capitular Vicar, introduced district conferences of clergy in the cities, not only to know better the needs of priests, but to increase solidarity and understanding among priests. Suddenly on January 11, 1921, the official news agency announced that the Holy Father had appointed the Capitular Vicar, Antonín Cyril Stojan, Archbishop of Olomouc. Endless joy and jubilation spread over the whole archdiocese. The newly nominated archbishop returned to Olomouc from the Nunciature in Prague on January 11, 1921 at midnight. Although his friends had prepared a welcome in his canonical house, the new archbishop arrived at his residence by electric trolley[1] without much fanfare. The next day numerous delegations came to offer their congratulations, among them the orphans of the Olomouc poor house. The new archbishop received the good wishes of the government, deputies and senators of both nationalities as well as of numerous offices.

On January 15, 1921, the new Archbishop departed to the Nunciature in Prague for an informative process where witnesses were Abbot Methoděj Zavoral and Jesuit Provincial Father Škárek. In the chapel of the Archbishop's residence in Prague Stojan made the solemn Confession of Faith before the Nuncio Micara in the presence of the Archbishop of Prague, Francis Kordač, and his master of ceremonies.

As Archbishop, Stojan also remained a senator. He went to Prague to defend some business concerning *congrua* on January 20. He was welcomed to the Club of the Senators of the Peoples party on January 24. There the new archbishop reaffirmed his intention to exercise his mandate in these chaotic and critical times. The next day the new archbishop was already at Velehrad, where he arrived incognito on foot from the station of Staré Město through the fields to Velehrad in order that he as the successor of St. Methodius might express his gratitude to God for this high priestly dignity. The students of the

Papal Institute at Velehrad were certainly pleasantly surprised when through the hall went the word: "The Archbishop is here!" He came to attend their play, "The Victory of Love." On January 25, Stojan went to Vienna to preside at the meeting of the Viennese Czechs[2] concerned with the pastoral care of the faithful. They chose a special congregation of priests and sisters to help in the spiritual care of, and Christian charity to, the Viennese Czechs. On February 27 Archbishop Stojan lead the Moravian delegation of 500 participants for the solemn consecration of three new Slovak bishops, M. Kmeťko, Msgr. Bláha and Jan Vojtašák by the Papal Nuncio Micara and Bishops Antonín Podlaha and Karel Kašpar in the Cathedral in Nitra. It was really a festive day for the Slovaks.

Even the Czechs in the United States were glad of the news about Archbishop Stojan, whose name they knew from the Velehrad activities and from the propagation of the *Apostolate of Sts. Cyril and Methodius*.[3] The Metropolitan of Lwov, Andrew Szeptycki, his long-time friend, took part in the funeral services of the Cyrilomethodian co-worker, Father Francis Snopek, in Olomouc, on March 30. On that occasion he had a conversation with Archbishop Stojan about future unionistic endeavors. The next day the funeral, presided over by Stojan with the assistance of Metropolitan Szeptyckyi, provided an opportunity to review the unionistic past of both these zealots, mourning the loss of the third one. On March 24 the new Archbishop went to Velehrad for retreat before his episcopal consecration, which was scheduled for April 3, 1921. This day became one of joyous demonstration in all Moravia, with the attendance of the Archbishop of Prague and bishops and prelates of Bohemia, Moravia, Slovakia, and guests from abroad, as well as government, public, secular and ecclesiastical authorities.[4] The Papal Nuncio of Prague, Archbishop Clement Micara, was consecrator with the assistance of Bishop Kmeťko (Slovak) and Auxiliary Bishop Karel Wisnar of Olomouc in St. Wenceslaus Cathedral, Olomouc.[5] Despite all this adulation, Stojan remained as humble as ever. This is perhaps illustrated by a story[6] told that the Archbishop immediately after his solemn reception went to visit the city poor house, where he hosted 662 to a dinner. In addition he hosted about 3,000 children at the institution of Religious Sisters on Marianská street and distributed the sum of 25,000 crowns to the poor. After that he hurried to see his beloved priests gathered at the seminary.

On April 4 Stojan invited all public officials, employees of public transportation, and all those involved in the festivities of his consecration to his residence for a supper, given in honor of the departing Papal Nuncio and all bishops who had attended the festivities. This was the truly original "Stojan's" event, which had a great impact on the public. It revealed his humility, gratitude and hospitality, for which he was well known. The *Union of Catholic Clergy* of Olomouc *(Jednota)* expressed publicly its appreciation for the new archbishop because its council voted to organize a collection for a new retreat house at Velehrad, to be called *Stojanov* in honor of their new shepherd. The collection succeeded so well that several years later *Stojanov* was built and stands as a historical monument that Velehrad and Stojan were always integral parts of each other. The meaning of Velehrad without Stojan is unthinkable and vice versa.

The first pastoral letter[7] of the new Archbishop, dated April 3, 1921, was a strong affirmation of Stojan's fatherly care for his sheep, for whom he took full responsibility, and that of a humble servant. On April 15 Stojan sent a letter of gratitude and appreciation[8] to Pope Benedict XV for entrusting him with this responsibility. As a manifestation of his love and loyalty toward this confidence, Stojan sent a letter[9] to the clergy and faithful of his archdiocese, to be read from all the pulpits. His first trip abroad as a new archbishop was on April 10 to Vienna where he gave a sermon and celebrated his first Pontifical Liturgy for Viennese Czechs in their church on Rennweg.[10] It is noteworthy that *Jednota Sv. Metoděje* (Union of St. Methodius) in Vienna was then in great financial distress and Stojan announced that the sum of 100,000 Czechoslovak crowns would be sent as a gift of the Archdiocese of Olomouc to alleviate the situation.

The new archbishop continued faithfully to serve all his apostolates as usual. On April 17 he took part in the jubilee convention of Catholic Farmers and Country Youth, *Omladina,* held at Brno[11] where he received a magnificent public ovation. The same day he went to Prague, where he made official visits to public authorities. His companion was the Jesuit Father Ludvík Štork. First in line was the Minister of Education, Professor Josef Šusta, in the Carmelites Street. Afterwards they rode in a coach to see the Papal Nuncio, living then at the Archepiscopal Palace. Stojan presented to him an album depicting his consecration. Next they visited the Prime Minister, officiating in the Institute of Nobles in Hradčany. On the way

The metropolitan church of St. Wenceslaus in Olomouc.

The Most Rev. Anthony Cyril Stojan, S.T.D.,
Archbishop of Olomouc and Metropolitan of Moravia.
This photograph was taken on the day of his episcopal consecration,
April 3, 1921.

they stopped at the tomb of St. John Nepomucene of St. Vitus Cathedral,[12] where he prayed fervently, and also at the Chapel of St. Wenceslaus. Stojan went promptly to see the Ministers of Justice and of Defense, both living at the military college. He also saw the official of Church affairs at the Ministry of Education on Letenská Street, and finally Abbot Zavoral at the Monastery at Strahov. Stojan brought a memorial gift to each of these authorities in appreciation, thus proving again his genuine concern and generosity toward everyone. Finished with official visits on the afternoon of the same day, he hurried to catch the train to Olomouc. Because of the speed with which he made his visits in Prague, Stojan was sorry but unable to see the Jesuit Provincial at St. Ignatius' and he apologized profusely for this to his companion, Father Štork. However, such speed in handling matters was characteristic of Stojan who never lost time for his own comfort or relaxation but followed a schedule he had determined.

Stojan was not only popular with the faithful, but also with all government authorities. Even the first President of the Czechoslovak Republic, Tomas Garrigue Masaryk (1850-1937)[13] invited the new Archbishop on May 3, 1921 to the Presidential Palace, where the President engaged him in a long talk about Church-State affairs. Masaryk, who otherwise did not care much for the Catholic hierarchy, liked Stojan very much for his outright honesty and had confidence in his programs.

On Thursday, May 5, the Feast of the Ascension, Stojan celebrated his first Pontifical Mass at his Cathedral and on the same day planned a trip to his beloved Kroměříž. But suddenly Stojan remained in Olomouc because of a rumor that members of a new Czechoslovak Church would take over Our Lady of Snow Church. The Catholic population of Olomouc naturally was disturbed. The Serbian Orthodox agitator of the Czechoslovak Church, Bishop Dositej,[14] wanted to have liturgical services at Our Lady of Snow Church. He requested permission from the Ministry of National Defense to have the memorial services (panichyde) for the fallen Serbian soldiers in Olomouc's military Catholic Church. Simultaneously it was planned that members of the Czechoslovak Church would take over the Church. When this was discovered in Prague at the last minute, the Orthodox liturgy in the Catholic Church was forbidden and Our Lady of Snow Church was closed in the early morning by military authorities and guarded by soldiers. Crowds of people came. The Catholic gymnastic organization, *Orel,* was ready to defend the Church against seizure by the Czechoslovak Church. Archbishop Stojan spent the whole day on guard and gathered the Catholic people in Catholic House, where several speakers informed them of the actual tense situation at Our Lady of Snow Church. This reveals clearly that Stojan was the faithful guardian of the Catholic Church, always ready to defend her.

When the turbulence was under control in Olomouc, the Archbishop visited his beloved city of Kroměříž on May 11, 1921 to administer the Sacrament of Confirmation. Crowds came to manifest respect for him who had done so much for them while he was there in canonical residence. About 6,000 adults were confirmed.

The new archbishop did not forget his beloved Hostyn, which he visited April 23-24, 1921 to express his devotion to the Blessed Mother, under whose protection he confidently placed his pastoral apostolate as shepherd. These public expressions show that simple popularity always harmonized well with Stojan's hierarchial dignity in such an appealing manner that all people spontaneously sensed his friendship. Perhaps the most interesting phenomenon was that Archbishop Stojan decided to continue his political activities as Senator. These he used very cleverly for the benefit of his large constituency. He returned to the Senate where he performed all his duties, especially those of secretary, responsible for the faithful keeping of records. Stojan felt that his presence on the political scene was vitally needed because the 1920's were turbulent years. He firmly believed that his personal involvement in public affairs could help to quiet the reformistic extremes and to keep them within the limits of order, discipline and law.

Stojan — A consolidator of a turbulent religious and cultural situation

Stojan did know well how to use his influence to counteract political, cultural and religious extremes of the 1920's in the new Czechoslovak Republic. Uncompromisingly loyal to both his nation and his Church, Stojan displayed his influence in keeping the people's sentiments in moderate tones. Perhaps an example of Stojan's shrewdness can be seen from his use of the solemn festivities at Velehrad, July 5-6, 1921, for the alignment of all segments of the nation toward their mutual awareness of a need for unity in the framework of a new Czechoslovak Republic.

The presence of Slovaks in an unusually great number with their leaders at the Velehrad festivities was an indication that they were fascinated with Stojan's care for a just and complete understanding of their national sentiments. At the same time, the presence of the whole diplomatic corps at Velehrad reaffirmed Stojan's beneficial consolidating efforts toward a much desired national tranquility. Stojan, with all his personal charm, knew well how to draw these diplomats to mutual understanding despite the different approaches and views of some individuals. At the public festivity held for these diplomats, Stojan gave public support to the President of the Czechoslovak Republic, Tomas Masaryk, and requested that the President's son, Jan Masaryk, who was present, convey the message from Velehrad to the President. One can easily realize from the turbulent religious situation what a beneficial impact on the ruling authorities of the new nation Stojan's gesture had. Even liberals were captivated by his goodness, sincerity and honesty, for no one could accuse him of political partiality despite his uncompromising defense of the Catholic Church and its valid role in the new Czechoslovak State.

All this, in turn, harmonized with the historical tradition of Moravia, for the Cyrilo-Methodian tradition of Great Moravia is by its very nature a unifying one. It began with the coming of the Byzantine teachers and missionaries, Sts. Cyril and Methodius, to Great Moravia in the year 863. This event was commemorated in the year 1963, not only by the Slav world, but also by the whole cultural world, even by UNESCO. And Pope John Paul II has proclaimed these Apostles of the Slavs the patrons of all Europe.[15]

Promoter of Slavic Solidarity

From the very beginning Stojan perceived in the Cyrilomethodian heritage[16] a powerful force toward a Slavic solidarity.[17] Against the background of the great resentment of the Germans,[18] against *Panslavism*[19] and his personal experience in difficulties he encountered with government authorities in Vienna while organizing the Neo-Slavic Velehrad festivities, Stojan rejected the exaggerated *Pan-Slavism and Nationalism*[20] by becoming a moderate *Neo-Slavist* and an active promoter of Slavic solidarity. In this sense he was also for Czechoslovak national independence in 1918 and the Cyrilomethodian heritage was for him an important component of Czechoslovak tradition.[21]

The most significant and most valuable aspect of the historical, philological, and ecclesiastical Cyrilo-Methodian researches,[22] so extensive and voluminous by this time, was the evidence they produced showing that the missionary and cultural activity of these Greek teachers were unifying, bringing all Slavs together. Methodius was to be the St. Boniface of the Slavs; his see at Velehrad, the metropolitan see for all the Slavs; and the Empire of Great Moravia, like a spiritual papal benefice, a crystal seed of a third power, situated between the Frankist West and the Greek East. This was a distant goal to be realized ages later, worked out by the two Thessalonian brothers and by the popes — Nicholas I, Adrian II, John VIII, and John IX. However, that goal lost its real foundation with the incursion of the Hungarians, who attacked Great Moravia and destroyed its governmental organization in the years 906 and 907.

When the bishopric of Great Moravia was re-established[23] in Olomouc, 1063, gradually there developed a return to the original idea of Moravia's mission to the rest of the Slavs. The need for Moravia's mission was brought to the fore by the separation of the Christian East, formally completed with the schism of Cerularius[24] in the year 1054. The Great Moravian bishop, reformer, and friend of Pope Eugene III, Jindřich Zdík,[25] journeyed as a missionary—in the footsteps of St. Vojtěch, St. Bruno of Querfurt, and others—to the Polabian (Trans-Elbe) Slavs in order to convert them to Christ (1144).

In the year 1147, Zdík was to go along as chaplain to the Crusaders of Conrad III and Vladislav II King of Bohemia, during the second Crusaders' expedition to Palestine. It seems that on this occasion, Eugene III entrusted Zdík with a commission to conduct negotiations with the Greeks. Zdík, however, preferred his duties in the crusade which was organized that same year, 1147. Anselm Havelberg, as Papal Legate, and Wibald of Stablo, Zdík's friend, also took part in this crusade. Otto, Bishop of Frisia, accompanied the crusaders.

Přemysl Otakar II, King of Bohemia, also a candidate for the office of Roman-German Emperor, and his adviser, Bruno of Schaumburk, Bishop of Olomouc, came up with the plan of re-establishing the Metropolitan See of Moravia for the Eastern Slavs. The two crusading expeditions to Prussia and Lithuania and the Baltic territories, in 1255 and 1267, were intended as a means of persuading Rome to re-establish Olomouc as a metropolitan see for all the Czechs and for all the newly christianized territories of the Slavic East. Pope Clement

IV, however, rejected this demand, probably out of consideration for the *Magdeburg* metropolitan, whose jurisdiction included Bohemia at this time, as well as out of consideration for the Gniezno metropolitan, whose interests were being promoted by Martin of Opava,[26] Papal Penitentiary who later became the bishop of Gniezno.

The idea of uniting all Slavs in the Catholic Church played a prominent part in the domestic and foreign policies of the Holy Roman Emperor and King of Bohemia, Charles I (known in Bohemia as Charles IV, Father of His Country). The basis for these policies was the Cyrilo-Methodian idea.[27] These Slav-oriented ecumenical and unionistic efforts were focused on Moravia and Velehrad, which was more resplendent with new glory when Pope Urban VI, on the recommendation of Jan of Středa, granted the abbots of Velehrad the privilege of the "pontificalia"[28] in the year 1379. From Moravia, the Cyrilo-Methodian spark jumped to Slovakia in the territory of Hungary, where as early as the fourteenth century the feast of Sts. Cyril and Methodius began to be liturgically commemorated on March 9th.

The essence of the Cyrilo-Methodian idea, the fostering of which, after the time of Charles IV, passed over to Moravia, as if back to its natural element, re-appeared unconsciously among the rebel Bohemian and Moravian Hussites[29] when they sought union with the Orthodox Slavs in the East and with the Orthodox Greeks in Constantinople. After the Council of Trent, (1546-63) during the Counter-Reformation in Bohemia, the great Cyrilo-Methodian idea came to life in the Moravian reforming bishops, not only in the context of internal renewal, but also in their missionary and unionistic work toward the Slav East.

This Moravian tradition was utilized by Pope Gregory XIII, who founded a pontifical institute in Olomouc, the Collegium Nordicum, for the purpose of training missionaries from the Orthodox East and from the Protestant North, who would then work among their own countrymen. The Collegium Nordicum was founded in 1578 and was confirmed by Gregory XIII on March 15, 1581. This Collegium Nordicum, brought into being by the foremost Jesuit missionary of the sixteenth century, Anthony Possevin,[30] was intended for 50 students. It was financed by Fugger of Augsburg.[31] This institute established the first practical contacts with the dissident Slav East. During the time of their studies, the students were brought closer to a Catholic spirit and environment, and were prepared for responsible functions in their Orthodox homes. The administration of the seminary as well as of the College[32] of Olomouc was in the hands of the Jesuits of the Czech province. This significant beginning of a practical coming closer together with the separated Eastern Christians was ideologically related to the Cyrilo-Methodian apostolate, not only in Moravia and in the see of the Olomouc Bishop as the successor of St. Methodius, but also throughout the whole movement to meet with the East.

In the year 1580, Stanislav Pavlovsky of Pavlovice, Bishop of Olomouc, petitioned Pope Gregory XIII for permission to transfer the bodies of Sts. Cyril and Methodius (then believed to be in Rome) from Rome to Moravia. His petition was not granted; but his successor, Francis Cardinal Dietrichstein (1599-1636), made another request for the relics in the year 1613. The pontifical seminary remained in existence until 1741. Many hundreds of seminarians completed their studies there; they came from many different countries and nations. Thus, in the course of not quite a hundred years, 1,145 students were educated there—according to the records in the archives of the Congregation of the Propaganda, the number finally was 1,253. Possevin's missionary and unionistic idea always had a living echo in Moravia, as demonstrated by the bands of foreign missionaries sent out. It can be presupposed that these missionaries from Bohemia recruited students for the Olomouc and Prague seminaries and thus were instrumental in bringing well educated men to the Catholic and Orthodox East.

The history of Moravia and Bohemia will always have a glorious chapter with the names of Eastern students who completed their studies with Czech Jesuits, Capuchins, Franciscans, and secular priests in Russia during the period of two Baroque centuries. They worked chiefly in Moscow, Petrograd, the Volga territories, and the Black Sea area. Through their writings they acquainted the West with Russian saints[33] and the Church situation. Most recent research,[34] to everyone's great surprise, has shown that even some of the foremost personalities of the Russian Orthodox Church at one time were students in Czech schools.

Varlaam Jasinskij, the Orthodox Metropolitan of Kiev, studied philosophy in Olomouc. Gedeon Odorskij studied theology there; he was the editor (1700-1704) of the *Duchovní Akademie* and later became a uniate Basilian monk. After having renounced union he finally died in exile in the Solovec Monastery. Palladij Rogovskij, a

convert, studied in Olomouc and in Rome where he earned a doctorate in theology. After returning to Russia, he again turned Orthodox
(1698) and became the rector of the Slavjanogrekolatinska Akademie
in Moscow. Active promotion, in the wider sense of the term, for the
conversion of the dissident East did not occur until the time of the
movement which is named after the scholarly Moravian priest, František Sušil (1804-1868) – the Sušil Movement[35] (Hnutí Sušilovské).

The essential element in Sušil's program was the ideal of Slav religious and ecclesiastical unity. This ideal traces its history back to
the 1830's. It has a double dynamic aspect. From Moravia it passed
over to Bohemia and Slovakia, where it was celebrated by the greatest of the Cyrilo-Methodian poets, Jan Hollý.[36] First they looked at
the glorious past of the Great Moravian Empire and would have liked
to call it back again. They then looked into the future of the Slavs,
which would be best insured for them by the protective home of one
Church of Christ, just as it was in the times of Sts. Cyril and Methodius.

With all this background, Stojan and his followers were conscious
of the command implied in the Moravian, Cyrilo-Methodian tradition: "Particularly the Czech nation is called to work for reunion;
for it was to us that Sts. Cyril and Methodius came; our nation has
been chosen by God to help with unity; and chosen in a special way
is Moravia, which, by Divine Providence, guards the tomb of St.
Methodius".[37]

Stojan – Unionistic Zealot

As the War (1914-18) had interrupted Velehrad's already well established tradition set by the previous Unionistic Congresses held in
1907, 1909 and 1911, Stojan as archbishop resumed his beloved
apostolate for Church unity. On August 4-6, 1921, he called a consultation about Unionistic projects which would have an informative
and practical impact on the future development of the Unionistic
Congresses. Because of the impossibility of convoking a Unionistic
Congress in 1921 due to travel difficulties among European States,
Stojan decided to hold a conference on closer attitudes and increasing understanding of the Slavic nations in the area of the Faith. This
was the first review of the work of the past and an affirmation of
the continuation of this greatly promising Unionistic endeavor. About
150 participants from various Slavic nations were present at the conference, over which Stojan presided, aided by his secretary, Rev.

Adolf Jašek. As spokesman for new visions in these Unionistic endeavors appeared the young priest, Francis Dvornik,[38] later sent by Stojan to study history in Prague and then to the Sorbonne in Paris. He became a respected authority on Byzantine affairs[39] and on Church unity. On this occasion the meeting of the most important organs, namely those of the *Velehrad Academy* and the Convention of the *Apostolate of Sts. Cyril and Methodius* and of the *Cyrilomethodian Association of Velehrad* were held and recommendations made about future endeavors and prospects of their success. Stojan was again the soul of all proceedings and his endless optimism greatly influenced others. The result of the preparatory meetings in 1921 was the convocation of the IV Unionistic Conference, attended by 114 delegates, held August 6-9, 1922 at Velehrad, again due mainly to Stojan's efforts, despite all his pastoral duties. Largely representing the Ruthenians from Subcarpathian Russia (Ruthenia) and the Uniates from Galicia were Dr. Jurij Šuba, Canon of Užhorod, Dr. Julius Hadžega, Professor of Theology, Spiritual Director Vasil Takač, Professor Victor Selyka, Seminarians Ivan Hromysk and M. Krvonyak, Rev. Met. Trčka, C.SS.R. of Stropkov, Igumen Josif Jeronym Malyckij, rector of the Seminary of Prešov, Msgr. Josef Gyulaj, Spiritual Director Emanuel Szedlák, Rev. Josef Zorvan, pastor of Klembuk, Dr. Josef Slipyj, Professor of Lwov, and Igumen Platonides Filas of Žokva. Russians also arrived: Editor and Orthodox writer N.K. Klimenko-Vitovtov of Split, students K. Vakitento, F. Piszatovskij, A. Jegorov, D. Trofim Siemiackij of Petersburg, and a Ukrainian of Kiev, Thomas Jakynčuk. Also present were Msgr. Francis Bobal of Chicago, Rev. Martin Bogar of Nebraska, Msgr. Sigbert Geržabek, Abbot and Professor in Gorica, P. Hilarian Gil, S.J., an editor of Madrid, Msgr. Gerdinand Hrdý, Apostolic Administrator in Nise, Serbia, Rev. Josef Janeček from Michigan as representative of the National Alliance of Czech Catholics in U.S.A., Dr. Juraj Magierec of Belehrad, Dr. Walter Vinnenberg, Theologian of Munster, Dr. And. Zivkovic, Chancellor of Diocese in Diakov, Croatia, Ing. C. Lojze Majče of Lublana. The Poles did not participate and Slovaks were few. Among them were Dr. Ed. Necsey and Dr. J. Hodonský. From Prague arrived Prior P. Arnošť Vykoukal, O.S.B., Rev. Ang. Galen, O.S.B. of Emausy, Theologian Cyril Ješ, S.J., Professor, Rev. František Pechuška, Rev. Antonín Stříž, Rev. Ant. Čulík. From Olomouc came Prelate and Canon Ledóchowski, Professor Richard Spaček,

Canon Jan Daněk, Professor Ad. Špaldák, Professor Vincenc Horák and several university students.

Archbishop Stojan was elected president; vice-presidents were Aug. Fischer-Colrie, Bishop of Košice, Dionysius Njaradi, Greek Catholic Bishop of Križevec, Croatia, and Josef Bocian, Greek Catholic Bishop of Podhorec, Galicia; secretaries were Professor Josef Vašica of Olomouc and Rev. Josef Lepka, S.J., of Prague, and as spokesman Professor Bohumil Spáčil, S.J., of the Oriental Institute in Rome was chosen. The Conference[40] began with an introductory talk by Stojan, followed by a Latin report from Professor Josef Vašica who explained how all preparatory work was done in 1921. Then supper was served for all present. Each day of the Conference at 6:00 a.m. Professor Spáčil, S.J., gave a moving spiritual meditation. Then at 8:00 o'clock the Congress began with the reading of telegrams by Archbishop Stojan followed by a lecture: *The Primacy and Infallibility of the Roman Pope* by Jesuit Father Spáčil. He began with this lecture purposely, because the Orthodox theologians held this as a principal objection toward Church unity. This was followed by another presentation, sent by Professor F. Grivec of the University of Lublana who was unable to come. It was entitled: *About the Primacy and Infallibility of the Pope According to Doctrines of the Byzantine and Orthodox Theologians,* which topic greatly interested all present, especially the Russians. This was a scholarly completion to Spáčil's Catholic exposition about the Primacy of the Pope.

At 3 o'clock in the afternoon the conference program continued. Stojan again read all telegrams and a special one was sent to the Holy Father. After this, Professor Julius Hadžega of Užhorod delivered a lecture concerning the *Primacy of the Roman Pope According to Writings of the Russian Church Historian Bolstov.* First he explained his teaching and submitted it to a critique. Then he showed how the difficulties regarding Primacy on the part of some Orthodox theologians could be removed if the doctrine about the Church could be revised a little. Debate was led by Russian academician, Alexander Jegorov, and Spanish Jesuit Father Gill.

The second lecture was given by Charles IV University's Professor Josef Kachník on *The Veneration of Sts. Cyril and Methodius in the East, of St. Vladimir and St. Olga in the West.* After the debate led by Bishop Fischer-Colbrie, the poet and Czech writer, layman

Jaroslav Durych[41] spoke about the role of the Czechoslovak Republic in Unionistic endeavors. He stressed it as providential in fulfillment of the Cyrilomethodian legacy and of its geographical position bridging East and West.

The second day of the Conference began at 8:00 o'clock with Msgr. F. Cinek's report on the Czechoslovak Church, in which he analyzed the doctrine historically and critically. Dr. Živkovic commented on Cinek's lecture by explaining a similar movement called "The Croatian National Church" and by affirming that the Czechs may have taken their example from this movement. This was followed by a report sent by the Russian priest, O. Gleb Verchovskij: *About the Meaning of the Liturgy for the Reunion of the Churches and the Possibility of Such a Union.* A report from Rev. Josef Zorvan-Karpaty of Klemberk on the *Church Discipline of the Catholics of the Eastern Rite according to the New Canon Law,* which was rather practical and lively and accompanied by long debate, was last on the agenda. In other lectures and discussions great attention was given to the religious situation in Russia, where after the fall of Constantinople in 1453, Orthodoxy became important. The Russian writer and editor Nikolai K. Klimenko-Vitovtov had a Croatian report about *"The Present Situation of the Russian Church at Home and Abroad."* Jesuit Father Sakač translated this lecture into Latin for the benefit of all. It was valuable because it came from a Russian Orthodox spokesman.

The third day of the Conference treated of more practical matters. In the morning Father Josef Janeček, representative of the National Alliance of Czech Catholics in U.S.A., commented on the absence of Poles and said that in the United States there is great understanding of the importance of the reunion of the Church. After him, a full-bearded Russian priest, Father Trofim Siemiackij reported in Russian about missionary activity in Russia. Debates in which all took part filled in the remaining time. Finally, thirteen resolutions were formulated and read. They dealt mainly with better prospects for successful Church reunion. The Conference had a great impact at home and abroad. Several foreign journals, like the Spanish *Razón y fé,* Ukrainian *Niva* or *Hrvatska Prosvjeta,* and others brought news and commentaries.

In a follow-up of the Conference, seminarians held a convention August 9 and 10th, together with meetings of all important organizations connected with Velehrad. Archbishop Stojan expressed gratitude to all participants and lecturers. With the veneration of the relics of Sts. Cyril and Methodius and prayers for the unity of the Slavs the Congress ended. No one dreamed that the inspiring closing talk of Archbishop Stojan to the seminarians was indeed his last one at the tomb of St. Methodius. As we now know, Stojan was then sick and dying, but as much as he suffered from exhaustion, he continued all phases of pastoral cares and apostolates. In retrospect A.C. Stojan, therefore, stands prominently in the ranks of those who led unionistic movements in Moravia: (1) To the centuries-old effort toward effecting a meeting and union with the dissident blood brothers, Stojan contributed popular fundamentals, broader by far then Slomšek's contribution. (2) He combined the various efforts into a single organization, the *Apostolate of Sts. Cyril and Methodius,* which laid stress on efficiency. (3) In addition to laying the foundations for the popular appeal generated by the *Apostolate,* he also laid the foundations for the scholarly appeal generated by the *Velehrad Academy.* (4) He was the first to bring about a practical meeting of the East and the West at the Velehrad Unionistic Congresses. (5) In this way he also renewed and insured for Moravia and Velehrad their former glory which they had in the days of the Great Moravian Empire; and to this was joined the duty of working for unity of faith among the Slavs. In the fulfillment of this Cyrilomethodian legacy, Stojan proved to be a worthy occupant of the see of St. Methodius.

NOTES

1. *Našinec* of Jan. 25, 1921.
2. The whole affair is detailed by F. Cinek, *op.cit.*, 950-958.
3. Hynek Dostál, "Apoštol Moravy," *Hlas* (St. Louis), Feb. 8, 1921.
4. Cinek, *ibid.*
5. Rudolf Šmahel, *Olomouc ve Fotografii* (Ostrava, 1965), 193-141; the naves of this Cathedral were built between 1265-1364, while towers were erected in 1885.
6. *Moravsko-slezský deník* of Sept. 30, 1923, detailed the solemn occasion by the parliament representative Spaček.
7. The full text is published in Cinek, *op.cit.*, 961-962.
8. Latin text is to be found in Cinek, *op.cit.*, 963.
9. This can be found in *Acta Curiae Archiepiscopalis Olomucensis*, no. 5, 1921, and is reprinted in Cinek, *op.cit.*, 963-964.
10. *Pravda* of April 15 and 22, 1921.
11. *Našinec* no. 89 (Olomouc) of April 19, 1921.
12. Jiří Burian, *Katedrála Sv. Víta na pražském hradě* (Prague; Odem 1975), VIII–XXXIV; Karel Plicka, *Prague en images* (Prague 1950), 14-31.
13. Otakar Odložilík, "T.G. Masaryk in the Past and Present" in Symposium: *Tributes to T.G. Masaryk* (London, 1950), 12-14; idem, *T.G. Masaryk, 1850-1937* (Chicago, 1950) 56 pp.
14. Frantisek Cinek, *K náboženské otácze v prvních letech naší samostatnosti* (Concerning religious question in the first years of our independence) (Olomouc, 1926) 87-95 and passim.
15. Ludvik Nemec, *Pope John Paul II, a Festive Profile* (New York, 1979). See Pope John Paul II Ap. letter "Egregiae virtutis" of Dec. 31, 1880, *L 'Osservatore Romano* of Dec. 31, 1980; Czech transl. in *Ochránci Evropy*, (Rome, 1981), 9-12.
16. Alois Kolísek, *Cyrillo-Methodějství u Čechů a u Slováků* (Brno, 1935) *passim;* Josef Kolejka, "Cyrilometodějská tradice v druhé polovině 19 století (Cyrilomethodian tradition in the second half of XIX century)"; *Velká Morava* ed. by Jan Böhm (Prague, 1963) 97-112.
17. Jan Kollár, *Rozpravy o Slovanské Vzájemnosti* (Discussions about Slavic solidarity) ed. by Miloš Weingart (Prague, 1929) passim; Adolf Jašek, *Výklad idee cyrillomethodějské* (Interpretation of the Cyrilomethodian idea) (Velehrad, 1909).
18. Pavel Kopal, *Das Slaventum und der Deutsche Geist, Problem einer Weltkultur auf Grundlage der Religiosen Idealismus* (Jena, 1914), passim.

19. S.H. Thomson, "A Century of a Phantom: Panslavism and the Western Slavs," *Journal of Central European Affairs*, XI (1951) 57-77; R.W. Seton-Watson, "Pan-Slavism," *The Contemporary Review* LX (1916) 419-428; Hans Kohn, "The Impact of Pan-Slavism on Central Europe," *The Review of Politics* XXIII (1961), 321-333; H. Hantsch, "Pan-Slavism, Austro-Slavism: The All-Slav Congresses and the Nationality Problems of Austria-Hungary," *Austrian History Yearbook* 1 (1965), 23-37.
20. Robert A. Kann, *The Multinational Empire—Nationalism and National Reforms in the Habsburg Monarchy 1848-1918*, (New Brunswick, NJ, 1950) passim; Václav Zácěk, "K dějinám austro-slavismu rakouských slovanů, "*Slovanské historické studie* 7 (1968) 129-180.
21. Otakar Odložilík, "Components of the Czechoslovak Tradition," *The Slavonic and East European Review* XXIII (1945), 97-106; Sis, Kramar, op.cit., pp. 153-190.
22. Ludvik Nemec, "The Recent Reinvestigation of Cyrillomethodian Sources and Their Basic Problems," *Czechoslovakia Past and Present*, ed. by M. Rechígl, Jr. (Hague, 1972) II, pp. 1151-1174.
23. Otakar Odložilík, "From Velehrad to Olomouc," *Harvard Slavic Studies* II (1962) 75-90.
24. Francis Dvornik—Arno Burg, *La Separazione tra Roma e Constantinopoli nel 1054 e l'Avvenimento del 7 December 1965* (Documentazione), *Concilium* 5 (1966).
25. Bohumil Zlámal, *Antonín Cyril Stojan*, (Rome, 1973), 94-99.
26. He wrote the world chronicle known as *Chronica Summorum Pontificum Imperatorumque ac de VII aetatis mundi*, covering world events up to the year 1277.
27. Milada Paulová, "L'idée cyrillo-méthodienne dans la politique de Charles IV et la foundation du monastère slave de Prague", *Byzantinoslavica* 11 (1950), 174-186.
28. Bohumil Zlámal, *Introduction to Rudolf Šmahel's Velehrad* (Ostrava 1969) passim.
29. Milada Paulová, "L'Empire byzantin et les tchèques avant la chute de Constantinople (L'Union Florentine et les Tchèques), *Byzantinoslavica* 14 (1953), 158-225.
30. Francis Dvornik, *The Slavs in European History and Civilization* (New Brunswick, NJ, 1962), 276.
31. Fuggers, the Augsburg financiers, dominated the banks of Antwerp, the greatest commercial center in XVIth century Europe.
32. Founded originally by Bishop Prusinovský of Olomouc in 1556.
33. Jiři David, S.J., *Synaxarium Ruthenicum, 1688, written for the Acta Sanctorum*—or with the Russian Cyrilo-Methodian script; idem., *Exemplar Characteris, Mosco-vitico-Ruthenici, Duplicis, Biblici et Usalis*, 1690—or with the religious and cultural conditions, idem., *Status Modernus Magnae Russiae seu Moscovitae*. The pioneer among Czech orientologists was a Jesuit from the diocese of Olomouc, Jan Fr. Milan, who journeyed through China and Tibet and then wrote about the life, culture, and religion of the Azov Kalmyks—*Missio Asophiensis et Taganrogensis*, 1700.

34. A. Ammann, *Abriss der ostslavichen Kirchengeschichte* (Vienna, 1950), passim; P. Pierling, *La Russie et le Saint-Siège,* 2 vols. (Paris, 1901).
35. Sušil is known for his collection of songs, which he included in his famous: *Moravské národní písně s nápěvy do textu vřaděnými* (Moravian National Songs, with music inserted in the text) (Brno, 1960); Jan Drábek, *Z časů nedlouho zašlých* (From times not long past) (Rome, 1967), 77-78.
36. Stanislav Meciar, "Cyrilometodska tema u Hollého a Hviezdoslava", *Most* X nos. 1-4 (Cleveland, 1963), 22-32.
37. As was reminded by František Žák, 1897.
38. Ludvik Nemec, ed. "80–František Dvorník", *Proměny* 3 no. 10 (New York, July 1973) 1-103 (multilingual Festschrift).
39. Ludvik Nemec, "The Festive Profile of Francis Dvornik, the Scholar, the Historian, and the Ecumenist," *The Catholic Historical Review* LIX no. 2 (July, 1973) 185-224; Cinek, *op.cit.,* 1000.
40. Detailed report by Professor Josef Vašica is in *Apoštolát* no. 10-12 of 1922, pp. 114 ff.
41. Cinek, *op.cit.,* 1059.

VIII
DEATH CAME FOR THE ARCHBISHOP

Stojan – Sick

The exhausting activities eventually undermined the strong body of the steadfast archbishop. In the fall of 1922 he first felt a grave loss of physical strength. In October the public became aware that the Archbishop was very weak. Stojan's problem was always that he seldom contacted a physician or was under one's care. If in some exceptional cases he submitted to an examination by a doctor, he frequently failed to follow the instructions given. It was difficult for him to change his way of living. He simply could not live without working. He was really—to use a modern word—a workaholic. Among his last business affairs was the nomination on November 26, 1922, of seven new metropolitan canons for Olomouc with a compromise from the Government authorities who gave up some of their rights (so-called regii) and with a certain understanding of the Collegiate chapter who had a right to elect three canons. This in itself was an achievement of diplomacy in view of the as yet unresolved State-Church relations at that time.

At the same time Pope Pius XI nominated Canon Josef Schinzl as the Auxiliary Bishop of Olomouc. In this case it can be demonstrated how sensitive Stojan was to the German minority of the clergy, and just to all in his archdiocese. On January 8, 1923, Stojan consecrated the new Auxiliary Bishop in the Cathedral of Olomouc and gave a reception in his honor in the seminary in the afternoon. Stojan became very depressed after receiving a telegram on January 11 from Rev. Oldřich Zlámal[1] of Cleveland, United States that Father Adolf Jašek, Stojan's most zealous Cyrilo-Methodian co-worker had died there. The following week, on January 17 and 18, Stojan conferred tonsure on 21 seminarians and performed minor ordinations for 18 others. This time he was really exhausted. His physician prohibited his delivering any speeches. Stojan, brokenhearted, submitted. Instead he sent his pastoral letter on the first Sunday of Lent, 1923, and published an appeal to Catholic Youth (Omladina).[2] On February 25 he ordained 21 seminarians subdeacons to whom he had dedicated all his loving care.

One of Stojan's most pressing worries remained the building of a retreat house in Velehrad, to be called *Stojanov*. He was constantly in contact with Mr. V. Zbořil, owner of a factory in Bystřice,[3] concerning his donation of 200,000 Czechoslovak crowns for Velehrad and 25,000 crowns for electrical installations at Hostyn. Stojan followed all news about the retreat house with great anxiety, hoping that he might consecrate it on July 5, 1923. He was kept informed about the development of the building by the rector of the Jesuits at Velehrad, Father Ostrčilík, who sent him copies of *Velehradské zprávy* (Velehrad's news) which delighted him.

On March 13, 1923 Stojan had a conference concerning the reform of theological studies, one of his overriding concerns. On March 17 he ordained 17 deacons in the seminary chapel and on Palm Sunday blessed palms with the assistance of the new canons in the Cathedral. During Holy Week Stojan's health became worse, but despite heart difficulties, he hosted the elders on Holy Thursday. The Papal Nuncio, Clement Micara, stayed then for several days in Stojan's residence. This caused the press to circulate a rumor about the possibility of Stojan's being named Cardinal. Unfortunately, these rumors never materialized even though everyone thought that such an honor would be most appropriately deserved.

On the Feast of the Ascension of the Lord, May 11, 1923, the agonizing Stojan suffered a stroke, and was given the Last Rites by the chapter's dean, Auxiliary Bishop Wisnar. He was still conscious but soon lapsed repeatedly into agony. For five months Stojan's strong body resisted the final attack. He took all suffering with exemplary resignation to God's will. During this prolonged illness there were five strokes before the end came. Extensive medical care was provided by Stojan's personal physician, Dr. Jan Glos and by Dr. F. Votruba, director of the State Hospital, who were always present during his last weeks. Stojan appreciated their care and frequently promised jokingly that if he should get well, all who served him would be invited to a banquet.

Just a few weeks before his death, he sent his blessing to the newly ordained priests on July 5, and thinking about Velehrad, with a cry

he sent the message: "I will not see Velehrad any more. . . Please
tell all seminarians that I beg them, as St. Cyril said to his brother
when he was dying. . .that they not abandon our good people."[4]
This was the last wish which Archbishop Stojan sent to the candidates for the priesthood—the desire he sent to Velehrad, the cradle
of Christian Faith. In spite of all this spiritual thought, Stojan remained himself even during his great suffering; he kept his humor very
much alive and with it surprised his friends and visitors, in whom he
caused laughter and joy. These were his constant companions until
his departure to eternity.

Stojan's Death

The lingering illness continued to worsen. Since September, 1923
it was clearly visible that the patient was weakening. He was frequently
in agony and slept almost all week. September 21 brought a complica-
tion, an inflammation of the lungs. September 22 and 23 he felt a
little better. He was delighted with a warm telegram from the Holy
Father, but after September 23 he spoke no more and on Saturday,
September 29, 1923, lapsed again into agony and at 1 o'clock in the
afternoon, Archbishop Stojan quietly passed away.

At his deathbed were relatives, members of the household with the
secretary, Msgr. K. Karlík, and the vice-president of the Senate, Dr.
Maurice Hruban who manifested his faithful friendship during the
whole illness. The bells of the churches of Olomouc announced the
sad news, which quickly spread over the land. Telegrams were sent
even to U.S.A.

His funeral was set for Tuesday and Wednesday, October 2 and 3.
It was also decided that the Archbishop should be buried in the Royal
Chapel at Velehrad, which was located on the left side of the Church
and restored by the Jesuits in 1898. In this chapel were buried the
Founder of the monastery, the Moravian Margrave Vladislav Jindřich (d. August 12, 922), benefactors and patrons of the monastery,
and the bishops of Prague, Daniel (d. 1215) and Andrew (d. 1224).
On Sunday, September 30, the Last Will was read, text of which
follows:

At Olomouc, February 2, 1923.
In the name of the Most Blessed Trinity, "Father, Son and the Holy
Ghost" I beg the Lord God, my Creator, for mercy and forgiveness. I
give my soul to Him. I beg my archdiocesan priests and friends that

they remember me in their prayers. Simultaneously I beg them to forgive me if I hurt them or in any way scandalized them.

I beg that at Velehrad, Hostyn, Stará Voda, Burkberk at Krnov and at all Churches which I helped to build or care for spiritually, the bells will ring after my death so that all the faithful may become aware and give me a remembrance in prayer. I beg my classmate—priests to have Mass according to agreement at the last dinner before departing from the seminary.

I am leaving the Foundation of Hostyn, the Apostolate of Sts. Cyril and Methodius under the protection of the Blessed Virgin Mary, the Cryilomethodian Association, Velehrad and the German boys seminary, which we intend to establish, an equal share in all that will be left after me, as universal heirs.

Grant, Lord God, that all be blessed!

I am appointing Very Reverend Father B. Hřiva, dean in Napajedla and Reverend Father Frant, Duda, chaplain in Šumperk, executors of this last Will.

Dr. Antonin Cyril Stojan,
Archbishop of Olomouc.[5]

All journals in the Czechoslovak Republic published devout memorials of the deceased Metropolitan, although this was not usual. Not only the Catholic, but also the secular press of all parties and nationalities, devoutly and unanimously appraised the true merits of this great Cyrilomethodian archbishop, an apostle of love on the throne of St. Methodius. The impact of the death of Archbishop Stojan on the entire populace was strong and deep. Perhaps there was no priest or bishop in any nation so far about whom so much was written with such spontaneous admiration, love and respect. Numerous telegrams of condolence arrived from all over the world. The President of the Czechoslovak Republic himself sent this telegram: "The Metropolitan Chapter in Olomouc. I am expressing to you, Sirs, on the occasion of the passing away of the archbishop, my sincere sympathy. I recognized early his fine humanitarianism, especially at the time we were both deputies. I always admired very much that in his high dignity he preserved his popular humor, sincere kindness and concern for the Moravian people. T.G. Masaryk."[6] Similar telegrams came from the Prime Minister and government as well as from military authorities.[7]

Stojan's Funeral

The embalmed body of the deceased Metropolitan was exposed a whole day in the archiepiscopal residence, decorated with an avalanche of flowers, one of which was from the President of the Czechoslovak Republic, T.G. Masaryk, with others from various institutions and individuals.

Monday, October 1, about 6 o'clock the train arrived from Prague bringing a new Papal Nuncio, Francis Marmaggi[8] with his secretary, Msgr. Arata; then Bishop J. Gross of Litoměřice, Auxiliary Bishop of Prague, J. Sedlák, who represented the Archbishop Francis Kordač of Prague, Canon Senator Dr. Reyl, representing the bishop of Hradec Králové, Karel Kašpar, Abbot of Strahov M. Zavoral and others. All were welcomed at the Olomouc station by the dean of the chapter, Msgr. M. Mayer, and dean of the Theological Cyrilomethodian Faculty, Dr. Josef Hejčl, ministerial Council J. Žáček and the delegation of the Czechoslovak Orel. The Square was full of people.

Tuesday, October 2, 1923, funeral services conducted by the Papal Nuncio began at 9 o'clock before the archiepiscopal residence. There was a procession to the Cathedral. All ecclesiastical, government and military authorities attended. The funeral Mass was said by the Bishop of Prague, Msgr. Sedlák; after the Mass the famous orator, Abbot of Strahov Methoděj Zavoral, gave an historical eulogy[9] reviewing in faithful fashion Stojan's personality and his mission as providential for national survival and spiritual renewal. Zavoral's beautiful eulogy faithfully mirrored the rarely found honesty and goodness of Archbishop Stojan. Following the sermon, Nuncio Francis Marmaggi performed the Rites *Libera* and the bishops, Sedlák, Klein, Gross and Jantausch, gave absolution. The body of the Cyrilomethodian apostle was then carried from the Cathedral, accompanied by the tears of all present. The huge procession followed the Avenue of the Czechoslovak Legions to the train station in Olomouc, from there to Uherské Hradiště, where crowds of Moravian Slovaks waited for their Stojan. Members of the Catholic gymnastic organization *Orel* bore the body from the train where a Liturgy of blessing was performed to the accompaniment of the choir "Svatopluk" with requiem hymns.

Stojan buried at Velehrad

From the city of Uherské Hradiště the funeral procession proceeded to its destination, Velehrad, arriving there about 7 o'clock in the evening. The faithful of Velehrad and the surrounding area awaited at the Chapel Cyrilka the arrival of the body of their beloved Stojan. Here the procession entered the church, where the Catholic *Orel* of the Velehrad district formed an honor guard until the Church was closed for the night. The morning of October 3 crowds of Moravian people came for the funeral. At 8 o'clock there was a Mass for the Catholic Youth Organization, *Omladina*, in Chapel Cyrilka. At 9 o'clock the general vicar, Msgr. Rusniak, celebrated Liturgy in Old Slovanic. After these devotions all went to the church where at 10 o'clock a Requiem Mass was celebrated by Prelate Ledóchowski with the assistance of the clergy. A deputy of Parliament, Father Rypar, delivered the sermon for the people. He described the beautiful, holy life and the outstanding merits of the deceased archbishop.[10] After Mass, a procession with the participation of organizations and Church, Government and Military authorities, and various bands followed by a crowd estimated at 50,000 led into the new square before the balcony of the Retreat House *Stojanov,* where there was a picture of Stojan. Here his friend and colleague from the Senate, Dr. Maurice Hruban, made the last lamentation upon the passing of the friend of all, as follows:

"The places where we are standing are sacred ones for their historical significance, for they are consecrated by the activities of the greatest men of our nation and of all Slavs, Sts. Cyril and Methodius. They are sacred because of the fire and zeal which enlightened and inspired enthusiasm, awakened the sleeping nation toward life with the Cyrilomethodian idea. The Royal Chapel, in which we today will lay this pilgrim, who in this world already reached a goal. A holy man, a good Christian, Antonín Cyril Stojan, will be doubly sacred to us.

"A very heavy, sad loss, his death affected especially the Church which is losing in him an exemplary bishop; Moravia, from which has departed its beloved Metropolitan; the archdiocese, crying out for its indefatigable shepherd. All have lost much, too much, but the loss which we have suffered, we who struggled with him for our people. A friend has departed from us, a leader, a counsellor, our best father.

"There is certainly today no need to speak about his activities, his merits—for his life lies before us as an open book and all know too well his impact and his life's work. A beautiful notice in the leading liberal Moravian journal related that 'behind the casket of the Archbishop, Dr. Stojan, the respect of the whole nation will follow.' And

I may add that not only the respect of our nation, but also that of other nations who knew his apostolic activity. Our great deceased loved above all the Church, the Fatherland and his people, and we cannot do otherwise than to give our love for a love; we are obligated to a devout love toward Holy Church, a Cyrilomethodian Faith, the guardian of the heritage of our Fathers, so much in our days vituperated, unrecognized and undermined; we are obligated to the love of a Nation, Fatherland and State if we wish to be worthy of the great and sacred legacy of Stojan. Let us promise upon his casket that we will defend the national freedom and independence of the State, which he has helped to build, and thus we will show gratitude and faithfulness to his mission and his work.

"The deceased, whenever he succeeded in any work, or when in Parliament he pushed a law which was important to him, used to say from his platform: 'How could I express gratitude better than with my great Lord God who repays?' Thus we cannot fail in this moment, when the bells of Velehrad which he helped to preserve in time of war, sing a sad song accompanying him on his last trip and inspiring our souls to cry, to express our gratitude in no better way than with the great 'Lord God, repay!' With the sacred promise of love and gratitude from the crowds we will come to his grave to beg that he in heaven intercede for us and for all, something he in his lifetime loved to do."[11]

Then a speaker, accompanied by the loud cries of the faithful, said the last: "With God" (Good-by) to the deceased shepherd. The funeral procession continued to the Royal Chapel in the church for burial. The Auxiliary Bishop of Prague, Josef Sedlák, performed the liturgy and during the singing of both national and papal hymns, the casket was placed in the sarcophagus.[12] After the funeral liturgy, Msgr. Andrej Hlinka in the name of Slovaks, Professor Josef Vašica for the Cyrilomethodian Faculty, the deputy of Parliament Mr. Joseph Šamalík, Dr. J. Daněk for the Czechoslovak Orel, Mr. Litomyšlský for the Viennese Czechs, Ing. Rostislav Sochorec for the Catholic students, Miss M. Lysonková for the Catholic Youth *Omladina*, Mr. Matthew Novák, Mayor of Staré Město, for all people of the Moravian Slovakia, and others expressed sad farewell eulogies of their beloved selfless humanitarian and humble servant of God.

BODY OF ARCHBISHOP STOJAN IN CASKET.
The entire Catholic Moravia participated in the funeral of Archbishop Antonin Cyril Stojan, with many distinguished people from Bohemia, Slovakia and from all Czechoslovakia, with many representatives of neighboring States.
The Administration of Railroads in Olomouc provided a great number of special trains so that people of the land could travel to give their last respects to their beloved Archbishop in Olomouc or in Velehrad.

Senator Dr. Mořic Hruban had a eulogy in front of the Retreat House Stojanov, whence the procession came to the place of burial: the royal chapel in the Church at Velehrad. Members of the Catholic Orel formed the honor guard.

FUNERAL PROCESSION OF OFFICIAL DIGNITARIES.
First line behind casket: Msgr. Jan Šrámek, minister of Czechoslovak
Government, then Senator Dr. Mořic Hruban and the Minister of
Justice, Dr. Jaroslav Dolanský; in center the Prime Minister, Dr.
Hodža, then Minister Rudolf Mlčoch, Minister Jan Černý, Minister
Dr. Mičura and Minister J. Mareš, Msgr. Andrej Hlinka representing
the Catholic Slovakia. Other participants are: Chairman of Senate,
J. Tomášek, Senator František Soukup, deputies J. Vičánek,
Dr. Novák, Dr. Řehulka, secretary general of the people's party,
J. Červinka, Senator Jan Pechanec, General of Army, R. Medek,
Professor J. Engliš, Professor Veyr, Deputy Alois Peter, Minister
Dr. J. Stránský, Deputies Cvincěk and Ursiny, Professor Adolf
Procházka, and a great number of city representatives from entire
Moravia, with large numbers of members of hierarchy, members of
religious orders, and Catholic organizations.

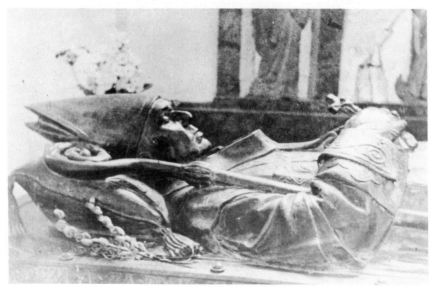

The royal chapel with the tomb of Archbishop Stojan in the
Velehrad Basilica — the bronze relief on the tomb
is the work of Julius Pelikan.

NOTES

1. Monsignor Oldřh Zlámal (d. 1955) was a prominent representative of the National Alliance of Czech Catholics, and also a pastor of Our Lady of Lourdes in Cleveland. He participated in several missions and political actions on behalf of the Czechoslovak Republic. He was active in cultural and religious Czech affairs in U.S.A. and in his memoirs he narrated this entitled: *Povídka mého života* (Story of My Life) (Chicago, 1953); concerning Czechs in Cleveland see Francis Dvornik, *Czech Contributions to the growth of the United States,* (Chicago, 1961) 41-46.
2. Text of this appeal was published in the journal *Hvězda* no. 1 of 1923 and is reproduced by F. Cinek, *op.cit.,* pp. 1075-1076.
3. *Bystřice pod Hostýnem* (Bystřice, 1933). This convenient booklet was published by courtesy of City Council for the information of tourists in the mountains around the Hostyn. Mr. Zbořil who was a great benefactor of Hostyn and Velehrad, was also a great friend of Archbishop Stojan.
4. Cinek, *op.cit.,* 1091.
5. The Czech text can be found in Cinek, *op.cit.,* 1151.
6. The Czech text is in Cinek, *op.cit.,* 1153.
7. Some are reported in Cinek, *op.cit.,* 1153-1157 by reproducing excerpts of journals in which these greetings were published.
8. He succeeded Clement Micara in May of 1923 and later had difficulties with the Czechoslovak government for tolerating all forms of attacks and disturbances. See *Osservatore Romano* of August 28, 1925; when the anniversary of Hus' death was celebrated with official attendance by members of the government, the Vatican recalled the Nuncio from Prague May 18, 1925; see S. Harrison Thomson, *Czechoslovakia in European History* (Princeton, NJ, 1943), 324; Orazio M. Premoli, *Contemporary Church History,* 1900-1925 (London, 1932), 242.
9. The full text can be found in F. Cinek, *op.cit.,* 1160-1163.
10. *Občanské noviny* of October 4, 1923.
11. *Našinec* of October 4, 1923 carries the Czech text of the speech; English translation is by the author.
12. This *sarcophagus* is simple in style, not elaborate as those in Ireland, England or elsewhere, which is greatly regretted by the author, hoping that in the future this may be rebuilt as it deserves to be.

IX
STOJAN'S ACTIVISM IN ITS
SPIRITUAL PERSPECTIVE

Looking at the enormous activity of Stojan, one must ask the question, was not this man a victim of the unhealthy fad of external activity? Was he not a captive of the error that Cardinal Mermillod calls "the heresy of the active life"? Was there not in Stojan a kind of spiritual neurasthenia, pressing him into activity, without which he could not live? Although this would seem to malign Stojan's spiritual motivation, it is good to follow this inquiry that all the truly noble spiritual characteristics of this man of God can be fully manifested. The fact that Stojan did not neglect his spiritual life at any time is evidence that he was not a workaholic by disposition but for his principal goal: to praise God and save souls. Even souls alienated from God felt that this priest lived for God, worked only for God, and that he sacrificed himself for God's concerns. Stojan's activism was motivated by St. Paul's admonition to be "all things to all men" (1 Cor. 9:22) in attempting to be as effective as possible in his all inclusive apostolate to safeguard the salvation of souls.

As a great idea influences not only its environment, but also its bearer, so it was with Stojan. The admonition of St. Paul inspired him with importance as well as humility; it urged him on to a strict life-long obligation, and subconsciously it unified all his activities and personal interests, pointing them exclusively in a single direction: the salvation of souls.

As one can see in retrospect, Stojan in his youthful student and seminary days manifested a lively interest in education for his own people. It was also in the blood of the Czech nation, which was just then trying to catch up with things which had been previously denied them. No other period of that nation's history witnessed a more feverish literary and educational activity. Poems, songs and music were utilized to express the whole nation's assertion of its right to an independent existence. This movement resulted in the founding or enlarging of several hundred libraries in the rural areas of Moravia—a movement in which Stojan played a very active role—funds being provided by the seminarians of Olomouc and Brno.

Like the majority of students in those days, Stojan was caught up in this stream of educational and cultural renewal. In Beňov he organized meetings and lectures; he was more effective in this kind of work than many others. He founded a school and parish library for the people of his home town, and also wrote a chronicle of the town's history. It was perhaps this activity that led some of the people to predict that this student named Stojan would some day be a nationally famous teacher.

Stojan actually remained interiorly attached to educational work. When compulsory military service made his ordination to the priesthood seem improbable, he decided to become a teacher. Later it was perfectly natural that he should choose teachers to be the first proponents of spiritual renewal when, in 1893, he assembled them for a meeting in Velehrad. The patronage for this meeting was provided by the Cyrilo-Methodian ideal: Sts. Cyril and Methodius were also teachers—they taught the Slavs.[1] It would have been surprising if Stojan had not been primarily concerned with schools and with every phase of education.

Not only was he zealously active in educational organizations, but he also went about zealously founding schools, or lending assistance to their building. Ample evidence of this can be found right in the city of Příbor, where he worked for the founding of several schools and adult education classes. He also organized a Sarkander Chapter (discussion club) to provide students with guidance in Christian spirituality. This was a daring initiative on the part of Stojan, for he was then only a curate in Příbor. But at this same time, he was also instrumental in building a school in the town of Myší (now called Mniši) not far from Příbor. In Svébohov, due to Stojan's initiative, the school was expanded, and in the mission attended from svébohov, in Václavov, a new school was built. Stojan was particularly active in education while he was pastor in Dražovice, where he organized the Hospodářské Besídky (agricultural clubs), the Hospodářské Kursy (agricultural courses), and "pokračovací školy" (continuation schools) for young people. Here he taught for six years, two class periods each week. He also obtained assistance for the city council's project of building a girls' school for domestic arts. The dedication of this public girls' school (1896), which was conducted by the Dominican Sisters of Vyškov, was a joyful occasion for Father Stojan. To gain support for this project, he founded the *Jednota Školního Družstva ve Vyškově* (The Federation of School Societies in Vyškov). Stojan's goal was always not only a Czech school, but also a Catholic school, as was specifically stated in the proclamation issued by the Katolicko-Národní Strana[2] (Catholic National Party) in Přerov in 1896. Very characteristically, in his address at the dedication of this school, Father Stojan spoke about Pope Leo XIII and Sts. Cyril and Methodius.[3] The climax of these educational activities was to be the founding of a Sts. Cyril and Methodius Catholic University in Moravia, a dream Stojan never realized.

Father Stojan regarded teachers and priests as principal agents for enlightening the people. As a member of Parliament, therefore, he manifested deep concern for educational and parochial matters. He was always a spokesman for educators; he spoke in their behalf in committee meetings and in sessions of Parliament; he promoted legislation to raise the teachers' salaries. He continued to do this even when it aroused political antagonism against himself. Some of the voters were disappointed in him on this account and threatened not to vote for him again. Stojan regretted this but his answer was: "Let them do as they wish. I am convinced that the teachers are underpaid, and I cannot act in any other way."

Father Stojan's second love was organizational activity, a characteristic of his times. Even in the most varied types of organizations, he saw the embodiment of unity in a small group, the opportunity for a meeting of minds, and particularly the means for carrying out concrete actions. He was convinced that societies, organizations and associations made it possible to create a greater impact and to carry out more decisive action than was possible for a single individual by himself. Every nation is, to a great extent, composed of a majority of average people; these, when supported by a chain of brotherly hands joined together in an organization, can rise to the level of effective activists, and thus goals can be more easily achieved.

Stojan seems to have believed something similar to this; and such a belief was not merely a figment of his imagination; rather, it was an enlightened method. In this light, one can understand why organizational activity remained one of Stojan's interests throughout his life. He founded almost a score of societies, alone or in collaboration with others; he organized temporary associations for various particular purposes—for building or renovating churches or schools, for charitable works, and for other similar purposes. He himself was a member or supporter of countless organizations. He had a collection of more than a hundred honorary diplomas conferred upon him by cities and organizations. Stojan's organizations operated on the principle expressed in the motto understood very well in ecclesiastical as well as in political circles; the motto which the Austrian ruling family adopted: "Viribus unitis" (with united strengths)[4] or in union there is strength.

Stojan was an organizational man. An organization was for him like a native home, where he sought to implant a useful idea and to anchor it permanently. In the history of the Church in Czechoslovakia, very few men founded as many professional organizations and church societies as did Father Stojan. He did not shy away from civic organizations when such organizations served a useful purpose. As a curate in Příbor, he became a member of the town's voluntary fire brigade; there he served as instructor, secretary and treasurer; he wrote the fire brigade's chronicle; he even wore the fireman's uniform and took part in rescue work whenever there was a fire in town. At the same time he was active in the Spolek sv. Mikuláše (Society of St. Nicholas) a charitable organization, and in the Bratrstvo sv. Josefa z Arimatie (Brotherhood of St. Joseph of Arimathea) which provided burial for strangers and derelicts, and in many other societies.

While he was still in Příbor, Father Stojan almost unconsciously entered the second, and more important, phase of his philanthropic and educational activities, which he carried out by means of participation in various organizations. This was his effective assistance to people in their everyday material and spiritual difficulties. The fire brigade to which he belonged had the motto: "Bohu ke cti, bližnímu ku pomoci!" (For the honor of God and help of neighbor), and the members of the fire brigade lived up to this motto in a very practical way. Later, as an archbishop, Stojan once remarked: "I know firemen: I was and I remain with those who have adopted as their motto that very beautiful phrase from Christ's teaching."[5]

The best help is self-help, and Stojan's times regarded organizations as a particularly effective self-help. The Church too did not over-look their importance. Stojan entered public life almost at the same time that Leo XIII was elected pope (1878-1903). This Pope, who "gained modern times for the Church and for the tiara"[6] did not fail to recognize the importance of modern media of communication, societies, congresses, organizations and mass demonstrations. He recognized such means as important in any ideological struggle; therefore, he approved and supported their use. With a sensitive ear turned to the voice of Rome, Stojan knew he was doing the right thing.

No biographer will presume to credit Stojan with any special literary talent. Yet, in his youth Stojan was very much attracted to writing. As a curate in Příbor, he wrote for the Brno *Hlas* (Voice) as well as for the *Škola Božského Srdce* (School of the Sacred Heart). The latter was edited by Father Placid Mathon, a Benedictine of Rajhrad Abbey, editor of several other publications. It was perhaps Mathon who encouraged Stojan to engage in journalistic work, just as it was again Mathon who later brought the needs of Mount Hostyn to Stojan's attention. Stojan wrote diligently about everything that transpired in the Příbor parish and its neighborhood. He wrote, not for the sake of entertainment, but rather to give instruction to all. Like the majority of his peers, he understood journalism primarily in its didactic aspects. In view of the poverty of Catholic publications in Czechoslovakia up to that time, Stojan believed that the absolute need of a good press imposed a heavy obligation on every priest. He had great praise for Rudigier, Bishop of Linz, for his understanding of the apostolate of the press and for his support of various publications, including the Czech periodical *Čech.* The Catholic press was a Cinderella. Understanding of the need for it was lacking; editors and writers were also lacking.

In content, Stojan's contributions were varied. Besides historical articles and chronicles, he wrote articles about various projects, such as Velehrad and Hostyn, or the Marian and Cyrilo-Methodian devotions. In other articles, he spoke out against alcoholism and other abuses; he also drew attention to the shortage of seminarians and priests. He must have been an alert and diligent reporter, because after he began reporting the Příbor local news, the people of that town were saying: "Watch yourself, or your name will make the newspapers!" Father Stojan was also requested to write for the German newspaper *Volksbote.*

His widening field of public activity soon left Stojan with no time for a personal interest in literary activity, but there is hardly any writer who wrote more extensively than he did. As the pastor of Dražovice and as a delegate to the legislature, he sent out sixty to a hundred letters every day. He had callouses on his hand from writing. But he never forgot that the press was the most important means for promoting any program. All of this reflected a belief in the axiom, "Good book—good reading." In this, Father Stojan was foremost with good example. He began as a seminarian; he organized a privately—supported project, the *Jednota pro Zakladání Venkovských Knihoven* (Association for the Founding of Rural Libraries) and soon after his ordination to the priesthood he conceived the plan of organizing a literary society, which would involve also laymen in "fostering literature in the spirit of the Church." He brought this plan to realization in the year 1907, when in Velehrad he founded the *Cyrilometodějský Tiskový Spolek* (Publishing Society of Sts. Cyril and Methodius), of which he became the chairman. The purpose of this organization was not fully realized for lack of co-workers; for this reason it merged (in 1920) with the *Apostolate of Sts. Cyril and Methodius.* The *Academia Velehradensis* was more successful, as has been previously mentioned.

While engaged in parish work, Stojan was also zealously active in the book trade and in promoting membership in the various Czechoslovak "Dědictví" (heritages, i.e., literary societies which distributed books as premiums, similar to book club dividents), such as the *Dědictví Sv. Jana Nepomuckého* (Heritage of St. John Nepomucene, founded in 1835), the *Dědictví Sv. Cyrila a Metoděje* (Heritage of Sts. Cyril and Methodius, founded in 1850), and the *Dědictví Maličkých* (Heritage of the Little Ones, founded in 1860). Generally, the clergy of his time were well informed, and many of them wrote extensively. Bishop Podlaha (1865-1932) in his bibliography of Czech Catholic literature,[7] has listed 73,700 works produced between 1828 and 1913; the authors of most of these were priests. Those who rose above the level of average authorship numbered 261 in Bohemia and 102 in Moravia. Father Stojan intended to arouse the Catholic layman to literary activity; at this time the Czechoslovak Catholic layman was making only a hesitant start in this field.

Father Stojan also planned to realize on a greater scale an idea with which he had great success as a seminarian. In the year 1880, he appealed to the public in Moravia with a proposal (published in the Brno periodical *Hlas*) that a centralized Cyrilo-Methodian library be founded in Velehrad, which would contain a collection of all the books, periodicals, magazine articles, and historical treatises on the subject of Sts. Cyril and Methodius. However, even to this day, it has been impossible to bring this idea to realization.

Stojan and the intellectuals: The terms *"Lidový panáček"* (people's little prince) or *"moravský panáček"* (Moravian little prince), as describing the simplicity of Archbishop Stojan and his attempt to provide leadership for the Czech intellectuals, seem to imply a paradox. But, really, there is no paradox. In what was said above, we have described how Stojan wished to instruct and to provide timely leadership by making use of organizations, newspapers and pamphlets. In doing this, he arrived at the conviction that a person working with educated classes achieves the best results if he acquires that professional consciousness which is considerably enhanced by the acquisition of an academic degree. Father Stojan, therefore, made an effort to obtain a doctorate in theology.

The urge to lead and exercise leadership in public life is demonstrated by the almost incredible fact that A.C. Stojan, soon after he came to the Parliament (Reichsrat) as a deputy, registered at the Law Faculty of the University of Vienna, and there passed the preliminary examinations in 1898. This was certainly also a mark of Stojan's conscientiousness; his desire to discharge the duties entrusted to him fully and responsibly; to develop in himself all his God-given talents. It cannot be denied, of course, that his youthful yearning to be educated and to educate constantly asserted itself. On the other hand, were it not for this instinct of the most popular priest in Moravia, the *Velehrad Unionistic Congresses*[8] might never have been conceived; for these congresses were primarily the concern of experts in the world of education. Likewise, the *Academia Velehradensis* might never have been organized; for he invited educated writers to contribute to the Academia: "If God has given you the talent of authorship, support the Academia!"

With all these activities Stojan never lost the balance between what may be called by theologians[9] action and meditation, i.e., activity and the spiritual life. On the contrary, the priest and archbishop Stojan was from the beginning of his spiritual career full of a deep spiritual interior life. In the simplicity and firmness of his deep faith and piety he showed how clearly he valued the weight of prayers and sacrifices. His activity was the result of his interior union with God and a devout appreciation of God's laws. To the priest and archbishop Stojan it was evident that God required apostolic labors and there is no sacrifice more acceptable to God than a zealous apostolate for the salvation of souls. Instinctively in his pure priestly heart he understood that while it is good to meditate about God's truth, it is better to spread this truth.[10] He certainly understood the great maxim of St. Alphonsus Ligouri: "I love Jesus Christ and therefore I am burning with desire to give him souls, especially mine, then a countless number of others!"[11] Stojan emphasized that priests must have concern for their own sanctification.[12] In fact, his enormous apostolic activity increased his concern for his spiritual life. How many times he was found, pressed and half exhausted, on his knees before the Santuary in the archepiscopal chapel when his work left little time for relaxation? He begged for prayers and aspired always toward prayers with devout anxiety. He always stressed piety in its principal forms: penance and prayer. Such apostolic work is pure love, manifested by works. He followed the way of the sacrifice of Jesus, the Worker and Shepherd, Missionary and Physician, the benign and indefatigable Helper in all need. He followed Christ's saying: "I am among you as he who serves." (Lk. 22:27) and "The Son of Man did not come in order to be served but to serve." (Matt. 20:20).

All his activity was rooted in lively, firm faith in God. Everything in him was rooted in faith. He was a man of Faith. Faith was for him the most precious treasure in addition to sanctifying grace and the purity of his priestly heart. Activity proceeds from thoughts and ideas. "If the tree is healthy, then also its branches." (Rom. 11:16). Priests find their strength for activities in a lively faith which usually honors the man of weak human faith. Here is the psychological key to the personality of this apostle of a full interior life, a man of prayer and activity, a man of works in extraordinary dimensions, a man of numerous initiatives and of exemplary productive activity replete with superabundant harvests. The foundation of the greatness of the priest and Churchman Stojan is in his profound, pure, deep faith. This deeply rooted faith was the cornerstone of his internal harmony, of Franciscan goodness, and of sunny joyfulness, by which he spread joy and confidence in God among people.[13]

Another principal source of Stojan's fruitful apostolate was his love of the Blessed Sacrament. In the Eucharist the Lord remains among us. It was Pius X who said: "To restore all things in Christ"[14] and this was true of Stojan. There was always a lively communing with Christ in the Blessed Sacrament, before which he made daily adoration.[15] An additional criterion of Stojan's pure and fruitful apostolate was his devout love of the Blessed Mother. The renovator of Hostyn[16] and the most popular Marian apostle of his times burned with love of the Blessed Mother, whom he wanted to have Queen of Moravia and Patroness of the great Cyrilomethodian renewal and unionistic trend in the family of the Slavs.

A special sign of Stojan's apostolate was his love for the confessional. He took confession so seriously that he used every opportunity to be a zealous confessor of his people. He had a predilection for the sacrament of penance. In confession the priest represents the Good Shepherd and the Father of the prodigal son. The confessor is, according to St. Ambrose (340-397), vicarius amoris eius![17] In connection with the sacrament of penance, Stojan had a special understanding love for the souls in purgatory, for whom he fervently prayed.

Another source of his apostolate was his love for the sick, whom he visited when he was pastor or in any other function. When he was unable to make visits, he wrote letters of comfort to the sick, expressing sentiments of his fatherly love. Last but not least was Stojan's love for children, with whom he felt at home and whom he understood well. St. Philip Neri (1515-1595) called children helpers of the conversion of sinners,[18] and the learned Jean Gerson (1363-1429), who taught children with a special preference, used to say that children through their prayers would open for him the gate of Heaven.[19] Stojan had a special pastoral love for children. They always had the front places in all devotions; rogation days, pilgrim days, spiritual retreats, or Stations of the Cross, especially at Hostyn and Velehrad. In this Stojan was a true follower of the great Pope Pius X (1903-1914).

With his spiritual loves, priorities, virtues and charisms, there is also room for a question about his failures. Even zealots have tendencies to be led by their nature, habits or excesses. Even virtuous people suffer much coping with their inequities. Stojan had tendencies to some excesses, beyond the limits of prudence. His zeal was difficult to hold in moderation. But errors of excessive love, as were Stojan's, do not take much away from their goodness. If he got angry, it was the anger of love. His workaholic tendencies can be explained by his adopted Biblical principle: to save the lost (Matt. 18:11). This meant quick action, without delay or thought of how far it was an obligation or responsibility, but who could be saved. Certainly Archbishop Stojan worked as shepherd of the archdiocese with great speed and prudence. Another weakness blamed on Stojan was that he was not a great economist; that he did not know the limits of generosity.

The executors of Stojan's estate calculated that all debts amounted to about 16½ million crowns.[20] This shocked the people. It should be kept in mind that this included claims of builders for the Retreat House *Stojanov,* claims of the Foundation of Hostyn, as well as all taxes, debts of the Central Directorate of the Archepiscopal Estates and debts from previous archbishops, Cardinals Francis Bauer and Leo Skrbenský. It should also be kept in mind that this financial transaction was conditioned by the 1918 transition from the Austro-Hungarian Empire into the new State of the Czechoslovak Republic. With the rescript of the District Court of Olomouc, August 9, 1928, the process was legally resolved and economical order was restored.

Indeed personal expenses of Stojan were always minimal. He was simple and personally deeply humble, disliking very much every kind of pomp. His incomes were moderate. He lived modestly but was generous where there was need for help. In his great love toward his neighbors, he frequently lost a practical sense for the limits of generosity. One thing, however, should be stressed—he never incurred debts for his personal profit, personal calculation, or personal welfare. A man of Stojan's type with such evangelical (according to some, primitive) views about money and worldly things was simply not sufficiently prepared for the economical and material requirements of the administration of an archdiocese. His concerns were directed entirely toward the spiritual needs of the faithful, to the spiritual treasures of the faith, which he saw endangered. Because of his magnanimity, he did not have time or interest for secondary things. Stojan was purely a Churchman par excellence. The Catholic Church benefitted greatly from his public career as a deputy of Parliament or that of Senator. He used his influence to get help for the building of Churches and to improve priestly compensation for better living conditions for priests and all ministers. There was a long list of the Churches and their spiritual administrations which Stojan was instrumental in building. This man, who was not concerned about his own material well-being, was deeply interested in improving the material welfare of others, especially of his peers in the priesthood.

The most important observation of Stojan's character comes from his reaction to his encounter with the most vicious anti-Catholic cultural struggle aroused by the propaganda of the new Czechoslovak Church in 1920. The offensive against Moravian Catholicism was then in its most radical and successful phase. About 22 communities of this church, 12 of which had independent pastoral care, (like Olomouc, Litovel, Kroměříž, Uh. Brod, Chudobín, Cholina, Vacanovice, Radvanice, Michalkovice, Petrvald, Poruba) were established.[21] Fraudulent manipulation of the Cyrilomethodian idea[22] for purposes of the Czechoslovak Church, as well as the abuse of the unionistic endeavors for encounters with the Orthodoxy, caused wide-spread confusion in some Catholic circles.

The Papal appointment of the man of God, Stojan, as leader of Moravia in this most critical moment was truly providential, for when he became archbishop, the strength of the anti-Catholic propaganda was broken. Stojan's merit in this regard can be clearly seen from a post-factum reflection, comparing the archbishop of Prague, Francis Kordač's uncompromising defense[23] and Stojan's handling of matters through his goodness and understanding. Kordač's approach increased resentment, Stojan's formed an atmosphere of conciliation[24] which eventually stabilized matters to the extent that the Catholic Church in Moravia successfully passed a dangerous crisis, while the Bohemian Church suffered much. Stojan's spiritual profile was effectively disarming to most reformers and all kinds of revolutionaries in the Church, and this in itself speaks in favor of the sanctity which he exemplified and for which he is remembered. Testimonials in this regard were so eloquent for the past half century since his death September 28, 1923, that the need for public Church recognition of his sanctity is felt even more with the increased urgency of time.

One of the most impressive testimonials came perhaps from the Papal Nuncio, F. Marmaggi of the Apostolic Nunciature in Prague, written on December 30, 1923, to the Metropolitan Archibishop Leopold Prečan, the successor of Archbishop Stojan:

"It would seem that in this historic moment Divine Providence is entrusting to the brave and disciplined Catholic faithful in this Republic a legacy of unusual importance. Perhaps by the grace of God this diocese was given the privilege that it should be the first to help our separated brothers, especially in the East, certainly unhappy, but still devoutly beloved, who wish to return to the Church, and to invite them by extending a hand to them. Nevertheless, in fulfillment of this goal which you began with such zeal and with the complete consensus of the whole Catholic world, you should not hesitate nor be misled. It is the sacred legacy of the holy man, your predecessor, Antonín Cyril Stojan. This magnificent spirit, who now shares a heavenly reward and a crown of immortality for his labors, will be here with you as an inseparable companion and he will always stay gracefully with you."[25]

Here Stojan gave an example to be followed by his successors and rightly so, for he was truly a Servant of God, who left a rich legacy to be fulfilled.

NOTES

1. Francis Dvornik, "The Significance of the Missions of Cyril and Methodius," *Slavic Review* XXIII no. 2 (July, 1964) 195-238; idem., "The Byzantine Mission to Moravia," *Czechoslovakia Past and Present*, ed. by M. Rechigl, Jr. II (Hague, 1964), 1107-1121.
2. Bruce M. Garver, *The Young Czech Party 1874-1901 and the Emergence of a Multi-party System* (New Haven, 1978), 224, 240, 286.
3. Bohumil Zlámal, *Antonín Cyril Stojan* (Rome, 1973), 17-27, especially pp. 19-20.
4. This was the motto of the Habsburg Monarchy; Jan Drábek, *Z časů nedlouho Zašlých* (From times not long past) (Rome, 1967).
5. Quoted by Cinek, *op.cit.*, passim.
6. René Fülöp-Miller, *Leo XIII and Our Times* (New York, 1936) passim; Eduardo Soderini, *The Pontificate of Leo XIII* (London, 1934).
7. "Půl století od. smrti Antonína Podlahy a Čeňka Zíbrta" (Half Century after the death of Antonin Podlaha and Cenek Zibrt", *Hlas Národa*, Feb. 27, 1982, p. 13.
8. Peter Esterka, "Toward Union: Congresses at Velehrad," *Journal of Ecumenical Studies*, VIII (Winter, 1971) 10-51; Maurice Gordillo, "Velehrad e i suoi Congressi unionistici," *Civiltà Catholica*, Anno 108 (1957), 677 ff.
9. Pascal P. Parenti, *The Ascetical Life* (St. Louis: Herder, 1944) 56-65 and passim.
10. This is also stressed by St. Thomas Aquinas, *Summa Theologica* 2a II, p. 188 cn. 6.
11. St. Alphonse Liguori's famous saying.
12. *Apoštolát* of 1913, p. 144, he writes: "We will be apostles. We will begin the apostolate first with ourselves. . ."
13. Vilém Bitnar, "O Stojanovi, českém Chudáčku Božím", *Lidové Listy* of May 22, 1931.

14. Igino Giordani, *Pius X, A Country Priest* (Milwaukee, 1954) passim; Catherine Burton, *The Great Mantle* (New York, 1950); Raffaelo Merry del Val, *Memoirs of Pope Pius X* (London, 1939) passim.

15. Dr. F. Snopek, *Ze Života nového arcibiskupa: Slavnost svěceni a nastoleni arcibiskupa Stojana.* (Olomouc, 1921) 10 and passim.

16. Ludvik Nemec, *Our Lady of Hostyn* (New York, 1981), 10-14.

17. Especially in his: *De paenitentia,* see M.J. Costelloe, "St. Ambroze," *Encyclopedic Dictionary of Religion* (Philadelphia, Pa., 1979) I, col. 135; A. Paredi, *Saint Ambroze: His Life and Times* (New York, 1964) passim.

18 M. Jouandeau, *St. Philip Neri* (tr. G. Lamb) (New York, 1960) passim; Louis Boyer, *Roman Socrates* (tr. by M. Day) (New York, 1958) passim; L. Ponnelle and L. Bordet, *St. Philip Neri and the Roman Society of His Times* (tr. R.T. Kerr) (New York, 1933).

19. J.C. Connolly, *John Gerson, Reformer and Mystic* (New York, 1928); J.B. Schwab, *Johannes Gerson, Professeur de Theologie und Kanzler de Universität Paris,* 2 vols. (Paris, 1958) passim.

20. See official proclamation in *Našinec* of October 18, 1928.

21. *Český zápas* no. 45.

22. Ludvik Nemec, *The Czechoslovak Heresy and Schism. The Emergence of a National Czechoslovak Church* (Philadelphia, 1975), 16-36 and passim; their abuse of the Cyrilomethodian heritage was to introduce a new Czech liturgy in *Český Misál* (Czech Missal) published by the Club of Reformistic priests in Prague, 1919-1920.

23. Ludvik Nemec, *op.cit.,* p. 13.

24. M. Pavlík-Gorazd, *O Krisi v Církvi Československé: Otázka Pravoslavné Cirkve v Československu* (Prague, 1924), pp. 15-29 and passim.

25. Czech text is to be found in Cinek, *op.cit.,* 1170, with the author's English translation.

X
THE FULFILLMENT OF THE LEGACY OF STOJAN

Stojan, an excellent spiritual economist diligently cultivated the "heritage of the Fathers", the Cyrilomethodian[1] one, and faithfully carried out the Velehrad idea. While there is a cause-effect relation between them. The former denotes the inheritance of the Fathers with a follow-up of its well established traditions. The latter is the result of a beneficiary use of the former. How much a certain idea is usable and practically workable is a reflection of its inherent goodness. Stojan, as a Cyrilomethodian activist knew well that a tradition must not only be preserved, but its legacy must be fulfilled. He worked so hard on this last that he eventually succeeded in reaping a harvest from the Cyrilomethodian crop by forcefully promoting unionistic endeavors toward a determined search for Church unity. For Stojan it was—to use Rahner's term—unity through love[2] that would bring about the reconciliation of the separated churches.[3] This was not merely conceivable in the abstract but had an inner dynamism of reality and a goal that could be victoriously attained. Inherent in this legacy was Stojan's preoccupation with the promotion of Slavic solidarity in the sense that the Slavs would have mutual understanding, support and concern. These he considered an integral part of the Cyrilomethodian heritage to be fulfilled simultaneously as a basis for the reconciliation of the separated Eastern—mostly Slavic—churches. He admitted this himself in a solemn proclamation of 1885: "The great Saint Methodius has made us heirs of that indivisible legacy, one dependent on the other. He preached the Faith to us, and through the Faith preserved our nationality for us; he preached it to us in the Slavonic language, in order to obtain our Faith for the exalted teaching of Christ!"[4]

The Cyrilomethodian program was not a splintering element; rather, it was a unifying movement. This is best recognized by the fact that it was accepted even by the metropolitan of Moravia, Friedrich Fürstenberg (1813-1892) who was of German extraction himself. He accepted it as the official program of his administration, in order that this very program would aid in solving the most delicate problems of the times. It was on a Cyrilomethodian basis that the Archbishop wished to resolve the problem of nationalism[5] especially in his archdiocese. He attempted to mediate the excessively vociferous expression of nationalistic feelings on the Czech side as well as on the German side. Not nationalism, but nationalistic chauvinism is un-Christian. The bishops of Olomouc were for centuries regarded as the successors of St. Methodius. But the Salonika brothers came to the Slavs and founded a national culture for them. According to their example, it was necessary to take a positive attitude toward Slav nationalism and not to oppose its development. This idea was to be the way, common to all members of the Church in Moravia, enhancing the cause of Faith, and at the same time bringing the two antagonistic nationalities closer together. It was to be a mutual bond uniting Czech and German co-regionists in a harmonious life together. This was to be effected through an exalted unifying function in the program. After all, they pointed out, Sts. Cyril and Methodius were shepherds full of love for both nations in Moravia, Slavs and Germans. One manifestation of the ecclesiastical community living in harmony in Moravia was to be the practice of going on pilgrimages—Czechs and Germans together—to the various places related to the Cyrilomethodian idea—Hostyn, and above all, Velehrad. For this reason, Fürstenberg, in his pastoral letter of 1885, invited the clergy and laity of both nationalities to participate in the pilgrimages to Velehrad, where sermons were delivered in the German language for pilgrims, the same as was done in the year 1863. Through Fürstenberg's efforts the feast of Sts. Cyril and Methodius, until then observed on March 9, was transferred to July 5, precisely for the purpose of facilitating the Velehrad pilgrimages. He made a personal contribution to the Velehrad Foundation to enable it to purchase the property on which Velehrad was located. At his own personal expense he renovated the Velehrad "Cyrilka."[6] Fürstenberg's fundamental concept of the Cyrilomethodian idea in both of its basic aspects, ecclesiastical and national, had great significance, not only for the sponsorship and development of the Velehrad pilgrimages, but also for the essence of Stojan's work. This was perhaps the most significant event in Moravian ecclesiastical history. No doubt, much credit for this was due also to the archbishop's counselors and vicars general, Königsbrunn and Poetting, who were influenced by the Cyrilomethodian idea and who professed to be Czechs—also to Tomáš Bečák, Ignat Wurm, Pavel Křížovský, and others.

Stojan, however, had a charisma of his own. Although he never claimed to be a professional scholar, he was certainly a student in his own right, well versed in theology and in Cyrilomethodian Church history. He certainly was acquainted with J.J. Středovský's basic Cyrilomethodian work, *Sacra Moraviae Historia; sive, Vita SS. Cyrilli et Methudii Genere Civium Romanorum... Velehradensium Archiepiscoporum... Universae Pene Slavoniae Zelantissimorum Apostolorum;*[7] and he was well versed in this and Moravian history. He seemed quite proud of his fellow Moravians and of the two priests who wrote the introduction to Středovský's book—both of them had been pastors near his birthplace. Sotinský, Pastor of Domaželice, concludes his elegiac distich with these words: "Through Středovský's efforts, Moravia will come to life in the world, and the restorer of its antiquity will be recognized. Therefore, applaud him, crown the author with laurel, for his work is worthy of your love!"[8] Stojan, therefore, consciously stepped into the footprints of his fellow Moravians of the Baroque era[9] and of more recent times. If Stojan was acquainted with Středovský's work and with Vincent Furch, how could he not know of another of his great countrymen, the dean and archpriest of Přerov, František Navrátil,[10] whom everyone regarded as a "milovaný stařeček" (beloved old gentleman) and a genuine "národu vlastimil" (country and nation lover). Stojan became acquainted with Navrátil when the latter was already advanced in age, and for Stojan this was already living history.

František Sušil (1804-1866) and his followers made a wonderful contribution to Church and nation. They effected a renewal in the Austrian Church which had been affected by *Josephinism.*[12] This they accomplished by deepening spiritual life through retreats, parocial missions, preaching and writing the Word of God. Zealously they aroused the people to a national consciousness and to a burning love for country, language, and national enlightenment. Without them, there would not have been such an early awakening of the country people, particularly in Moravia and Silesia. With great fervor, they extolled the national unity of the Czechs and Slovaks as a "Cyrilomethodian order," as a Cyrilomethodian spiritual whole," as a "Cyrilomethodian archdiocese."[13] But at the same time, they were opening the windows to world Catholicism, and they were strengthening the bonds of faith around Peter's See. Stojan was among them and leading them. He inherited an old estate, but like a young master he developed it. He joined the romantic roots together to produce a realistic stem of a gigantic organization. In the *Apostolate of Sts. Cyril and Methodius,* he organized a people's Cyrilomethodian program, with the clear goal of a spiritual mission. He eliminated as unrealistic the German aspect of the program when not enough interest was manifested. For the *Apostolate* he opened up new views into the Slavonic world. All this was not a particularly original concept. The same idea of uniting all the Slavs into one true Faith was proposed as early as the year 1841, by the *Bratovščina Sv. Cirila in Metoda* (Brotherhood of Sts. Cyril and Methodius) organized by Anton Martin Slomšek, Bishop of Maribor, as an echo of the ancient Cyrilomethodian tradition among the Slovenes. But the action was supplied by Stojan! After the idealistic Sušil and the spiritual Slomšek, came the realistic A.C. Stojan, who took their program synthesized it, preserved it, and began to put it into practice. All the followers of Sušil joined Stojan's *Apostolate of Sts. Cyril and Methodius* in a body. Thus they made possible a concentration of united effort and a single mass movement. Into this program, Stojan incorporated, not only a solicitous concern for his own countrymen, but also a universal concern, even for the emigrated Czechs and Slovaks, in order that they too might become bearers of the Cyrilomethodian apostolic idea. This broad foundation of interest among the Slav Catholics later became a bridge to his most daring projects—initiation to and continuation of unionistic congresses[14] in Velehrad.

The daring of these unionistic congresses at Velehrad is more immediately realized when one recalls that the spirit of the first decades of the twentieth century was deeply affected by the disruption of the *away-from Rome Movement,*[15] and the stimulation of the so-called *Catholic Modernism*[16] condemned by Rome in 1910. The result was a divided Czech nationalistic mind which tenaciously fought for the Czech word and book[17] while seeking political disassociation from the official Austrian policy—problems eventually resolved by the events of World War I (1914-18). The Orthodox-Catholic discourse was in time impregnated with nationalistic sentiments. It was not easy to maintain a triangular balance with Vienna, Prague, and Rome, and still keep the idea of unionism alive without loss of appeal to the diversified Slav nationals at a time when political forces strongly tended to disrupt it. Fortunately, Velehrad, an eloquent testimony to the glories of the Slavic past, was able to satisfy national feeling and to keep the national mind in harmony with the religious factor and the Church, thus preventing much of the cultural and spiritual damage that might have been caused by national but irreligious radicals. The Catholic priests who bore the brunt of these turbulent times recognized the historic mission of Velehrad as providential, and were more than ever ready to share in the activities connected with the Cyrilo-methodian heritage. Unionistic endeavors, interrupted by World War I, were soon reactivated under the direction of Stojan, then Secretary of the *Apostolate of Sts. Cyril and Methodius,* and also a Senator. He resumed contact with other Slavic groups and advanced the cause in many directions. In 1919, following the death of Dr. Pospíšil, Canon Stojan became President of the *Apostolate,* and the office of Secretary was assumed by Father Adolph Jašek.

In 1921, Church Unity received a most generous patron determined to continue the Congresses when Monsignor Stojan was named Archbishop of Olomouc and successor to the See of St. Methodius. From the viewpoint of contemporary days and needs, which call for the unity of Christians in the world-wide struggle to preserve the Faith, the Velehrad Unionistic Congresses, dedicated to this same exalted purpose, appear as a most valuable contribution made by the Moravian Cyrilomethodian movement. They are, indeed, the precious fruit of apostolic efforts, at the head of which we find in every instance the man of Divine Providence, A.C. Stojan. One could see from the first Unionistic Congresses, held in 1907, 1909 and 1911, what great benefit could be hoped for and expected from these apostolic efforts and endeavors. Subsequently, post-war unionistic conferences, presided over by Stojan in 1921 and 1922, referred to the pre-war congresses and stressed their practical aspects. To increase their impact the following resolutions were formulated: (1) that the *Apostolate of Sts. Cyril and Methodius* would be extended to the Church universal. (2) That the feast of Sts. Cyril and Methodius would be solemnly observed in all places. (3) That chairs of Eastern theology would be established at Western Catholic universities and in seminaries. (4) That Catholic educational institutions would admit Orthodox theology students. (5) That theological schools would admit laymen as students. (6) That Catholic religious orders and societies would train some of their members for work in the Orthodox East.

(7) That in the Catholic West, new institutions and religious societies would be founded for the training of unionistic workers and missionaries. (8) That Russian refugees would be given material as well as spiritual assistance. Such were the resolutions of the 1921 conference. Does this not sound like the recommendations for unionistic work and practice as proposed at the Second Vatican Council in 1963? Pope Benedict XV in his apostolic letter of November 30, 1921 whole-heartedly approved the resolutions of the 1921 Velehrad Conference much the same way as Pope Paul VI enthusiastically ratified the proceedings of the Second Vatican Council on the same subject. No wonder then that Archbishop Stojan's unionistic idea and work not only survived in 1923, but continued to flourish and prosper under his successors because the beneficial impact of unionism was already felt and God's blessings clearly manifested in Stojan's legacy.

The *Fourth Unionistic Congress,*[18] scheduled for 1923, was postponed for one year due to the death of Archbishop Stojan on September 29, 1923. His successor, Archbishop Leopold Prečan, received from Pope Pius XI special praise[19] for resuming the unionistic efforts of his predecessor and in fulfilling his legacy. This Fourth Velehrad Congress became a reality July 30 to August 8, 1924, under the chairmanship of the new Metropolitan of Moravia, Archbishop Leopold Prečan (1923-1947). This congress attracted attention all over the world, first because it had official representation from the Holy See with the apostolic letter of Pope Pius XI; secondly, because the participants included twenty-four archbishops and bishops as well as many representatives from religious orders far and wide. Pope Pius XI, in his apostolic letter, praised the invitation extended to the East, its history, customs, liturgical rites, and its designation as a proper way toward reunion: "Therefore, we repeatedly exhort, and we wish it for the future, not only that Catholic men, outstanding in piety and in leadership, and enkindled with the desire for a more abundant salvation of souls, be present at this Congress, which is being convened at the tomb of St. Methodius, and that they would conscientiously participate in its work, but also that the schismatic clergy would come to the Congress. . ."[20]

Clamorous applause followed the address of the Russian Orthodox writer, Nikolaj Klymenko of Paris, who proclaimed that it is above all else necessary to demolish the wall of psychological and historical misunderstanding, suspicions and lack of love—the wall which Constantinople built between the Eastern and the Western Church. After that, mutual understanding will not be difficult. This was accepted so well that the Czech writer, Jaroslav Durych, characterized it fittingly as "the answer to the Russians"[21] in their spiritual search. Even Pope Pius XI commended it in a Secret Consistory held on December 18, 1924, as an important contribution.[22] At this Congress, the ideas stressed by Slomšek and Stojan's legacy were not forgotten, that is, that the work of reunion will not be the result of merely human effort. The influential unionistic leader (and later Bishop) Michael d'Herbigny, S.J.,[23] on three different days led meditations (in Latin) before the Most Blessed Sacrament exposed. Several eminent Russians living in Parish sent messages of greeting to the Congress: S. Bulgakov, Kartaschev, Trubetskoj, Berdǰajev, and others. The debates, at times rather heated, like the ones about papal infallibility, were moderated with insight and a conciliatory attitude by Archbishop Prečan, whose concluding remarks deserve to be brought to the attention of modern times: "There will come a time when it will become evident to the whole world that your work was not in vain, but that it prepared the way for future ages, for happier days."[24]

This Fourth Velehrad Congress seemed also to light numerous smaller lamps. In the year 1925, the Slovenians convoked a "congress for Eastern questions" which was held in Lubljana, July 12 to 16, and was attended by a scholarly delegation from the Orthodox Church. Proceedings were conducted by L. Prečan, Archbishop of Olomouc, who was by this time experienced in unionistic congresses. The Pontifical Oriental Institute[25] was represented by three professors with Michael d'Herbigny as their leader. Pius XI did not overlook sending a letter of warm greetings to this meeting. In Lubljana it was resolved that the *Apostolate of Sts. Cyril and Methodius* would prepare an Eastern unionistic section for the Eucharistic Congress to be held in Chicago.[26] This resolution was put into effect the next year, 1926. The publicity was handled by delegates from the *Ústřední Apoštolát Sv. Cyrila a Metoděje* (The Central Apostolate of Sts. Cyril and Methodius) in Olomouc and by two missionaries, František Jemelka and Lev Pospíšil.

Unionistic congresses on a smaller scale were also attempted by the Germans in Vienna (May 25 to 27, 1926) and in Litoměřice, Bohemia (August 19 to 22, 1926); the Poles did likewise in Vilno. Of greater significance was the founding of a Jesuit mission station of the Greek-Slavonic Rite in Albertyn, in Eastern Poland, in the year 1926. During these same years the Apostolate of Sts. Cyril and Methodius took root in other Slav countries. One chapter of the *Apostolate* was established in Rome, and in this way the goal of earlier years (since 1864) set by the Society of Sts. Cyril and Methodius of Rome was actually realized. In Holland, a kind of unionistic apostolate was founded, with material support from the Uniate Ukrainians. In Belgium, an important center of Unionistic work was developed at the Benedictine Abbey of the Eastern Rite in Amay (now Chevêtogne). This center publishes a very influential periodical, the *Irenikon*.

The idea of the Apostolate and its goal of church unity became popular especially in America, supported by the Czech and Slovak immigrants there. The first contacts with them in this apostolate were made by A.C. Stojan. That same year, 1926, at the suggestion of Franc Grivec, a society of priests was formed, the *Apostolate of Unity—Apostolatus Unitatis*-whose members were obliged to pray for unity and to promote it. Especially Czech Benedictines of St. Procopius Abbey in Lisle Illinois, took Stojan's legacy seriously, particularly after Pope Pius XI entrusted them to work on the reunion of the Church.[27] Their abbot, Procopius Neužil[28] not only made available members of his abbey for this apostolate, but created another center[29] in U.S.A. His successor, Abbot Ambroze L. Ondrák (189-1962)[30] embraced entirely Stojan's legacy. He not only revived the Velehrad tradition by making his abbey the "American Velehrad."[31] but reconstructed a kind of continuation of the Unionistic Congresses[32] held at the abbey in 1956, 1957 and 1959. He was fortunate to use the beneficial services of Stojan's one-time protegé and follower, the renowned historian, the late Professor Francis Dvornik (1893-1975), who by his authority in Byzantine History was greatly instrumental in acting not only as a vehicle of the Velehrad tradition, but of serving as a bridge to its transfer to America. Even Rome was quick to see the importance of his unionistic endeavors[33] as an extension of Stojan's legacy.

Another important event belonging to the Stojan legacy was the Prague Congress, convened in the course of the St. Václav millenium year, 1929. A special letter was addressed to this Congress by Pope Pius XI.[34] In Poland, a center for a practical unionistic apostolate developed in Pinsk, where, under the leadership of Bishop Lozinský, pastoral unionistic conferences were held almost every year since 1930 up to the time of World War II. Poland also had a periodical, *Oriens*, edited by a Polish unionistic worker, P. Jan Urban, S.J., who took part in Velehrad Congresses, with the purpose of propagating a correct understanding of the idea of church unity. The unionistic movement took root also in Italy, where a beautiful tradition developed—the "week of prayer and study of the Christian East"-held in Palermo 1930, Syracuse 1931, Venice 1934, Rome 1937, Florence 1938, Milan 1940, etc. In Germany the movement called "Una Sancta,"[35] founded in the year 1938, and other manifestations of interest in the reunion of the Catholic West with the Orthodox East, are evidence that the Moravian Stojan had sown the seed of the future, and his originality comes into prominence when viewed against this background of universal interest.

The Fifth Velehrad Unionistic Congress, July 20 to 24, 1927, was held in the eleventh centennial year of St. Cyril's birth (827). A great number of experts and writers attended. Even though the Orthodox were not officially represented, many friends of the unity idea did attend. The letter of Pope Pius XI addressed to this Congress indicated Rome's closer participation in this Congress.[36] Rome's representative was the president of the Pontifical Oriental Institute, Bishop d'Herbigny, who, after Archbishop Prečan, was the foremost activist at the Congress. The Slavonic Liturgy was celebrated on the first day by the Metropolitan Andrej Szeptycky of Galicia; the second day a Solemn Liturgy according to the Syro-Chaldean Rite was celebrated by the Egyptian Bishop for the Chaldean Catholic Church, Peter Aziz Hoh. On the third day, a requiem Mass was offered in memory of the deceased Archbishop Stojan. The Eucharistic procession concluding the Congress was led by the Polish Bishop Przezdziecki of Podlesí. Countless pilgrims in Velehrad for the St. Cyril centennial thus had an opportunity to become acquainted with Eastern liturgies. In addition to the 720 Holy Masses in the Latin Rite, there were also more than 30 Holy Masses in the Greek-Slavonic Rite.

Papers read in the course of this Congress gave a broad picture of the development of the unionistic movement and of the various activities being conducted in Europe and in America. This was the first of the Velehrad Congresses to hear a paper by František Dvorník,[37] who spoke on *Saints Cyril and Methodius in the light of Byzantine history*.[38] A. Böminghaus, a Jesuit, treated of spiritual exercises as a means toward unity, a theme that was certainly close to Stojan's heart. The Czechoslovak government was officially represented at this Congress.[39] After the tempestuous upheavals of the post-war period, this government began to show interest in assuming a more favorable attitude toward the Catholic Church. The Sixth Velehrad

Unionistic Congress, July 13 to 17, 1932, was scheduled for the silver anniversary of the first Congress, 1907. The proceedings of this Congress left no doubt that one of the principal ideas binding every Christian, "ut omnes unum sint!" had extended itself to become the desire of the universal Church. An expression of this fact was the encyclical of Pope Pius XI, *Rerum Orientalium*[40] of September 7, 1928. In all its content, this encyclical conferred the highest sanction on the Velehrad efforts for church unity. One echo of this international event was the Sixth Velehrad Unionistic Congress, dedicated to promoting Christian unity. This Congress had twenty outstanding speakers, representing many nations, and about 300 professionally interested participants. This was the first of the Velehrad Congresses to schedule learned discussions between Catholic and Orthodox experts on controversial ecclesiastical questions, and these were conducted in the spirit of a rare conciliatory understanding. The Evangelical scholar of Vienna, Hans Koch, came to this Congress; so did the first representative ever sent to such a meeting by Hungary.

One of the communications sent to this Sixth Velehrad Unionistic Congress deserving serious attention was the letter of the famous Orthodox theologian, Sergej Bulgakov, who was unable to attend in person. In his letter, he stated that the martyrs' blood of his church would be the seed of new faith and renewal. But that renewal can be realized only when the various Christian confessions free themselves of the sin of fragmentation, carried over from their ancestors, and when they unite under the roof of one ecumenical, apostolic Church. Bulgakov explained further, that among other obstacles, the greatest dogmatic obstacle between Catholicism and Orthodoxy is the question of the primacy of the Roman pope as defined by the First Vatican Council (1870). Writing in this vein, he noted, almost prophetically: "Nothing else can be done but to wait for a further explanation of a hastily adopted dogmatic definition and to wait especially for its eventual completion, which had not been realized because the Vatican Council was interrupted, and thus to hope that by this means a bridge can be found to that kind of an understanding of the ecumenical character of the Church in which the East and the West at one time were in agreement." However, in the deepest mystical sense, the Catholics and the Orthodox are not divided, when "the two churches are indivisibly united through the unity of the altar in the sacrament of the Eucharist as well as in the fullness of all the other mysteries. The division concerns only the canonical and empirical surface, but the Eucharistic Christ has not been divided in us."[41]

Three addresses at this Congress were delivered as if in the spirit of Stojan. Rev. Placid de Meester, O.S.B., of Rome, chose as his theme the liturgy as the principle of preservation and propagation of the Faith in the theological concepts of the separated East. Severin Salaville, an Assumptionist from Rome, spoke on the liturgy as the support of the unionistic movement. George Maklakov, a Russian professor from the Catholic University of Lille, spoke on how the separated East regards the liturgy and the symbol of Faith.[42] It was here that Dvorník made a telling point—strange to the West but substantiated in the East—concerning the position of civil authority in the Ecumenical Councils.[43] The Orthodox Bishop Seraphim of Vienna was on his way to this Congress, but for unknown reasons was detained by the police in Breslau and was forced to return. However, many Orthodox periodicals published reports that were positive, factual, and fair in evaluating this Congress. The Russian periodical *Naša Réč* (Our Language)[44] expressed its conviction that the Catholic Church and the Orthodox Church would find a way of coming closer together against constantly growing irreligion. The resolutions adopted at this Congress stress the need for a new generation of unionistic experts, especially in unionistic centers like Olomouc. Gifted young men should be sent to the Pontifical Oriental Institute. Reports should be presented during unionistic congresses concerning the activities of the Apostolate of Sts. Cyril and Methodius. This Apostolate should be the means of spreading the veneration of Sts. Cyril and Methodius, who were outstanding apostles of ecumenical unity. The remaining resolutions were devoted to stressing prayer, Catholic as well as Orthodox, Holy Mass, and Holy Communion offered for the intention of unity. The votive Mass "ad tollendum schisma" ought to be offered regularly by secular priests, also in seminaries and monasteries, for "the Eucharist is the sacrament of unity." Recommendations were made once more that educational institutions establish chairs of Eastern studies and that seminaries include unionistic subjects in their curriculm. The Sixth Velehrad Unionistic Congress was a greater success than the previous Congresses—in the number of experts present, in the active participation of the Russian Orthodox, in the topics discussed by the experts, and in the friendly conversations with separated Christians.

During the Congress, the Spanish Jesuit and professor, Rev. M. Gordillo,[45] preached stirring sermons and appeals in the course of the devotions and during the exposition of the Blessed Sacrament.

Also at this time it was Dvornik's constant insistence on a critical historical basis for all Cyrilomethodian questions and for East-West relations, and in turn corresponding efforts on the part of Slavic schools in European universities, stimulated interest in the verification of the historical background of ancient Velehrad. Archeologists attempted to resolve the controversy by extensive excavations in Moravia.[46] To this day[47] competent scholars anxiously await, scrutinize, study, and discuss the significance of their discoveries. The claim of some authorities for other possible locations[48] of the original Velehrad, and the prestige envisioned for the present Velehrad, lend impetus to the work. Political implications indirectly assumed a motivating role when on the occasion of the Pribina celebrations August 10-15, 1933, commemorating the eleven-hundredth anniversary of the first Church in Nitra, the Slovaks attempted to assume the role of exclusive recipients of the Sts. Cyril and Methodius heritage.[49] To maintain interest in the search for ancient Velehrad, a special Museum was established under the guidance of Dr. K. Guth, Director of the National Museum in Prague, and Dr. Jar. Boehm, Commissary of the Archeological Institute in Prague. It was administered by Antonín Zelnitius, a school teacher, who later assumed responsibility for a similar Museum in Staré Město, site of the historic excavations.

The international significance of the Velehrad efforts for a meeting and union of dissident Christians was re-affirmed at the Seventh Velehrad Unionistic Congress,[50] July 15 to 19, 1936, which was the last such congress to be held in Velehrad. In the meantime, the framework within which the two previous congresses were held also gained in international prominence. With the increased significance of Velehrad the Church authorities decided that the Velehrad Basilica should be raised to the dignity of a pontifical basilica, "basilica minor,"[51] as it was already in 1928; and on April 13, 1932, Sts. Cyril and Methodius were designated as co-patrons of this shrine of Our Lady. This action emphasized the whole of Stojan's Cyrilomethodian legacy under the patronage of these two saints. A precise statement of this fact occurs in the papal decree: "Velehrad is the place at which the veneration of these saints is blossoming and is particularly cultivated, so that the glory of their names spreads from here beyond the boundaries of the Olomouc Archdiocese."[52] In the brief of December 2, 1933, František Sal. Bařina, the Augustinian Abbot of Brno,[53] was named the honorary abbot of Velehrad; and thus its glory of ancient times was restored to Velehrad, that is, the distinction conferred on Velehrad by Urban VI in 1379. Furthermore, in the year 1935, a thorough renovation of the interior of the Velehrad Basilica was undertaken. In the succeeding years, the "underground" Velehrad was archaeologically authenticated[54] and made accessible with its massive stone work and refined architectural structures of the original royal buildings from the first half of the thirteenth century.

The Seventh Congress had a considerable representation from various spiritual learned societies working for church unity. Interest in the work shown in other countries and the participation of such a large number of representatives from foreign countries had such a profound influence on the Czechoslovak government that it extended its protectorate to include the Congress and arranged to be represented by a minister. Msgr. Jan Šrámek was appointed to this post. A letter sent by the papal secretary of state, Eugene Pacelli, praised that which deserves our closest attention, "that is, our union with the dissident East," and expressed the hope that this Congress would help prepare the way for this desired goal. The central theme of the papers read at this Congress was the unionistic significance of the Cyrilomethodian work. Among several Slavists taking part in the Congress was F. Dvornik, whose lecture[55] which, because of an official assignment, he was unable to deliver in person, was read by Professor J. Matocha of Olomouc. The circumstance that the major part of papers dealt with Cyrilomethodian heritage and Stojan's legacy was very appropriate for the one thousand fiftieth anniversary of St. Methodius's death. These papers were divided into three categories: dogmatic, liturgical, and historical.

Eastern dogmatic theology was discussed by an authority in the field, Bohumil Spáčil, S.J. Contributing to the discussion was the French Jesuit, Rouet de Journel, this being the first Velehrad Congress that he attended. Ch. V. Bourgeois spoke about the unionistic activities in Estonia. Every day while the Congress was in session, solemn pontifical services were held according to the Eastern Rite; the evening devotions, hours of adoration, were conducted in Latin by the Slovak Assistant General of the Society of Jesus, Rev. Prešeren.

The resolutions of the Seventh Velehrad Unionistic Congress consisted of ten points, specifying the agenda for the next Congress to be held in the jubilee year of the Florentine union, 1939. At this Eighth Congress, the discussions were to examine the practical and pastoral questions. The Seventh Congress exhorted the bishops to

give their faithful the opportunity to become more intimately acquainted with the Byzantine-Slavonic liturgy, at least in the seminaries and in the cities. It adopted the plea of Tomažič, Bishop of Maribor, for the beatification of the pioneer and supporter of the Cyrilomethodian unionistic idea, Anton Martin Slomšek. In every seminary
in the Republic of Czechoslovakia, a chapter of the *Apostolate of
Sts. Cyril and Methodius* was to be established. Finally, the Congress
petitioned the Holy See to introduce feasts commemorating the death
of St. Cyril (February the 14th) and the death of St. Methodius
(April the 6th) for Czechoslovakia, Jugoslavia and Poland. Archbishop
Prečan, who presided over the four last Velehrad Congresses, ad-
journed the Seventh Congress with these words: "We know not the
hour of the day when the unification of the Church will come; but
we firmly believe that it will come. For this we must work and for
this we must pray. May the number of those participating grow,
especially in the ranks of the younger clergy."[56]

The Eighth Velehrad Unionistic Congress was never convened.
World War II (1939-1945) broke out, more terrible than the First. But
even the further, post-war turn of events did not afford an opportunity to convoke a unionistic congress at Velehrad. In the year 1946,
only minor conferences were held there. The fortieth anniversary of
the First Velehrad Unionistic Congress (1947) brought about seventy
guests from Czechoslovakia and other countries to Velehrad (September 11 to 12, 1947), to confer about means to be used in continuing the work of reunion; but these conferences of experts are not
considered as unionistic congresses in the strict sense of the term.
The Eighth Velehrad Unionistic Congress is still waiting to be realized.

The originator of the Velehrad Unionistic Congresses, Antonín
Cyril Stojan, has been laid to rest in the Royal Chapel of the Velehrad Basilica, under a tombstone donated by the priests of Moravia
in the year 1936.[57] However, the foundation he laid for unionistic
work has not died—the principle is still alive, as vital as it was in 1910
when he formulated his legacy. "I compare schism to the separation
or divorce of two married people. As long as the divorced spouses do
not speak to each other, everything is in vain. As soon as they begin
to talk to each other, even if they should begin to argue, there is hope
that they will come together once more, that they will belong to
each other. We are divorced from our intimate friends. And we must
begin talking with them in our publications. Perhaps this will lead to
fights, but this will already mean hope that we shall begin a conversa-

tion and further negotiations."[58] This statement of Stojan about the continuing slow and delicate process in the reunion of Churches is an indication in itself of how his unionistic legacy is an open, slowly developing and never ending task to be fulfilled only if that wholesome and all embracing love of Stojan be its constantly motivating force.

In view of the fact that Church unity itself as promised by Jesus Christ, that "All may be one" (John 7:23) was providentially guaranteed, Stojan shared Christ's assurance firmly and implicitly. Yet his legacy is on rather a limited scale in a sense that he was concerned primarily about the reunion of Churches[59] in the framework of what Karl Rahner calls *ecclesial Christianity*[60] and its awareness of the historicity of the Church, in which he firmly believed as "one, holy, catholic and apostolic" and institutionally to be reflected in the Roman Catholic Church as the Church of Christ, able to serve as a cornerstone for a possible corporate reunion of other schismatic Churches.

In this sense, the Stojan legacy was a concrete and well thought-out program for the Orthodox-Anglican-Catholic encounters while leaving a wide open door to all other Protestant and Evangelical Churches still searching for their connection with a biblical Church of Christ to find their place eventually in the Universal Church. Stojan always a practical man knew well how to set his priorities, where the Church unionism was to be the opening stage for modern ecumenism. In this, Stojan's legacy stands out as that of an apostle of Church unity.

NOTES

1. Alois Kolísek, *Cyrillo-Methodějství u Čechů a Slováků* (Cyrilomethodian heritage of the Czechs and Slovaks) (Brno, 1935) passim; Josef Kolejka, "Cyrilometodějská tradice v druhé polovině 19 Století" (Cyrilomethodian tradition in the second half of XIX century) *Velká Morava*, ed. Jar Böhm, (Prague, 1963), 97-112.
2. Karl Rahner, *Concern for the Church* (transl. by Edward Quinn) (New York, 1981), 154-172, especially p. 157: "Unity through love."
3. Steven Runciman, *The Eastern Schism* (Oxford, 1955), 157-170.
4. Bohumil Zlámal, *Antonín Cyril Stojan* (Rome, 1973), 55-56.
5. Mořic Hruban, *Z časů nedlouho zašlých* (From the Recent Past) (Rome and Los Angeles, 1967), 66-68; the author has a valuable chapter, "Olomoučtí arcibiskupové" pp. 66-100, in which he deals with the archbishops of Olomouc from the view of his personal experiences.
6. This was the original parish church built around 1250 in the style of early Gothic. This church is now used mostly for Eastern liturgy and perhaps for this appropriately called Cyrilka, i.e., little church dedicated to St. Cyril. See Bohumil Zlámal, in introduction, "Velehrad" Rudolf Šmahel's book about Velehrad.
7. Quoted by Bohumil Zlámal, *Antonín Cyril Stojan* (Rome, 1973), 54 ff: Stojan quoted Středovský in his address before the Catholic Congress in Olomouc in 1911 in reference to Marian devotions. Středovský authored also, *Sacra Moraviae historia* (1710) and *Rubinus Moraviae* (1712).
8. Quoted *ibid* p. 54.
9. Josef Vašica, *České Literární baroko* (Czech Literary Baroque) (Prague, 1938) passim.
10. Mentioned by Moric Hruban, *op.cit.*, 190.
11. Václav Flajšhans, *Písemnictví české*, 2 vols. (Prague 1900-1901).
12. Edward Winter, *Der Josefinismus und Seine Geschichte: Beiträge zur Geistes-Geschichte Oesterreichs 1710-1848* (Brno–Vienna, 1943) passim.
13. Alois Kolísek, *Cyrillo-Methodějství u Čechů Slováků* (Brno, 1935).
14. Anton Kasalaj, "Das Cyrillo-Methodianische Velehrad und Seine Unions Kongresse", *Slovak Studies* XII (Rome–Cleveland, 1972) 153-191.
15. Franz Stauracz, *Los von Rom* (Hamm v Wertl, 1901) 16-17 and passim; T.G. Masaryk, *Los von Rom* (Boston, 1902) 100-102 and passim.
16. Pius X, Encyclical, *Pascendi* of Sept. 7, 1907 in *A.S.S.* 40 (1908) 38 ff; Pius X, *Motu Proprio* of Sept. 1, 1910 in *A.A.S.* 11 (1911) 655-580; J. Godrycz, *The Doctrine of Modernism and Its Refutation* (Philadelphia, 1908), 121.

17. Augustin Neuman, *Katolíci a naše národní svobození* (Catholics and our National Independence) (Olomouc, 1922) passim.
18. *Acta IV Conventus Velehradensis Anno 1924* (Olomouc: 1925) cf., F. Cinek, *Velehrad viry* (Olomouc, 1936) 499-515.
19. Epistola pii PP. XI *A.A.S.* 16 (1924) 326-7.
20. Pii PP. XI *A.A.S.* 16 (1924) 327.
21. Jaroslav Durych, "Odpověď Rusům" *Rozmach* 2 (Prague, 1924) 266-73.
22. *A.A.S.* 16 (1924) 490.
23. Hansjakob Stehle, *Eastern Politics of the Vatican 1917-1979* (transl. by Sandra Smith) (Athens, Ohio, London, 1981), 6, 73-83, 113, 185 and passim. This author is rather negative to d'Herbigny's approaches in dealing with the East.
24. Bohumil Zlámal, *op.cit.,* 84.
25. Established by Pope Pius XI for the promotion of Church unity and for a study of related problems.
26. Charles Kolek, O.S.B., "The Twenty-eighth International Eucharistic Congress in Chicago" in *Czech Catholics at the 41st International Congress,* ed. by Ludvik Nemec, (Philadelphia, 1977), 76-77.
27. Claude G. Victora, "The Apostolate for reunion at St. Procopius Abbey," *Proceedings of the First Unionistic Congress,* Sept. 28-30, 1956 (Lisle, 1956) 19-25.
28. On Nov. 3, 1961, the one hundredth anniversary of the birth was observed as *Abbot Procopius Neužil Day* by proclamation of the Governor of the State of Illinois. See English section of *Národ* of Nov. 11, 1961. Public and ecclesiastical celebrations were held in Chicago and on this occasion the Benedictine Abbey Press published a booklet on this Abbot, although a much needed biography still awaits the pen of a skillful historian.
29. Emil Petřík, "Opatství Svatoprokopské mohutný středem apoštolské práce (St. Procopies Abbey an influential center of Apostolic Work), *Národ Calendar of 1961* (Chicago, 1961), 127-131.
30. Emil Petřík is preparing a long awaited biography on this abbot.
31. Ludvik Nemec, "American Velehrad," *The Byzantine Catholic World* (BCW) 7 (nos. 14-15, 1962) 6-14.
32. *Proceedings of the First Unionistic Congress, September 28-30, 1956* (St. Procopius, Lisle, 1956) and the *Proceedings of the Second and Third Unionistic Congresses* (St. Procopius, Lisle, 1960). These *Acts* are detailed documentary about these congresses.
33. "II 3° Congresso Unionistico in America," *L'Osservatore Romano,* July 18, 1959, p. 3, contains a detailed description of the proceedings of the third congress with accompanying photographs. In specific reference to Dvornik's lectures is the following: "Il Prof. Dvornik ha tenuto una seconda conferenza, illustrando i suoi nuovi studi sui rapporti tra Roma e Bisanzio, documentando la supremazia della Sede di Pietro, riconosciuta dall'Oriente, oggi dissidente, fino al IX secolo..." *L.Osservatore Romano,* October 24, 1961, p. 3; cr. NC News Service, October 25, 1961; cf. *The Byzantine Catholic World,* December 24, 1961, p. 1.

34. *De Millenaria Celebritate Sancti Wenceslai Ducis, Martyris,* apostolic letter of Pope on this occasion, see *A.A.S.* XXI, (1930) 129-37, and the occasion of the Oriental Congress Pius XI sent a letter of August 2, 1929, see *A.A.S.* XXI (1930) 598.
35. Leonard J. Swidler, *Ecumenical Vanguard: The History of the Una Sancta Movement* (Philadelphia, 1966), passim; see J.R. Fang, "Una Sancta Movement," *Encyclopedic Dictionary of Religion* (Washington, DC/Philadelphia, 1978) III, col. 3597-3598.
36. *A.A.S.* XIX (1928) 93-96.
37. He delivered his paper "De Sancto Cyrillo et Methodio in luce Historiae Byzantinae," *Acta V Conventus Velehradensis* (Olomouc, 1927), in which he emphasizes that East and West have to take responsibility for the Schism. The same pursuit Dvornik stressed in the paper, "Quomodo incrementum influxus orientalis im imperio byzantino s. VII-IX dissensionem inter ecclesiam Romanam et Orientalem promoverit," *Acta Conventus Pragensis pro studiis orientalium* (Olomouc, 1930), pp. 159-172. In the sixth congress at Velehrad he wrote a paper, "De Audtoritate civili in conciliis oecumenicis," *Acta VI Congressus Velehradensis* (Olomouc, 1933), in which he shattered the traditional view of the great scholar Funk. In the seventh Velehrad Congress in 1936 Dvornik delivered a lecture on the historical background of the Byzantine Empire in the time of SS. Cyril and Methodius; cf. Cinek, *Velehrad* (Olomouc, 1936) pp. 733-736, which, because of a previous official assignment, he was unable to deliver in person, but which was read by Professor J. Matocha of Olomouc.
38. Cinek, *Velehrad víry* (Olomouc, 1936) 528-29.
39. *Acta V Conventus Velehradensis* (Olomouc, 1927) 151 ff.
40. *Brief* of Sept. 7, 1928, see *A.A.S.* 20 (1928), 277-278; see F. Cinek, *op.cit.,* 561-563.
41. Bohumil Zlámal, *Antonin Cyril Stojan* (Rome, 1973) 88 and passim.
42. *Acta VI Congressus Velehradensis* (Olomouc, 1933).
43. "De auctoritate civili in conciliis oecumeninicis" published in *Acta VI,* ibid., see its English text: "The Authority of the State in the Oecumenical Councils," *The Christian East* 14 (1934) 95-108.
44. Quoted by Zlámal, *op.cit.,* 89.
45. He also wrote a history of the Congresses titled: "Velehrad e i suoi Congressi unionistici," *Civiltà Catolica Anno* 108 (1957) II, 577 ff.
46. Summed up by Cibulka, *op.cit.,* 5-10.
47. Cinek, *op.cit.,* 656-70. cf. J. Poulík "Výsledky výzkumu na velkomoravském hradišti "Valy" u Mikulčic" (Result from the exploration in the Wall at Mikulčice) *Památky Archeologické* 48 (1957) 274-97.
48. F. Robenek, *Moravská Metropole. K dějinám její lokalisace* (Moravian Metropolis. Concerning history of its location) (Kroměříž, 1934) cf. Michael Lacko "The Cyrilomethodian mission and Slovakia", *Slovak Studies* 1 (Rome, 1961) 23-49; cf. Peter Ratkoš "K otázce sídla panonsko-moravského metropolity" (Concerning the question of panonian Moravian metropolitan) *Verbum* 2 (Kosice, 1948) 342-45; cf. L. Zachar, *Der hl. Cyrill and*

Method in Devin (Theben). Devin die Haupt-und Residenz Stadt des Gross-mahrischen Reiches. (Bratislava, 1929).

49. Otto Polach "Metropolitní sídlo sv. Metoda a Nitra," *Historický Sborník Matice Slovenské* 4 (1946) 274-97; cf. M. Weingart "Pribina, Kocel a Nitra v zrkadle doby cyrilometodějské (Pribina, Kocel and Nitra in the mirror of the Cyrilomethodian period.) *Sborník Riša Velkomoravská* (Prague, 1933).

50. *Acta VII. Conventus Velehradensis* (Olomouc, 1937) 160-73.

51. John A Abbo and Jerome D. Hannan, *The Sacred Canons,* 2 vols. (St. Louis, 1952) II, 435-450.

52. Zlámal, *op.cit.,* 89.

53. This is unique title for the Augustinians, who regularly have a superior Abbot, but General Provincial and superior at this Abbey at Brno is well known, because the famous biologist Gregor Johann Mendel (1822-1884) was once Abbot here. See J.R. Aherne, *Encyclopedic Dictionary of Religion* (Philadelphia, 1978) II, 2333.

54. Purpose of these excavations is the search for the connection of the present Velehrad with that of history. Professor Nevěřil initiated these in 1911 and excavations continue to the present. There is established evidence that the location of ancient Velehrad was in the vicinity of the present Velehrad.

55. Titled "Historical Background of the Byzantine Empire in time of Sts. Cyril and Methodius. See Cinek, *op.cit.,* 723-4.

56. Quoted by Zlámal, *op.cit.,* 91.

57. Tombstone with inlaid bronze figure of the deceased Stojan is the work of Julius Pelikan, and the three partial reliefs of Our Lady of Hostyn with Sts. Cyril and Methodius were produced by Joseph Axman.

58. Quoted by Zlámal, *op.cit.,* 92.

59. Francis Dvornik, *National Churches and the Church Universal* (Westminster, 1944), 48-50; L. Nemec, "Father Dvornik's Views on the Reunion of Churches," *Perspectives* 6 No. 2 (1961) 15-19, cf. idem, "Dvorníkovy názory na sjednocení církvi" (Dvornik's Views on Churches Reunion) *Katolík* 67 (Nov. 4, 1960) 3-4; E.F. Hanahoe, *Catholic Ecumenism* (Washington, DC, 1953) 43-167. Details the various movements having ecumenism as a specific goal, and contains a well-selected bibliography (pp. 13-19). cr. Y.M.J. Congar "Oekumenische Bewegung" *Lexikon fuer Theologie und Kirche* (ed. 1962) VII col. 1128-1137; B. Schwitze "Orthodoxe Kirchen" *Lexikon fuer Theologie und Kirche* VII (ed. 1962) col. 1246-1255; Henry St. John, *Essays in Christian Unity* (Westminister, MD, 1955), 1-24.

60. Karl Rahner, *Concern for the Church* (transl. by Edward Quinn) (New York, 1981).

XI

THE LOYALTY OF STOJAN TO
THE VICAR OF CHRIST

As Stojan's legacy was concerned about the Church of Christ in the framework of the ecclesial Roman Church, his loyalty to the Popes was also tied to the latter because the Vicars of Christ are an indispensable bond and a vitally important connection of the mystical Body of Christ. Stojan was truly 'semper fidelis' in every sense of that word and in everything the Pope represented and stood for in his role as Vicar of Christ. He had a filial relationship of obedience to the Apostolic See as well as great reverence and love for the person of the Holy Father in Rome. He identified with the Pope's struggles and sufferings. He had a profound understanding and docility toward his counsels, directives and commands. They became the guiding principles of A.C. Stojan as priest and ecclesiastical dignitary. He controlled his progress and plans according to Rome's wishes and directives. This stand of unconditional loyalty to the Papacy was not only needed but greatly appreciated against the background of liberalism[1] so evident in the Habsburg monarchy in the second half of the nineteenth century when the situation of the Roman Catholic Church became precarious.

All was set in motion, and the year 1848 witnessed the first indication of freedom for the whole society of nations and individuals. Their cry became the catchword of the time. Some measures were also attempted against the central government in Vienna. The new Emperor Francis Joseph tried to control the revolutionary movement, but even the so-called absolutism of Bach (1851) was a complete failure. Set in motion by the Emperor's directives of 1855, concordats with the Holy See were made. Concordats became the pattern by which the relationship between Church and state[2] were regulated. The Habsburg dynasty recognized the full validity and power of canon law and gave the Church extensive jurisdiction and influence in education.[3] The Church thus should have become the central point of the whole empire which was practically disintegrating, and should have been the main support for the authority of the dynasty. Some thought this would necessarily follow, but a real psychological reaction became evident in increased defiance toward the dynasty.

All national groups began expressing claims and making demands, especially after 1867, when dualism was introduced into Austria-Hungary.[4] Czechs were represented by the movement of the old Czech party (František Palacký, František Brauner, František L. Rieger) who wanted trialism.[5] The Prime Minister of that time, Count Karel Sigismund of Hohenvart, by his federalistic concept of nations in Austria-Hungary, was inclined to favor the demands of the national groups. But he was succeeded by Count Adolf of Auersperg and the attitude of centralism prevailed. Later, Minister Beust confirmed this policy. After dualism was settled, the relation between Church and state suddenly changed. Austria opened an attack on the concordats.[6] The constitution of December 21, 1867, and the bills of May 25, 1868, which regulated laws about marriage, education, and interdenominational affairs provided ammunition against the concordats. Rome turned its attention toward them, and Pope Pius IX called these bills *leges abominabiles, vehementer reprobandae et damnandae*[7] in an allocution characteristic of the times. It was delivered in a private consistory, June 22, 1868.

The document indicated that the validity of the *Concordat* was short-lived. By this it can be seen that the Habsburg dynasty was not consistent in its relationships with the Church. The dynasty formed attitudes according to her needs, and used the Church as a means to her own ends. In the meantime, anti-Catholic groups exerted greater pressure. Czech Protestants, supported by the so-called "Protestant Patent" of 1861, and led by Pastor F.W. Kossuth of Prague and the Protestant minister, Rev. Ruzicka,[8] tried to unify Czech Lutherans and Czech-Moravian Brethren. Their model was the work of John Amos Comenius. Kossuth, extracting ideas from the history of Palacký, proclaimed a doctrine based on the program of John Hus, formulating it as a unifying factor for all Czechs. The trend was marked by the *Kutná Hora Epistles* of Karel Havlíček and by the excommunicated priest, Augustin Smetana (1814-1850),[9] who wrote many pamphlets against the Church.

The ecclesiastical magazine, *Časopis katolického duchovenstva,* which had been edited since 1848 by Bishop V. Jirsík, and the review, *Blahověst,* edited since 1846 by Vyšehrad Canon Václav Štulc, strove to face the movement of mass apostasy. The Vatican Council (1870) with a dramatic procedure[10] made clear the attitude of the Church concerning Enlightenment in the impending struggle. It also showed its attitude towards Gallicanism, Febroianism, and Joseph-inism[11] by proclaiming the dogma of the infallibility of the Pope,[12] thus strengthening the authority of the Holy See. Among later nations and among Catholics throughout the world, this dogma found accept-ance. But in Germany and Austria-Hungary, opposition to it was strong. Even during the council sessions the following very ardently expressed their opinions against the dogma: Cardinal Schwarzen-berg of Prague, Cardianl Rauscher of Vienna, Archbishop Haynald of Kolscza, Hungary, and Bishop Strossmayer of Diakov. They were known as "non-opportunists."[13] They were influenced by the Gun-therians who were on principle against the proclaimed dogma. The Cistercian priest, Salesius Majer of Osek, A Gunther adherent, was an adviser to Cardinal Schwarzenberg and exerted great influence everywhere.[14]

The wave of resistance against the proclaimed dogma began to spread throughout all Germany. Chief representatives of this group of dissenters were Professor Schulte of Prague and the well-known ecclesiastical historian, Ignatz Doellinger. Furthermore, Pope Pius IX's (1846-1878) great battle for the Church's freedom took place while Stojan was too young to experience it personally, but the shock wave created in Moravia by this "Roman question"[15] was important for the success of Stojan's life-work. This tragedy of the papacy had a considerable echo even in Austria, which was then lethargic in matters Catholic and weakened by ill-willed Josephinism. The Roman question moved minds and aroused sympathy toward the oppressed Pope, who on three different occasions had considered the possi-bility of flight from Rome and from Italy to Austria.

The Moravian action in support of the Pope, whether in the form of fund raising, addresses of salutation, subscriptions to papal loans, recruitment for the papal army, or the activities of the Brotherhood of St. Michael, met with understanding. From the beginning, the government supported all these; but later, these activities were carried on contrary to the government's will and in spite of its pro-hibition. Behind all these expressions and actions, stood the young

Archbishop of Olomouc, the Landgrave Friedrich Fürstenberg (1813-1892), who deserves respect for his answer to the governor of Moravia, Prince Lažanský, in the year 1860: "I have always believed, and I still believe, that it is the sacred duty, as well as the right, of every good Catholic Christian, and all the more of a Catholic bishop, to lend assistance to the Supreme Head of the Church in time of danger and suffering, and to help by such means as the individual has at hand; and this, all the more certainly when it is not only a question of the Holy See's rights, but at the same time a question of the most sacred thing we have, the Church and religion."[16]

The deviation away from the papacy of Austrian politics occurred for internal reasons. This was the opposition leveled against the Austrian concordat (1885-1870). Unfortunate consequences followed but there was also a good effect. That opposition became perhaps the most important factor contributing toward an arousing of ecclesiastical and national consciousness in the Moravian rural areas, which had never been awakened up to that time. Stojan was then a young student and later a seminarian who had an opportunity to experience some of it. As a young priest he became aware of the real situation when he often heard his friend, Father Joseph, but the solution to this question was never reached. Leo XIII had also taken a stand on social problems in his encyclical *Rerum Novarum.*[24] The development concerning Austria made the necessity for a solution urgent. The converts of Mecklenburg, Franz of Florencourt and Karl Knight of Vogelsang, established a conservative movement called Christian-Social.[25] The main magazine for it was *Vaterland,* which was supported by Count Egbert Belcredi and Prince Liechtenstein. Thus the Conservative-Catholic party was established.

These attitudes of meeting national and social demands were stressed by Austrian Catholics led by the devoted and capable Dr. Karl Lueger (1844-1910),[26] who was a personal friend of Pope Leo XIII. In his practical view of social problems, Dr. Lueger adhered to the ideas of the Catholic priest Ambrosius Opik who as early as the second half of the nineteenth century was proclaiming in Warnsdorf the urgent necessity to change and socially rearrange the so-called "Catholic Days" (*Katholiken Tage).*[27] This reinforced Stojan's love for the Holy Father, to whom in the course of his first pilgrimage to Rome in 1881, he had presented a Latin petition for the blessing of pictures for Hostyn, Prague and Radhošť. Stojan always recalled this occasion with deep emotion whenever he urged the faithful to pray before those pictures for the union of the Slav nations with the Holy See. He re-echoed the pope's call for unity. The *Association of Mount Hostyn* at the Přerov parish decided to organize a pilgrimage of thanksgiving to Hostyn and there to dedicate the picture blessed by Pope Leo XIII as a symbol of unity. He issued a proclamation for this pilgrimage, which re-echoed the emotions of that Roman papal audience (1881) and the words of the Holy Father: "Be diligent, dear sons, that unity with the Roman Church be preserved, and that, day after day, it be increased and strengthened. Praying together, we wish to beseech Cyril and Methodius that from heaven on high they protect the Slavic people, that they obtain from God perseverance for some, the regaining of health for others; that they enkindle mutual love in the hearts of all, that they deliver Christ's heritage from all discord and jealousy."[28] Stojan seized every opportunity and marshalled every argument to remind the people of their duty of devotion, loyalty, and love toward the successor of St. Peter, not only in feeling, but in works of love, by fulfilling his wishes.

He himself was the best example of this. Even to the point of most generous personal sacrifice, he responded to the call of Leo XIII for apostolates conducted through organizations, publications, newspapers, congresses, political parties, social justice, and, of course, spiritual exercises and eucharistic devotions, which Leo's successor, Pope St. Pius X, (1903-14) stressed so much.

As Leo XIII appealed to the Slavs, Stojan turned this around and appealed to Rome. He wished to demonstrate for the people of Moravia that the Holy Father had a tangible interest in the life and efforts of Catholic Slavs. He wished to gain a concrete Roman interest for his work of renewal and unification among the Slavs and for the two centers of that work, Hostyn and Velehrad. In the year 1904, he brought the Holy Father's representative, the Nuncio to Vienna, Genaro Granito-Pignatelli di Belmonte, to Hostyn and Velehrad for the first time. Any previous visit of that nature (for example, the jubilee celebrations in the year 1885) was made impossible by Vienna politics. The people gave the Nuncio a great ovation, and he was so impressed by the Moravian piety that he said he had witnessed nowhere else such devotion and such a gigantic demonstration of Faith. Stojan was evidently pleased with the Nuncio's appreciative reports on his country. He regarded it as good diplomacy to bring the attention of the highest ecclesiastical authorities to the unionistic endeavors of Velehrad and the affairs of the Czech nation.

Several years later, Stojan himself went to petition Pope Pius X to grant permission for the crowning of Our Lady of Hostyn, and requested him to bless two crowns. The coronation of the miraculous statue in the year 1912 was the most splendid Marian celebration[29] in Moravian history. This was a joyous occasion for Stojan because not only was it a time of spiritual benefits for about 300,000 pilgrims, but particularly it attracted once more the attention of Rome and gained Rome's benevolence for the Cyrilomethodian idea.

In retrospect, one has to wonder why Stojan was so anxious to manifest loyalty to Rome, the Pope and the Church. This was for Stojan much more than a matter of faith, conscience and personal priestly integrity. It was greatly conditioned by circumstances surrounding the situation of the Church in Bohemia and Moravia and most of Austria toward the end of the nineteenth and the beginning of the twentieth century, which showed a great decline. The Catholic modernist movement[30] was especially typical of the time. It was liberal emphasizing the personal adjustment of the individual, thus accounting for a great decline of religious beliefs and an increase of religious indifferentism. The very existence of Catholic modernists indicated that their attitude was favorably received and hailed as progressive. But this "progress," to use the words of the poet Victor Dyk, was "progress to the point of stupidity."[31]

Meanwhile progress was being advanced according to the plan of the antithetical "Reformation—Counter—Reformation." The indifferentism of Czech Catholics, supported by another catchword, "Prague-Vienna," aimed to achieve the stand called "Religio depopulata."[32] Herein lay the roots of the Czech movement, "Away from Rome." Meanwhile, the Austrian *Los von Rom* movement was in the organization process. This sought to prove that the Catholic Church had committed "crimes" against the Czech nation throughout its history. Admittedly, a motive of retribution can be taken for granted, since the Church in her attempt to re-Catholicize Bohemia was supported by the Habsburg dynasty. It is sad, however, that all the merits of the Catholic Church recorded in various histories were wilfully forgotten and overlooked. This was the result of the relentless work of those Czech priests who had adapted themselves to progressivism. Propaganda for the movement was spread in the name of national demands, and Stojan, a practical man, was determined to offset this anti-Catholic propaganda.

At the beginning of the war of 1914, the Czechs were in an unusual situation. They were forced to fight for Austria, despite their sympathies for Russia, Serbia, and the Western Allies.[33] This was a critical point in the relation of the Czechs with Austria. The tactful stand of Palacký[34] ceased, and under T.G. Masaryk an open fight began. An all-out persecution of Czech traditions, the introduction of the German language into schools, the arrest of Czech and Slovak patriots even in the Czech districts, the arrest of the Young Czech leaders Karel Kramář and Alois Rašín in 1915—all these events accelerated the decision of the Czechs to raise the flag in the fight for national independence with the aim of destroying Austria-Hungary. The patriotic Stojan understood this situation well and without hesitation took the side of the nation. During the stormy era following the revolutionary change in government in the year 1918, when the Austrio-Hungarian monarchy disintegrated into the five separate states that replaced it, among which was the Republic of Czechoslovakia, Stojan was again subjected to a statesman's test of loyalty to the Holy See.

The crisis involving the Czech clergy was two-fold. First, many of nationally conscious priests and laymen thought that the Church was allying itself for life and death with a state which appeared to be more Catholic than it really was, and that in this way it was indirectly giving its approval for any oppression of nationalities. Critical internal conditions could not be sufficiently exposed by a relatively fictitious distinction between a Catholic emperor and a liberal government. The former was praised; the latter was condemned. This dilemma affected the Czech Catholic intellectuals too; they manifested a dislike for the Church, opposition to it, and even outright apostasy. Though overstating the issues somewhat Father Karel Dostál-Lutinov wrote in 1906: "Consider this! For fourteen years, with the support of the State, the Czech intellectual is trained in Catholic religion; after graduation he is usually an atheist or an opponent of his Catholic Church; and he does not even know the catechism. This proclaims the urgency of a reform in teaching, in education, and in Catholic theology."[35]

Secondly, the Church in Austria was ridiculed by the liberals as "Kaiserlich-königlich-katholische Kirche" (Imperial-royal-Catholic

Church) – scandalous, in the opinion of the Sušil nationalists. The crisis was aggravated by several unfortunate public events. The chief of these was the forced resignation in 1904 of Theodor Kohn,[36] Archbishop of Olomouc, a Czech by nationality, who was hailed as the "first successor of St. Methodius by reason of both office and nationality;" he was succeeded by Francis S. Bauer (1841-1915) and later, after his death, the crisis was further aggravated by the postulation, forced by the Vienna government, to have Lev Skrbenský, Cardinal of Prague, made the Archbishop of Olomouc (1916-1920), who was the last elected archbishop. Even the struggles against Modernism were used by some ecclesiastical officials of an Austrian frame of mind to suppress the Czech-Catholic tendencies among seminarians and priests. This especially affected one genuine renewal movement among the priests, the so-called *Katolická Moderna.*[37]

The First World War (1914-1918) brought the Czech Catholics, particularly the priests, not only moral difficulties of conscience, but also a political crisis, the consequences of which later appeared in the form of an apostasy movement, which took place after the change in government. A great dike trying to stem this flood was the patriotic and loyal A.C. Stojan, and only from today's vantage point can we realize how effective he was. Fortunately he was placed at the head of the Olomoucká *Jednota Duchovenstva* (The Olomouc Union of Clergy), organized on November 7, 1918. Stojan was a firm crystallizing element in this organization, while Cardinal Skrbenský, who was Austrian, remained passive. The fact that conditions in Moravia became more favorable toward loyalty to the Church and to priestly ideals was largely due to Stojan.

In Bohemia, the crisis led to the forming of a schismatic Czechoslovak Church on January 8, 1920, which also involved many Moravian priests by reason of its nationalistic basis, elimination of celibacy, and slogans of modernism.[38] Like a solicitous father, Stojan sent out a plea to the apostates even in his first pastoral letter of April 3, 1921: "Return to the Lord, shepherds of souls. . . . The Church with its altars and pulpits, even with its Latin for which you reproach her, has saved our nationality and language for us. . . . With love we wish to adhere to Christ's Vicar, the Holy Father."[39]

As the chairman of the *Jednota Duchovenstva* (Union of Clergy), he used all his influence to defend the authority of the Church, and he would not allow any schismatic and anti-Church activities. To counteract such tendencies, he explained the revised requisites and regulations governing the priesthood. When he published them in the *Věstník Jednoty Duchovenstva* (Journal of the Union of Clergy) of Olomouc and Brno, in 1919, he did it in a legal way and used a tactful manner. The firm and just stand of the Church was explained by the Canon A.C. Stojan in his proclamation, which was also published in the Roman *Osservatore Romano*, July, 1920. Stojan also personally attended the stormy meeting of the schismatic *Česká Jednota Duchovenstva* (Czech Union of the Clergy) on October 26, 1920; and there he adjured the participants to heed the voices of the bishops and the pope.

One of the demands made by the radical priests in Bohemia was the establishing of a Czech patriarchate. It is certainly noteworthy that A.C. Stojan, then Archbishop of Olomouc, was proposed by them as the one to be named patriarch. Stojan, however, reacted by publishing a proclamation in the newspapers on April 5, 1922, saying: "I have read in the newspapers that the *Jednota* recommended to the government that I be named a patriarch. Anyone who knows me is certainly convinced that as a faithful priest of the Holy Church, I will not do anything contrary to the will of the Holy See and of the Holy Father."[40]

During the pilgrimage to Rome, on October 18, 1921, Archbishop Stojan, together with the other bishops, solemnly renewed his promise of loyalty to the Catholic Faith and to the Holy Father. He informed the people of his archdiocese about this in a special pastoral letter of October 13, 1921: "Holy Father, from the new Republic of Czechoslovakia, we come to you that you may encourage us and strengthen us for fighting the battles of the Lord. We wish to be your loyal sons, to remain such, and to also preserve our loyalty to the Holy See. We grieve together with you over the unfortunate schism of some of our nation, who fell away from the rock of Faith and who strive to lead others astray. We, however, wish to pray earnestly, and by means of the example of a truly Christian life, to do everything possible to build a dam to stop the schism; in fact, we wish to do everything possible to bring back into Peter's Bark those of our brethren who have suffered shipwreck."[41]

Many voices of loyalty were raised by the Moravian theologians, so dear to Stojan, over whose conventions in Velehrad he presided almost every year. In the year 1921, he met them as an archbishop.

They showed their gratitude to him by adopting a most realistic slogan: "Velehrad—our program. In aeternum iuxta Roman." This was an answer to the taunting cry of those who had fallen away, who said: 'Pryč od Říma!'" (Away from Rome). This struggle of Czech Catholicism[42] was complex and very difficult indeed. It demanded skillful diplomacy on the part of Catholic politicians and Church authorities to offset the hostile attacks on all fronts of the restless nation. Stojan not only survived all these crises but handled the affairs of the nation and of the Church in the true conscience of a real patriot and a diligent observer of the national scene. In this he proved himself to be a faithful disciple of another patriot, Father Francis Sušil and his program: "For the Church and nation!" People of all walks of life accepted him in complete confidence and trust because of his past wonderful activities on their behalf. Even in times of intense animosities it was Stojan's goodness, his great heart, his priestly integrity, and a complete loyalty as Churchman to the Vicar of Christ which was constantly silencing all discordant voices and trends in his beloved nation. Through his ever faithful loyalty to the Vicar of Christ he showed himself also a worthy successor on the throne of the see of St. Methodius.

NOTES

1. Johann Kirsch and Ludwig A. Veit, *Kirchengeschichte,* 4 vols. (Freiburg im Bresigau, 1930) IV, 61-63 ff.
2. Pii IX, *Acta,* pars prima, Vol. II, 465-484. Cf. Mercati, *Raccolta di concordati su materie ecclesiastiche fra la Santa Sede et le Autorita Civili,* 821-844.
3. Felix John Vondráček, *The Foreign Policy of Czechoslovakia 1918-1935,* 91. It was decreed that the state should preserve the Roman Catholic religion "with all its rights and prerogatives according to God's order and the Church's laws." Thereby the Church had been granted control over all matters pertaining to marriage, morals and education.
4. Kamil Krofta, *Stará ústava Česká a Uherská* (Prague, 1940) 72.
5. Franz. Lad. Rieger, *"Ein Charakterbild aus Boehmens Neuester Geschichte,"* 633-651; 734-752.
6. Kirsch-Veit, *Kirchengeschichte* (Freiburg im Breisgau, 1930) II, 301.
7. *ASS,* IV (1868), 10-13; Papae Pii IX. Allocutio habita in consistorio secreto die 22 Junii 1868.
8. Winter, *Tausend Jahre Geisteskampf im Sudetenraum* (Salzburg, 1938), 350.

9. T.G. Masaryk, *Moderní člověk a náboženství* (Modern Man and Religion), 187-224.

10. Joseph Cardinal Hergenroether, *Handbuch der Allegemeinen Kirchengeschichte*, III, 976-977; idem., *op.cit.*, 978.

11. Joseph Schmidlin, *Papstgeschichte der Neusten Zeit. (Papstum und Paepste gegenüber den modernen Strönungen. Pius IX and Leo XIII, 1846-1903)*, Vol. II, 255-283.

12. *Ibid.*, 275-283.

13. Beiser J. Ryan, *The Vatican Council and the American Secular Newspapers*, 1867-70, 10. Most of the adversaries accepted papal infallibility as a dogma but were opposed to its definition on various grounds.

14. Winter, *op.cit.*, 380.

15. Thomas P. Neill and Raymond H. Schmandt, *History of the Catholic Church* (Milwaukee, 1957) 519-525, J.F. Maguire, *Rome, Its Ruler and Its Institutions* (London, 1859) passim; G.F.H. Berkeley, *Italy in the Making* (Cambridge, 1936), passim.

16. Quoted by Bohumil Zlámal, *Antonín Cyril Stojan* (Rome, 1975), 66 and passim.

17. *Ibid.*, 67.

18. *Grande Munus* of Leo XIII.

19. Leonis XIII, Pontificis Maximi *Acta*, V, 1-7. De collegio clericorum bohemorum in urbe condendo.

20. Theodor Grentrup, *Volk and Volkstum im Lichte der Religion*, 151.

21. Grentrup, *op.cit.*, 150; cr. Schmidlin, *op.cit.*, 479.

22. Leonis XIII, *Acta*, XXI, 137-144; 164-165; XXII, 239-240. Congratulations for the successful absolving of the episcopal conference in Olomouc.

23. Winter, *op.cit.*, 383.

24. Leonis XIII, *Acta*, XI, 91-144.

25. Wiard Klapp, *Leben und Wirken des Sozialpolitikers Karl Freiherr von Vogelsang* (Nach den Quellen bearbeitet).

26. Franz Stuaracz, *Dr. Karl Lueger*, cf. Adolf Hitler, *Mein Kampf*, 99. 55. Hitler writes about him with great admiration, commenting especially on his political works.

27. Winter, *op.cit.*, 384.

28. Quoted by Bohumil Zlámal, *op.cit.*, 68.

29. Antonín Janda, *Papežská korunovace matky Boží svatohostýnské* (The Papal Coronation of the Blessed Mother of Holy Hostyn) (Brno, 1913) passim.

30. Pius X, *Motu Proprio*, Sept. 1, 1910; in *AAS*, II, 655-680.

31. Viktor Dyk declared that atheists and Socialists are anti-Catholic to the point of insanity. His statement is well-known. NCWC., May 4, 1925. Cf. Hanuš Jelínek, *Viktor Dyk* (Prague, 1932).

32. J. Godrycz, *The Doctrine of Modernism and Its Refutation* (Philadelphia, 1908), 121.

33. Von Luetzov, *Bohemia, an Historical Sketch* (London, 1939), 335.

34. Zdeňka and John Munzer, *We Were and We Shall Be,* 81-86. Cf. Beneš, *Le Problème Autrichien et la Question Tchèque* (Paris, 1908), Beneš and Masaryk realized the necessity for the Habsburg monarchy before the war, but were against it after the war.
35. Quoted by Bohumil Zlámal, *op.cit.,* 70 ff.
36. Mořic Hruban, *Z času nedlouho zašlých* (From recent Past) (Rome-Los Angeles, 1967) 68-72.
37. Ludvik Nemec, "The Czech Jednota, the Avant-Garde of Modern Clerical Progressivism and Unionism," *Proceedings of American Philosophical Society,* 112 no. 1 (1968) 74-100.
38. Frant. M. Hník, *Duchovní Ideály Československé Církve* (Spiritual Ideals of Czechoslovak Church), the Contribution towards the analysis of her social structure (Prague, 1939) 160-165; see idem., *Za Lepší Církev* (For the Better Church) (Prague, 1930), passim. Father Mattias Pavlík, later Bishop Gorazd, was mostly responsible that the Czechoslovak Church found supporters among some Moravian priests.
39. Bohumil Zlámal, *op.cit.,* 71.
40. *Ibid.,* 72.
41. *Ibid.,* 72.
42. Jaroslav Pecháček, "Politický Katolicismus v parlamentní demokracii," (Political Catholicism in the Parliamentarian Democracy), *Studie* I-II (Rome, 1976), 1-18; Miloš Trapl, *Politika čaského katolicismu na Moravě 1918-1938* (The Policy of Czech Catholicism in Moravia 1918-1938) (Prague, 1968) passim.

XII

THE UNIONISM OF STOJAN AND THE
SECOND VATICAN COUNCIL

The goal of the Unionism that Stojan advocated was a search for Church unity through the reunion of the Eastern churches with the ecclesial Christian Church of Christ in Rome. As such it was a foreshadowing of the ecumenical movement[1] as a dramatic symbol of modern Christianity.[2] During the twentieth century inevitably human society everywhere was affected by the communication revolution. The churches of Christendom felt the impact and were challenged to repair their broken unity. Ecumenism widened its concern to include all churches and religious associations searching for a placement in the universal church. Since schism[3] and heresy[4] were the principal causes of Christian divisions, Unionism was a limited form of ecumenism which in turn is a completion of the former with an inclusive world-wide framework for all churches,[5] mostly protestant and evangelical, and any other religious association rooted in Christianity.[6] Stojan had primarily a concrete scope and goal for his Church Unionism, namely a reunion of the Slavic Orthodox Churches with Rome. In this aspect he opened a new page in Church history by stretching out the hand of reconciliation and leaving a legacy of love that "All may be one." He paved the way for the second Vatican Council of 1962.[7]

The Second Vatican Council (1962-1965) is like a mirror, in which we see to what heights of world-wide actuality the thoughts of this Cyrilomethodian Moravian apostle of church unity among the Slavs attained—thoughts of which he spoke and put into practice half a century earlier. It becomes like a spirit moving the Council; the same spirit which was the sum total of the life and work of Archbishop Stojan. This signifies primarily the idea of the living role of the Church's liturgy in reaching all levels of people. The Council legislated a liturgical reform,[8] which popularized sacred liturgy; decreed that certain portions be performed in the vernacular to enable the people to understand it. The faithful, on the other hand, are urged to participate in worship, and to follow attentively what the priest-liturgist is doing. The Consilium for the implementation of the *Constitution on the Sacred Liturgy,* December 4, 1963, which Pope Paul VI established by the Motu Proprio *"Sacram Liturgiam"*[9] of January 25, 1964, has energetically set about the task confided to it, namely the faithful execution of the prescriptions of the *Constitution* and of the Motu Proprio, their interpretation and implementation. In its *Instruction*[10] it is a pleasure to read the recommendation of the vernacular and the extension of pastoral care of migrants. One can easily sense in this an echo of similar concerns of Stojan.

Stojan as a practical man also promoted the popularization of the liturgy. He understood liturgy as the harmony of hearts and lips, which in his day was incorporated by means of popular sacred hymns. Enthusiastically he taught the people to sing during worship, in order that, through the words of the text, properly sung, the faithful would participate intelligently in worship with their minds as well as with their emotions—particularly in the holy sacrifice of the Mass. No devotion conducted by Stojan was held without community praying and singing. In this, he reached for a vehicle of expression which is characteristic of his people. Generally speaking, the Slavs are a singing people. Their national songs and hymns form a counterpart to the colorful, ornate and artistically wrought national costumes. Songs and costumes were regarded by the Sušilites[11] as resources for a national rebirth.

Stojan similarly incorporated the song as an element in his program of spiritual and moral rebirth. The folk-song[12] in the liturgy, of course, could be only a religious song. He drew from the ancient tradition of spiritual folk-hymns, sung in the language of the people. As early as the time of Charles IV (1346-1378), four Czech hymns were allowed in churches.[13] The Cyrilomethodian idea[14] was well at home in Prague and actually exerted considerable influence. More effective however was the popular Hussite movement which introduced into religious services liturgical hymns sung in the vernacular as did the Moravian Brethren.[15] Influenced by the Hussite songs, the Czech Brethren developed their own spiritual songs. These were collected into hymnals called *Kancionál*[17] in the care of literary brotherhoods who provided liturgical songs and music for their churches. *Kancionál* also influenced and encouraged the composing of Protestant lyrics.[18] as soon as Catholics became aware of how attractive and intelligible the liturgy could be, and what spiritual value melodic songs could have, they incorporated many of the hymns and songs already written into their hymnals. In the Catholic Baroque,[19] a multitude of emotionally boisterous liturgical[20] and Marian songs appeared. The lyrical element in church hymns fell somewhat into disuse in the succeeding era of Josephinian Enlightenment. However in Stojan's day, sacred hymns were revived. Stojan himself was largely responsible for the revival.

Czech liturgical hymns, accompanied by musical instruments, resounded especially in famous Moravian churches in Hostyn and Velehrad. They constituted an essential part of the popular religious and national celebrations which Stojan organized. The people became so accustomed to these "Stojanese" celebrations that if they did not have devotional songs they would feel that something was missing. To give church celebrations the greatest possible solemnity was always Stojan's persistent concern. However, he did not dwell exclusively on mere externals. At the Hostyn and Velehrad pilgrimages, his concern was not merely an external demonstration. He constantly pointed out that in making a pilgrimage to the Cyrilomethodian cradle of the Faith, everyone should renew himself spiritually, become more devout and strengthened in Faith. For this reason above all he stressed the reception of the sacraments. Anyone who would neglect this, according to Stojan, was not a genuine Velehrad pilgrim.

He had a similar understanding of the Hostyn pilgrimages. As the spokesman for the *Matice Svatohostýnská* (Mount Hostyn Foundation) with its 15,000 members, he said in 1919: "The *Mount Hostyn Foundation* will continue to fulfill its mission and its purpose, so that in this place it will afford the crowds a place to stay for spiritual rest, for spiritual refreshment and rebirth, as well as for zeal in matters of temporal and eternal happiness."[21] Stojan's liturgical program had a far-reaching significance. Here Stojan, for the first time, organized popular devotions on a large scale and a permanent basis; he enlivened the liturgy by introducing the singing of spiritual hymns; and in that way he transferred the effects of the liturgy into everyday life, because melodies so impressed themselves on the memories of the people that they sang them in their homes and in their fields. This, of course, Stojan did not originate, but he did take this historical heritage and give it new life. He introduced a national element into the liturgy of the Latin Church—that of singing as a means of participation by the faithful in that which is being done on the altar. Hostyn and Velehrad are testimonials of Stojan's efforts to make the sacred liturgy accessible to the people; to make it understood and enlivened by Mass hymns. In this way, Stojan's pilgrimages to Hostyn, and especially his apostolic work at Velehrad, became "model spiritual renewals," and at the same time "popular national religious festivals."[22]

In a similar way, the Second Vatican Council searched for means by which the people could be intimately united to the liturgy. To a great extent it has adopted the same means which Stojan found so effective—participation in community prayer and community singing. Stojan's zealous personal efforts and sacrifices for people's pilgrimages to the two most important shrines in Moravia were motivated by his belief that people who came to know their liturgy, came to understand and love it, would themselves become renewed. They would also be more likely to understand the character and values of the liturgies of the separated Christians of the East[23] —liturgies in which there are so many popular elements and chants.

Since 1891, Stojan saw to it that the Slavonic liturgy according to the Eastern Rite was celebrated every year during the pilgrimages which were arranged by the *Apostolate of Sts. Cyril and Methodius,* and during various other Cyrilomethodian celebrations. This gave Velehrad an all-Slav character, but also a unifying influence. Through the liturgy of the Eastern Slavs, the seeds were planted for an understanding and a practical relationship on the part of the common people, who had no other way of experiencing contact with the separated East. The Apostolate provided them with a personal explanation of Old Slavonic liturgical ceremonies in a printed booklet.[24] The Old Slavonic Mass was celebrated at Velehrad according to the Eastern Rite. It was not possible to have the Slavonic Mass according to the Western Rite, even though many Southern Slav priests (Glagolitic priests) came to Velehrad—their privilege of saying the Latin Rite Mass using the Old Slavonic language was only a local privilege. At first the Eastern Rite Masses celebrated at Velehrad were simple, for there were not enough priests for solemn services, nor an "iconostas," nor enough vestments. But it would not have been like Stojan, if he had not thought of some way to show the Eastern liturgy in all its splendor.

The first solemn Old Slavonic liturgy in Velehrad was celebrated in the courtyard,[25] during the First Velehrad Unionistic Congress in 1907. Andrew Szeptycky, the Uniate Ukrainian Metropolitan of Lwov, attended that Congress and was a frequent participant in others. The theology students of the Olomouc seminary learned the Eastern Rite liturgical chants; and later, in 1911 and 1915, they again acted as the choir for a solemn Slavonic Mass. During the war years, Old Slavonic priests exiled from their own countries used to offer Mass in Velehrad according to their own Rite.

A large iconostas[26] was finally erected by the *Cyrilometodějské Dědictví Velehrad* (Cyrilo-Methodian Heritage Velehrad) in 1913. Pope Pius X granted special permission for placing the iconostas into a Latin Rite Church in Velehrad on solemn occasions. However, there was no suitable place for it in that church; therefore, another iconostas, smaller in size, was erected in the "Cyrilka," a chapel in Velehrad formerly used as the original church since the middle of the thirteenth century.

For thirty years, Stojan was tireless in seeing to it that this beautiful and significant custom of having the liturgy celebrated according to the Eastern Rite would not be abandoned. It was really the Old Slavonic language[27] that proclaimed the liturgical legacy of Sts. Cyril and Methodius; that legacy which has been preserved among Eastern Christians. The Eastern form of worship was like a spokesman for the movement to bring about a brotherly reunion based on a Cyrilo-Methodian foundation,[28] which in its day had not known painful division. Velehrad, with its headquarters for the mission of Sts. Cyril and Methodius among Slavs, was to become the place where the Slavs would again become brothers in the common embrace of one Mother, the Catholic Church.

At the opening of the Second Vatican Council, in the year 1962, the Cyrilo-Methodian Old Slavonic language and chant resounded in the Archbasilica of St. Peter. In this, there was an echo of the Moravian Velehrad and of the man who built it with a holy faith in reunion, Anthony Cyril Stojan. His emphasis on vernacular liturgy, his zeal in promoting popular songs and his predilection for church music made a great impact on the deliberations concerning liturgical reforms at the Council because his ideas are reflected in the instructions outlined in "The Constitution of the Sacred Liturgy".[29]

In that document active participation[30] of the faithful in the vernacular liturgy is encouraged. Religious singing by the people was to
be skillfully fostered and sacred music[31] cultivated to enhance the
splendor of divine worship. All this stimulated lively discussion about
popular music[32] and which types were suitable for sacred liturgy.[33]
Subsequently regulatory norms were established. The motivation for
these was mainly a concern for an increase of participation on the
part of the faithful and an aid to ecumenism. Again Stojan's ideas
came to the fore especially that the Eucharist was the most essential
source for Church unity.[34] Eucharistic ecclesiology[35] would be a
bridge for all Christians. By it an atmosphere of dialogue[36] via love
and understanding instead of polemics would be created. The Council
Fathers diligently utilized a reservoir of good will in ecumenical
theology to facilitate the understanding of all alienated Christians.
Pope Paul VI's *"Decree on Ecumenism"* issued November 21, 1964,
further safeguarded all previous unionistic endeavors by marking the
full entry of the Roman Catholic Church into the ecumenical movement.[37] The Coundil moved into action in the concise spirit expressed
thus: "All have an obligation to pray and work for the restoration
of unity; all are called to dialogue according to their ability, in prayer
and in social action. These are not mere words and plans. This is a
call to action. And one is always to remember the one thing essential:
change of heart." All this certainly echoes the spirit of Stojan.

For Stojan, the Cyrilomethodian idea was truly ecumenical. In
contrast to the verbal enthusiasm of many Cyrilomethodian roman-
tics and in contrast to the Brotherhood founded by Slomšek as pre-
marily a prayer association, Stojan's program, in addition to prayer,
also promoted action; it was practical. It is possible to go even further and to say that in Stojan's idea there was less theory and more
of a practical aspect in his concept of Cyrilomethodianism. This is
evident in his choice of subject for a doctoral dissertation, written in
1896. Here for the first time he had the opportunity to speak at
length on the Cyrilomethodian theme, which is evidenced in the
title: *Concerning the Union of the Slav Nations with the Roman
Catholic Church According to the Intentions of the Holy Father
Leo XIII.*[38] This reveals Stojan's heart and the striving of his will,
love and yearning for the final goal of reunion.

Accordingly, reunion meant completing the work of Sts. Cyril and
Methodius. Stojan's biographer put it as follows: "Sts. Cyril and

Methodius incorporated the Slav nations into the Mystical Body of Christ and assembled them around the Rock of Peter. Through various intrigues and political influences, a great number had separated themselves from this Rock. The Slav nations still have the greatest fund of faith. Who would not feel a yearning to have this fund preserved and to have all the Cyrilomethodian peoples once more united in Faith?"[39] "Is this a vain effort?" Stojan asks. "The unionistic movement is not Utopian; for the contemporary situation was by no means anticipated. . . A work undertaken out of love produces wonders." The principal means of reunion is effective Christian love; "a truly Christian life, a life which in all its thinking and acting is permeated by the truths of the Gospels. If the separated nations will recognize the wonders produced by our effective love, the walls which are like barriers separating us from them will be demolished. . . Wherever the separated brethren will see the deeds of effective love, there happy results will appear."[40]

Pope John XXIII[41] used the same kind of language of love for our separated Christian associates when he expressed the great yearning of his heart for a meeting and eventual union of all who invoke the name of Christ. He established a special *Secretariat in the Second Vatican Council* to deal with questions of Christian unity. "The love of Christ impels us"[42] is always his pervasive argument and forceful motivation. Again in his apostolic letter, *Magnifici Eventus* of May 11, 1963, he said: "You know, venerable brethren, that with fervent desires we have striven and labored so that the Orientals who glory in the name of Christian, separated from the communion of the Apostolic See, may be zealous towards re-establishing it, and that by gradually fulfilling the prayer of Christ, the unity of one flock and one shepherd may be realized. The desires of the Second Ecumenical Council of the Vatican, at which—bringing pleasures to the heart and promise of fair hope—even observer delegates of the separated churches have been present, reach out toward the same end. . . . Now both must prepare the roads which will be of solid construction and which, if there will be mutual understanding and fraternal charity, will lead to the desired success. This eagerness to fulfill the Will of God strengthens all things, hopes all things, sustains all things."[43] And it was Pope John himself who singled out the Cyrilomethodian unionism in its historical connection with the Council, when he stated in its opening words:[44] "In the hidden designs of God's Providence, the centennial celebration of a glorious event is taking place at the moment when the Second Ecumenical Council of the Vatican is being held. It also seems to be closely connected with the purposes of this general council. It was just eleven centuries ago this year that the two noble Apostles arrived from Constantinople to Great Moravia."[44] In the rest of the apostolic letter, Pope John XXIII then writes at length on the thought which he expressed in conversation with Cardinal A.G. Cicognani, then Papal Secretary of State, regarding the possibility of finding the relics of St. Cyril. He did not live to see the finding of these relics and to express his joy over the way his desire was fulfilled. At that time, the Secretary of State informed Pope John that the American Benedictine Abbot, the Rt. Rev. Ambrose L. Ondrak, O.S.B., of St. Procopius Abbey in Lisle, Illinois, requested that in the jubilee year of 1963 a search be made in Rome for the relics of St. Cyril.[45] At that time, the Holy Father noted that the finding of these relics would bring a great contribution and impetus to the labors of the ecumenical council which he had convoked.

Even though he did not give any further explanation, Pope John's words are clear to us today. He had in mind the heavenly intercession of Sts. Cyril and Methodius for the success of the unionistic actions which were to be discussed at the Council. The finding of the relics of St. Cyril, the great saint and apostle of the East, was to shine forth like a symbol of hope that the separated Greek and Slavonic East would understand the holy invitation and would not reject an offer to come together.

In the course of extensive archival research, the Rev. Leonard Boyle,[46] a member of the Dominican monastery of St. Clement in Rome, discovered that the relics of St. Cyril, who had been buried in the church of St. Clement, were in the possession of a noble family, the Antici-Mattei in Recanati near Loretto. There were no records of these relics since the year 1798. After authentication, Princess Antici-Mattei donated the relics to the Pope, on November 15, 1963. This relic consisted of a piece of bone, considerably damaged.

Pope Paul VI, who continued the program of Pope John XXIII, especially regarding the aims of the Council, hailed this discovery of St. Cyril's relics as a welcome introduction to the Council's deliberations on ecumenism, which had just begun at that time. When the relic was returned to Rome, he exhorted everyone to work and pray for the unity of Christians—as he did once before, on August 17, 1963, during his visit to the Greek-Catholic Abbey of Grottaferrata. The address delivered by Pope Paul VI over the newly-discovered relics of St. Cyril was naturally directed to the Orthodox separated brethren.

On Sunday, November 11, 1963, Pope Paul was present at an Old Slavonic Mass in St. Clement's Basilica. Both in word and in deed he showed his charity to the united as well as the separated associates. He pronounced his blessing in the Old Slavonic language—*"Mír vsjem!"* (Peace be to all) and *"Blagoslovenije gospodnije na vás!"* (May the blessing of the Lord come upon you!)[47] By this action he set the proper tone for the discussions in the Council during the following days.

On November 18, 1963, one of the most important schema of the second session of the Council came up for discussion—"On Ecumenism," that is, on Christian unity. During the discussion of Chapter Two, "On Ecumenical Practice," two Czechoslovak bishops requested leave to speak, Bishop Eduard Necsey and Bishop František Tomášek.[48] Tomášek's suggestion for convoking a Catholic-Orthodox council aroused universal interest. For making this proposal, he was distinguished by Alexej, the Orthodox Patriarch of Moscow, who conferred on him a memorial medal.

"From the Roman Church, the center of the communion of all Christians," Pope Paul VI said at St. Clement's Basilica, "comes the example and invitation to an ever closer unity." Speaking over the relic of St. Cyril, the Apostle of the Slavs, he greeted the uniate Eastern churches; he assured the Orthodox Church of his benevolence; and he concluded with a touching and earnest prayer for the unity of all Christians.

It is not without significance that the new Holy Father, Pope Paul VI, soon after his election addressed himself to Czechoslovakia, then celebrating the Cyrilomethodian jubilee, in his apostolic letter of July 4, 1963, exhorting the people toward perseverance in the Cyrilomethodian Faith: "May your holy patrons, Sts. Cyril and Methodius, whose coming to Great Moravia you are now celebrating, help to fulfill this our hope. Those who brought the Gospel into your country will certainly accord you powerful protection, in order that you may preserve for yourselves that precious treasure of their legacy, to lead a Christian life, rich in good works."[49]

At this time, as we seek to acquaint the world with a laborer in the vineyard of reunion, Antonín Cyril Stojan, the Catholic world has already experienced the joy of witnessing the historic meeting between Pope Paul VI and Athenagorus I, (1886-1972) the Patriarch of Constantinople.[50] which occurred in Jerusalem, January 5, 1964. Perhaps we may allow ourselves to express joy over the happy circumstance that this meeting with its touching kiss of peace, the prayer of Christ the Highpriest, and the recitation of the Our Father in Greek, took place in the Czechoslovak Peace Chapel on Mount Olivet. This chapel, with statues of Sts. Cyril and Methodius, now belongs to the Apostolic Delegation in Jerusalem. It was like a kiss of peace between the spirit of Rome and the spirit of Velehrad. They are joined by the mysterious bond of working together for the reunion of associates in faith, whom the spirit of the world has separated. And the guardian angel, the spirit of Velehrad, during his lifetime as well as after his death, is A.C. Stojan, who has been accorded well-deserved recognition as a pioneer of the chief interest of all Christendom, in having Pope John XXIII speak of him by name in the apostolic letter *Magnifici eventus.* It was in this spirit that the *Decree on Eastern Catholic Churches*[51] of November 21, 1964 be considered a complement to the *Decree on Ecumenism,* was published. The Decree has brought most valuable clarifications in several fields concerning the Catholic Eastern Churches. (1) It expresses unequivocally the position and the rights of Eastern communities in the Catholic Church and re-establishes privileges and customs which were abolished in the past.[52] (2) It clearly manifests the hope of the Council for a corporate reunion of the Eastern Churches presently not in union with the Church of Rome. Thereby Stojan's unionism not only found Rome's appreciation, but it was considered a worthy historical contribution toward Church Unity. Furthermore, this decree was also opportune and timely for several reasons: [1] because the very existence of the "uniate" Eastern Catholic Churches has always been considered by the Orthodox as one of the obstacles[53] to any sincere theological confrontation with the Roman Catholic Church; [2] that some Orthodox churches undermined the existence of the *Uniates* because of a lack of free dialogue in the past and considered reunion as an event under pressure;[54] [3] others blamed Rome for excessive Latinization[55] once they were absorbed by the Roman Catholic Church. Stojan never had these difficulties, for he rightly recognized all *Uniate* churches for their historical endeavors toward unity on one hand and on the other implicitly trusted Rome's motivation to handle their affairs justly. Here his loyalty to Rome becomes even more obvious. For him, Church unity was always a sacred biblical design of God's providence and not a kind of human maneuvering of Church politics. Subsequently the Vicar of Christ could not fail in it but had to be concerned about it as an entrusted Divine mandate, which was to be fulfilled by him.

Thus Stojan's spirit was reflected in a new spirit that pervaded the Second Vatican Council and for which it will always be remembered. The epochal importance of this fact is stressed by almost all observers from non-Catholic churches and religious bodies. It is a spirit of peace, understanding, forgiveness, and universal love toward the baptized as well as toward the yet unbaptized members of the human race. It is a spirit whose profundity and breadth was outlined in the encyclical of Pope John XXIII, *Pacem in terris* (1963), which was so well received.[56]

"We are working for a church of love!" proclaimed his successor, Pope Paul VI. There was nothing further removed from the spirit of Archbishop Stojan than a lack of charity which seeks to condemn. This is evident in everything he did, particularly in the work of the *Apostolate of Sts. Cyril and Methodius.* We have noted his written statements and his documentation for his program, in which he speaks in modern terminology. Perhaps he never suspected, when he wrote these statements, the painful situation that would arise, compelling him to demonstrate the genuine character of this principle of effectual neighborly love.

The national, political and moral crisis confronting the Czech Catholics under the two-headed Austrian eagle came to a head after the year 1918, when almost three quarters of a million Catholics as well as three hundred priests fell away and joined the newly-founded "Czechoslovak Church,"[57] or the Orthodox Church, or professed no religious affiliation. The anti-Austrian and anti-Roman sentiment came like a hurricane, sudden and strong. It threatened to lay low the Church in Bohemia and Moravia, to level it down to its roots. The hierarchy, bound to the old regime, generally assumed an attitude of rejection taking a legalistic stand; that is, not to negotiate with the disloyal but to afflict them with canonical penalties. However, no serious measure was taken to check the agitation for apostasy. Stojan, then a canon and soon to become archbishop, took a different approach, but that old spirit of resentment caused many to criticize him, saying that his kindness and forbearance toward fallen and erring priests only made the situation worse. It created confusion in the ranks of those who persevered. Some said that he lacked the ability to give a commanding word and to form a plan for ordering his own ranks. Such accusations were leveled even by a few worthy priests. Rebukes of this kind were deserved rather by those Churchmen, many of them in high positions, who were committed to the old regime who took a passive attitude toward tirades directed against the Church, and who disdainfully condemned Stojan's efforts to ease the situation—well-meant efforts which he exerted with the best of intentions and at the cost of extreme sacrifices.

When thunder is rumbling and the storm is tearing down everything, it is hard to decide what to do and hard to foresee the outcome. At first Stojan did not know either what stand the highest church authorities would take regarding the demands for vernacular in the liturgy and concerning certain problems of the priests. But right from the beginning, he strove by kindness and love to keep the faltering from departing; to lend a helping hand to the erring, to regain those who fell away and to ease their return into the Church. Finally, a decision came from Rome, with permission for repeating the reading of the Epistle and Gospel in the mother tongue and in Church Slavonic during Holy Mass in several places in Bohemia and Moravia. But Rome's decision rejected demands for the relaxation of the laws governing clerical celibacy.[58] When this decision came, Stojan gave it his complete and uncompromising support and began to put it into effect immediately. As Stojan always manifested his loyalty to the Pope, he likewise displayed it to his priests especially in their times of crisis. In this he was greatly misunderstood. He was frequently accused of allowing his priests excessive freedom, to the detriment of ecclestical discipline, and of failing to wield sufficient authority during his pastoral conferences with priests. That was usually how those people spoke who did not know the realities of priestly life and did not comprehend how grave and complex was the situation. Archbishop Stojan understood the spirit of his times better than almost anyone else did, and he knew the thinking and internal sorrows of his priests. He was aware that he would spoil everything if he exercised his authority without any consideration. He wished to show his priests that he trusted them; he gave them opportunity to express their minds freely and he was amenable to their suggestions and advice. In this way, he relieved interior tensions, of which, in those days, there were many in the souls of priests and he channeled the excessive energy of the critics into constructive work. In doing this, he did not surrender his authority, nor did he lose it. He was the personification of the moral authority of great love and self-sacrifice; and this had incalcuable significance in those times. He did not employ harsh official commands and prohibitions, but he did have the ability to make requests like a father. Even in the erring man, he recognized a human being who is in need of help and can thus be saved. In this Stojan was similar to Pope John XXIII who seemed to follow the same pattern of goodness, kindness and love with a full understanding of a soul extremely sensitive[59] toward others.

As already described, love was for Stojan not only an idea but an action with full compassion for others by doing good deeds, exhibiting generous public service to all in need and helping the poor. Even for this he was rebuked for excessive generosity, accused of being imprudent to the point of squandering church property. They were anxious lest on account of his extraordinary goodness of heart, he would not do well in governing and administering the wealth of the archdiocese. In short, Stojan, with his charity and kindness, was in his time a stumbling block for many. However, we must not forget that Archbishop Stojan became a successor to the heritage of St. Methodius in one of the most difficult periods of Czech and Moravian church history. He was to set in order those things which were the sad legacy of the preceding times, which he himself fully experienced. He was confronted by nationalistically agitated, dissatisfied, sensitive, and often morally tainted clergy, who had lived through the First World War (1914-18) and its moral quagmire and did not survive without blemish—clergy who were in the midst of an agitation for apostasy, which instigated disobedience and incited them in that direction. Stojan wished to set all this in order, but he could not do so in any other manner than the one to which he was accustomed throughout his lifetime, that is, his own virtues of reconciliation and charity. Through these virtues he became a participant in the Second Vatican Council, the council of conciliatory charity toward all Christian denominations and toward all nations. In spite of his proverbial goodness, Stojan's courage in dealing with contemporary problems and challenging them, no matter how unpopular they were, reflected somewhat the courageous initiatives and actions of the great Pope Paul VI.[60] At the same time his simplicity matched up with that of Pope John Paul I.[61] His successor, John Paul II, finds Stojan's Church unionism very consonant with his own ecumenical thought. He gave the world an early and open sign of ecumenism when he stood on the balcony of St. Peter's on the evening of October 16th and crossed his hands on his chest, his fists closed. This is the ancient gesture of Eastern Orthodoxy, repeated endlessly in its history and in its icons, heavy with the significance of unity and perseverance until death in belief in Jesus and His salvation. Already on January 17, 1979, the Pope announced:

> "I wish to mention now that the Catholic Church and the (Eastern) Churches of the Byzantine tradition are about to open a theological dialogue aimed at eliminating those difficulties which still impede Eucharistic celebration and full unity. We have been holding dialogues with our brothers in the West—Anglicans, Lutherans, Methodists, and the Reformed. On themes which in the past contributed great differences, consoling convergences have been made. The voyage is not yet finished, however, and we must speed up our pace to reach our goal."[62]

With such ecumenism in mind, it is not hard to discern policies and actions which may finally accomplish the reunion of Eastern Orthodox Churches with Rome, for which so many efforts were made by Stojan, together with another saintly apostle of Church unity—none other than Metropolitan Andrew Szeptycky[63] of Lwov. By this Pope's estimate the reunion with the Eastern Churches[64] is attainable without much difficulty owing to the Cyrilomethodian tradition[65] which has been the common heritage of all Slavs,[66] a circumstance certainly dear to this first Slavic Pope.

From past experiences with Polish Communists Wojtyla has a special understanding of the oppressed Christians behind the Iron Curtain, a sympathy one can feel in his warm relationship with all the bishops of these countries, his friendship with the late Stephen Cardinal Trochta,[67] bishop of Litoměřice, and especially has it been so with Cardinal František Tomášek of Prague, whom he assured: "We are very close to each other and now shall be even closer, because from now on I am also entrusted with care for you. I assure you that I shall do all I can for the growth of spiritual life in your country. I shall give you a special place in my prayers. Please give my greetings to your bishops, priests, members of the Holy Orders, and all the faithful. Also I shall count on your prayers very much."

Later he said with special emphasis: "We in Poland are especially grateful to you, the Czechs, for having introduced the Christian faith into our country. Yes, it was the first bishop of Prague of Slavonic blood, Saint Vojtěch and the Przemyslid Princess Dobravka who had founded it here. And you are the successor to Saint Vojtěch. It is therefore also thanks to you, the Czechs, that today the Church has at its head a pope of Slavonic blood."[68] This is not only a true testimonial of the Pope's spirituality of compassion for his suffering friends, but his expression of real spiritual concern, keeping in mind its historical dimension.

In reflecting on all this, one can understand why he embraced the Cyrilomethodian legacy as the most valuable and effective vehicle for the Church unity among the Slavs. He refers to Sts. Cyril and Methodius quite frequently. During his trip to Poland,[69] while visiting the historical city of Gniezno on June 3, 1979, the Pope said: "Is it not Christ's will, is it not what the Holy Spirit disposes, that this Pope should in a special way manifest and confirm in our age the presence of these (Slavic) people in the Church and their specific contribution to the history of Christiantiy? Is it not Christ's will, is it not what the Holy Spirit disposes, that this Polish Pope, this Slav Pope, should at this precise moment manifest the spiritual unity of Christian hope?"[70] On December 31, 1980, this Slavic Pope issued his apostolic letter *Egregiae virtutis*[71] on the centennial anniversary of the famous encyclical of Pope Leo XIII, *Grande Munus,* of September 30, 1880, designating Sts. Cyril and Methodius the co-patrons of Europe besides Saint Benedict, in a time when both Churches, Roman Catholic and Orthodox, entered into decisive dialogue, which began on the island of Patmos tied to a tradition of St. John, Apostle and Evangelist.[72] This further symbolized the unity of Christian Europe with both the Western tradition (St. Benedict) and the Eastern one in its making.[73] It was also to express public sorrow upon the disruption of Christianity and the dividing of Christendom[74] plus the resulting disunity of Europe. In a spontaneous reflection Pope John Paul II sees the apostles of the Slavs, Sts. Cyril and Methodius, not only as the restorers of Christian Europe but also as rebuilders of Church unity. Thus the Cyrilomethodian heritage with the Stojan legacy for Church unity came to their full meaning and significance after having been singled out as the most effective historical forces in unifying the nation, Europe and the Church. It is, indeed, a striking anomaly that, despite their many political differences, all Slavs revert with enthusiasm to this common heritage which, whether directly or indirectly, has enriched every Slavic nation. Perhaps the most conspicuous characteristic of this inheritance is the unifying spirit, ecclesiastically evident in the unionism of Velehrad,[75] and nationally apparent in the Neo-Slavic Solidarity,[76] which always refers to the Cyrilomethodian mission as its foundation. That the national revival of each of the Slavic nations draws upon its Cyrilomethodian heritage is ample testimony not only of the strength of its source, but also of its enduring influence through the ages.

From this wellspring of the Cyrilomethodian heritage[77] the religious, national, linguistic, civilizing, cultural and idealistic vitality of the Slavs is maintained and invigorated. Undoubtedly ancient in its foundation on the Cyrilomethodian sources, it nonetheless continues with striking newness as it draws refreshment from the same source. Similarly the Second Vatican Council certainly benefitted from the wellspring of Stojan's Unionism by influencing with the same striking novelty the Church and liturgical reforms with their ecumenical convergence toward Church unity.

The Most Rev. Josef Karel Matocha, Archbishop of Olomouc, who died in Olomouc, November 2, 1961, petitioned the Holy See in 1948 for Archbishop Stojan's beatification. Since the archiepiscopal see of Olomouc was left vacant after his death, it was not possible to proceed with the preparatory work for the beatification.

Metropolitan Andrew Szeptycky Archbishop of Lwov (1865-1944), Servant of God, faithful associate of Stojan.

NOTES

1. W.A. Visser't Hovft, *The Meaning of Ecumenical* (London, 1954) 21-27.
2. John A Hardon, *Christianity in the Twentieth Century* (Garden City, NY, 1971) 418 and passim.
3. *CIC* 1325 par. 2, Coronata, *Institutiones juris cononici,* 5 vols. (Turin-Rome, 1935-1939) II, 911; see Henri de Lubac, *The Church: Paradox and Mystery* (Staten Island, NY, 1969), 1-30.
4. Karl Rahner, "What is heresy?" *Theological Investigations* 5 (Baltimore, 1966) 488-512 idem., *Gefahren im heutigen Katholicismus* (Einsiedeln, 1955), 63-80.
5. František Hník, *Duchovní Ideály Československé Cíkve* (Spiritual Ideals of Czechoslovak Church) (Prague, 1939), 160-168.
6. Ludvik Nemec, *The Czechoslovak Heresy and Schism.* The Emergence of a National Czechoslovak Church (Philadelphia, American Phil. Society, 1975), 3-9; see "meaning of heresy and schism" and the quest for the Church; see Richard P. McBrian, *The Church: The Continuing Quest,* (New York, 1970), 67-83.
7. Austin Flannery, O.P., ed., *Vatican Council II. The Conciliar and Post-Conciliar Documents* (Northport, NY, 1975) with Preface of John Cardinal Wright; passim.
8. Walter M. Abbot, SJ, ed., *The Documents of Vatican II* (New York, 1966), see *Constitution on the Sacred Liturgy* (Sacrosanctum Concilium), pp. 137-179, with introduction by C.J. McNaspy, SJ, pp. 133-136 and a response by Protestant theologian Jaroslav J. Pelikan, pp. 179-182.
9. See Latin text in *AAS* 56 (1964), 877-900, transl. into English by Austin Flannery.
10. *Instruction on the proper implementation of the Constitution on the Sacred Liturgy. S.C.R.* Inter Decumenici of September 26, 1964, in *Vatican Council II,* ed. by Austin Flannery (Northport, NY, 1975), 45-56.
11. Francis Sušil, *Moravské písně s nápěvy do textu vřaděnými* (Moravian songs with the melodies inserted into text) (Brno, 1860) passim.
12. M. Eileen Bednarik, Ss.C.M., "Slovak Music," *Slovak Studies* XV (Cleveland-Rome, 1975) 177-194.
13. Zdeněk Nejedlý, *Dějiny předhusitského zpěvu v Čechách* (History of the pre-Hussite Song in Bohemia) (Prague, 1904); Roman Jacobson, *Nejstarší Duchovni písně české* (Oldest Czech religious hymns) (Prague, 1929; M. Weingart, "Vznik první české duchovni písně" (Origin of the first Czech religious song) *Byzantinoslavica* II (Prague, 1930), passim.

14. M. Paulová, "L'idée cyrillo-methodienne dans la politique de Charles IV et la fondation du monastère slave in Prague", *Byzantinoslavica* 11 (1950), 174-190.

15. Otakar Odložilík, "Z počátku husitství na Moravě (Šimon z Tišnova a Jan Vavřincův z Račic", *ČMM* 49 (1925), 1-170; idem., "Jednota bratři Habrovanských", *Č.H.C.* 39 (1923) 1-70; 201-364.

16. Zdeněk Nejedlý, *Počátky husitského zpěvu* (Origins of the Hussite Song) (Prague, 1907); idem, *Dějiny husitského zpěvu za válek husitských* (History of the Hussite song during the Hussite wars) (Prague, 1913).

17. Hubert Doležil, "Česká píseň reformační a vývoj protestanského chorálu," (Czech Reform Song and development of Protestant hymn) *in Co daly naše země Evropě a lidstvu,* ed. by Vilém Mathesius (Prague, 1940), 96-101; Václav Novotný, *Náboženské hnutí řeske ve 14 a 15 století* (Religious Czech movement in the 14th and 15th centuries) (Prague, 1915), passim.

18. Rudolf Wolkan, *Das deutsche Kirchenlied der Böhmischen Bruder im XVI Jahrhundert,* (Prague, 1891).

19. Josef Vašica, *České Literárni baroko* (Prague, 1938), passim.

20. Vladimir Helfert, "Průkopnický význam české hudby v. 18 století" (Pioneering significance of Czech music in XVIIIth century) in *Co daly naše země Evropě a lidstvu,* ed. by Vilém Mathesius (Prague, 1940), 216-221.

21. Bohumil Zlámal, *Antonín Cyril Stojan* (Rome, 1973), 103.

22. Cinek, *op.cit.,* passim.

23. Herman A.J. Wegman, *Geschichte der Liturgie im Westen und Osten* (Regensburg, 1979), passim. Reviewed by Andrew D. Ciferni in *CHR* 68 (Jan., 1982), 58-59.

24. J. Pospíšil, *Mše Svatá podle obřadu církve Východni* (The Holy Mass according to the Rite of the Eastern Church) (Velehrad, 1907) had several editions; see Stephen Smržík, S.J., *The Glagolitic or roman-slavonic liturgy* (Rome-Cleveland, 1958); see also Basil Shereghy, *The Divine Liturgy of St. John Chrysostom* (Pittsburgh, 1965).

25. Located in front of the Church and Jesuit monastery on one side and of the Papal Institute on the other. This courtyard was and is used in all solemn occasions and to accomodate crowds of faithful gathered on these occasions.

26. *i-co-no-sta-sis* = the screen dividing the sanctuary from the main body of an Eastern Orthodox Church (From Late Greek eikonostasion, shrine, "place where images stand."

27. Michael Lacko, *Sts. Cyril and Methodius* (Rome, 1963), 83-87.

28. Michael Lacko, SJ., "East Meets West in Sts. Cyril and Methodius," *American Ecclesiastical Review* CXLI (Washington, 1959), 241-245.

29. Promulgated on December 4, 1963 by Pope Paul VI. See English text in Walter M. Abbott, SJ., *The Documents of Vatican II* (New York, 1966), 137-178.

30. See especially II part of the *Constitution:* The Promotion of Liturgical Instruction and Active Participation, and III part: Reform of the Sacred Liturgy with its norms to regulate it, see *ibid.,* pp. 144-152.

31. See especially Chapter VI titled Sacred Music, of the *Constitution, ibid.*, pp. 171-173.

32. Gino Stefani, "Does the liturgy still need music?" *Concilium*, vol. 42: *The Crisis of Liturgical Reform* (New York, 1969), 76-86.

33. Helmut Hucke, "Musical requirements of Liturgical Reform," *Concilium* vol. 12: The Church Worships (New York, 1966) 45-75; *idem.*, "Jazz and Folk Music in the Liturgy", *Concilium* vol. 42: *The Crisis of Liturgical Reform* (New York, 1969), 139-172.

34. Cardinal A. Bea, "L'Eucaristia e l'unione dei cristiani," *La Civiltà Cattolica* 116 (4 September 1965), vol. 1765, pp. 401-413.

35. Hans-Joachim Schulz, "The Dialogue with the Orthodox," *Concilium: The Church and Ecumenism* 4 (New York, 1965), 131-149.

36. Walter Kasper, "The Dialogue with Protestant Theology," *Concilium: The Church and Ecumenism* 4 (New York, 1965), 150-173.

37. Decree on Ecumenism of November 21, 1964 by Pope Paul VI in Abbott's *Documents of Vatican II* (New York, 1966), 341-366.

38. As mentioned previously.

39. Bohumil Zlámal, *Antonin Cyril Stojan* (Rome, 1973), 107.

40. *ibid.*, 107.

41. Giancarlo Zizola, *The Utopia of Pope John XXIII* (Transl. by Helen Batolini) (Maryknoll, NY 1982), 76-77.

42. See Pope John XXIII's "Message to Humanity," issued at the beginning of the Second Vatican Council on October 11, 1962; see English text in Abbott's *Documents of Vatican II* (New York, 1966), 3-7.

43. Zlámal, *op.cit.*, 108.

44. cf. his apostolic letter *Magnifici eventus* of May 11, 1963; quoted by B. Zlámal, *op.cit.*, 109.

45. E. Petřík, "Opat Ondrák a hledání ostatků svatého Cyrila" (Abbot Ondrak and search for the relics of St. Cyril) *Se Znamením Kříže* (Rome, 1967), 41-45.

46. Leonard Boyle, O.P. "Osud ostatků svatého Cyrila" (Destiny of the relics of St. Cyril), *ibid.*, pp. 45-16.

47. Zlámal, *op.cit.*, 110.

48. Now he is Cardinal and archbishop of Prague and Primate of Bohemia.

49. Apostolic letter of July 4, 1963, *A.A.S.* (1963), Zlámal, *op.cit.*, 111.

50. H. Georgiadis "Athenagoras I" in *Encyclopedic Dictionary of Religion,* 3 vols. (Philadelphia, 1978) I, 301; the meeting with Pope Paul VI in Jerusalem in 1964 took place on his initiative.

51. *Decree on Eastern Catholic Church,* November 21, 1964, *A Æ.S.* (1964).

52. Two commentaries on this decree have been published in English, the first by Meletius Wojnar, O.S.B., in *The Jurist* XXV No. 2 (April, 1965) and the second by Victor J. Pospishil, published in New York, John XXIII Center for Eastern Christian Studies. There are six main Eastern Catholic rites: the Chaldean, Syrian, Maronite, Coptic, Armenian and Byzantine. There are about one million Catholics of Eastern Rite in U.S.A.

53. Alexander Schmemann, "A Response" to the Decree in Abbot's *Documents of Vatican II* (New York, 1966), 387-388; Donald Atwater, "Facts that make reunion with the Orthodox Church difficult." *The Catholic Mind* XLII (October, 1944).

54. Hansjakob Stehle, *Eastern Politics of the Vatican, 1917-1979* (transl. by Sandra Smith) (Athens, Ohio, 1981), 106, 143, 220, and passim.

55. Basil Boysák, The Fate of the Holy Union in Carpatho-Ukraine. (Toronto, New York, 1963), passim.

56. Encyclical *Pacem in Terris* of 1963, see Richard P. McBrien, *Catholicism*, 2 vols. (Minneapolis, 1980) II, 647, 665, 1045-1047.

57. See for precise account Dr. Josef Hanuš, *Religious Chronicle of Czechoslovakia*, (Washington, DC, 1921), *NCWC* Release of April 5, 12, 1921. 7, 2, Blažej Ráček, *Československé Dějiny* (Czechoslovak History, Prague, 1933), 694 ff.; Dr. Ant. Boháč, "Přehled nejdůležitějších výsledků posledního Sčítání Lidu." *Statistický Obzor* 14 (June, 1933), 175-180. (This is a review of the most important results of the last census of the people according to religion and nationality); Aug. Neuman, *Katolíci a naše osvobození* (Olomouc, 1931), passim.

58. Pope Benedict XV's letter to Archbishop of Prague, asking him to convoke all bishops of Moravia and Bohemia to hear their suggestions. In this letter, Pope designated the demands of the Jednota as unwise and he gave certain instructions; see *A.A.S.* XII (1920) 33-37.

59. Pope John XXIII, *Journal of a Soul* (transl. by Dorothy White) (New York, 1964), passim.

60. Philip S. Land, "The Social Theology of Paul VI", *America*, May 12, 1979, pp. 392-394.

61. John Paul I. *The Message of John Paul I.*, ed. by Daughters of St. Paul (Boston, 1978); "Pope John Paul I (1912-1978)", *The Pope Speaks* (Washington, DC). Special Winter issue of 1978. Peter Hebblethwaite, *The Year of Three Popes* (Cleveland, 1979).

62. *Osservatore Romano*, Jan. 22, 1979; The Pope spoke in general audience on the theme: "Charity is a gift of God."

63. Genge J. Perejda, C.SS.R., *Apostle of Church Unity: Metropolitan Andrew Sheptycky* (Yorkton, Sask., 1960), passim.

64. George Huntson Williams, *The Mind of John Paul II* (New York, 1981), 329 and passim.

65. Francis Dvornik, *Byzantine Missions among the Slavs* (New Brunswick, NJ, 1970); idem., *Byzantské misie u Slovanů* (Prague, 1971).

66. Ludvik Nemec, *Pope John Paul II, A Festive Profile* (New York, 1979), 172, 181-182.

67. Ludvik Nemec, "Stephen Cardinal Trochta, an Educator, a Churchman and an Ecumenist," special offprint of *Bohemia*, vol. 17 (Munich-Vienna, 1976).

68. "Close to us." Cardinal František Tomášek delivers the Pope's message to the Czechoslovak faithful, see *Hlas Národa* (Voice of the Nation) (Chicago, Dec. 22, 1979), 23-24.

69. John Paul II, *"Pilgrimage of Faith,"* (New York: A Crossroad book, 1979), 90-98, especially 92.
70. *ibid.*, 92.
71. See *A.A.S.* (1921).
72. It was translated in Czech as "Svatí Cyril a Metoděj patrony Evropy," and published by Czechoslovak Academy Velehrad in Rome as *Ochránci Evropy* Rome: Velehrad, 1981), pp. 9-12.
73. Christopher Dawson, *The Making of Europe* (London, 1945); Francis Dvornik, the *Making of Central and Eastern Europe* (London, 1949) 11-38 and passim.
74. Christopher Dawson, *The Dividing of Christendom,* (New York, 1965), 19-40 and passim.
75. Antonin Salajka, "K odkazu sv. soluňských bratří" (Concerning the heritage of the Brothers of Thessalonica) *Katolické noviny* (Prague, September 15, 1963) 2; Ludvik Nemec, "Unionistic Endeavors in Velehrad," *Byzantine Catholic World* (BCW) 7 no. 10 (1962) 6, 18; no. 11 (1962) 6, 19; no. 12 (1962) 6, 14.
76. J.F.N. Bradley, "Czech Pan-Slavism before the First World War," *Slavonic and East European Review* 40 (1961) 184-205.
77. F. Graus, "Velkomoravská říše v české středověké tradici" (Great Moravian Empire in Czech Medieval Tradition) *Československý časopis historický* 40 (Prague, 1963) 289-305.

EPILOGUE: Give me Souls; Take the Rest, O Lord

With this motto Stojan lived, died and is remembered for his saintly legacy: "The foundation of his power as priest and archbishop is his intense, authentic and heartfelt faith. He was an effective, blazing torch of faith, an apostle motivated by faith, a Christian promoter completely rooted in God through an extraordinarily alive faith. He lived and worked in the light of a living faith; consequently he had very clear vision; his demands were just and his steps firm. Such a profound faith was the foundation of his internal harmonious Franciscan constancy and for the cheerfulness which diffused joy and confidence in God as well as in people. This radiant faith enriched all his deeds with merit, and called down upon each of his projects the blessings of God. All his undertakings flourished even after his death and grew into praiseworthy works, which led to gigantically extensive actions, attracting the attention of the whole Catholic world for a long time. Faith supplied him with a great strength which precluded despair in the face of the greatest obstacles. It made him plunge into projects which others considered impossible or visionary; strengthened his confidence in prayer and really made of him an apostle of prayer. His astonishing activity in the service of neighborly love as well as in the incomprehensible sacrifices in which he was totally consumed[1] could only be achieved by a very deep faith in the omnipotence of God. He was also a beautifully human person. His closest friend and political and associate, Dr. Mořic Hruban, verifies this in the following tribute: "After reading certain descriptions of Stojan, a person who did not know him would go away with the impression of 'God's simpleton.' He was nothing of the sort! There was an unpretentious attraction which radiated from Stojan's whole personality. He gained anyone to whom he spoke, or at whom he looked with his wise, guileless eyes. He was a man of great learning, universal and admirable scholarly interests. Dr. A.C. Stojan is our most eminent modern high-priestly personality. . . Stojan was a democrat through and through. A certain rusticity in his appearance and a kind of awkwardness and coarseness at times startled those who met him for the first time or did not know him well. This unfavorable impression would last only a moment, and it would melt quickly under the warming touch of his innate goodness and heartfelt love, radiating from a golden interior under a Hanak [Moravian peasant] rough shell. . .

With Stojan as deputy, and later, under the Czechoslovak Republic, as senator, I traveled much, criss-crossing Moravia; and I was an eyewitness of his affection for people, a love such as never distinguished any other political representative of great sections of the nation.

"His speeches and addresses were composed like exhortations; they manifested profundity of faith in the spirit of a Cyrilomethodian and apostolic self-dedication to the people whom he represented in legislative bodies. He was forebearing to an extreme and a patriot of the purest minting. He was a sincere guardian of the national tradition, a lover of native costumes, ancient usages and customs, and national songs."[2] Stojan's spirituality is admirable and most praiseworthy against the background of the grave consequences of a century-long Josephinist[3] system, reflecting a spiritual lethargy which spread like cancer and made its appearance even in the Church. Providence had prepared a way for him, a way that is always most characteristic of the servants of God and always proves itself effective, the way of internal renewal, the way of a true reformer of the Church, the way that is fundamental for every saint. A movement to deepen spiritual life by means of closed retreats and parish missions was then current in all of Europe. However, there was need for it particularly in Austria. Cardinal Fürstenberg of Olomouc, together with Bishop Schaffgotsch of Brno, initiated a very timely and important program—the renewal of priests through retreats, which they also attended themselves. Generally, these retreats were conducted by Jesuit Fathers—at first by the Jesuits of Vienna (Schlör), while the retreats for the people (parish missions) were the specialty of the Viennese Redemptorist Fathers who had a strong contingent of Czech members, mainly due to the apostolate of the "apostle of Vienna," St. Clement Mary Hofbauer (1751-1820), whose fame in pastoral work grew to a point where his influence thwarted the effort at the Congress of Vienna

(1814-15) to separate the Austrian Church from Rome.[4] Indeed it was to Clement Hofbauer perhaps more than any single individual that the extinction of Josephinism was due. The external yoke of Josephinism was not unshackled until the year 1848. Its influences lasted much longer, leaving behind much religious apathy.

Stojan reacted with a revolt of the spirit. He tried to spread the idea of retreats and parish missions to arouse intellectuals as well as common people from sloth and spiritual lethargy, to give them a vivid awareness of spiritual values for which to live. Stojan knew well that even the most beautiful idea can remain superficial and not penetrate to any depth, conviction or action, if the person's interior is not prepared for it. Even though arranging spiritual exercises for priests and for laymen was not Stojan's invention, he did grasp the significance and importance of retreats and was ahead of his time in carrying out this spiritual "mandate." Only 50 years later did retreats for laymen become the common practice and accepted pastoral exercise in Moravia or in any number of other countries, especially among the Slavic nations. For this reason, Archbishop Stojan deserves to be called the pioneer of retreats for laymen among Slavs in general. He was ahead of his time, promoting retreats and providing practical guide-lines for internal renewal.

Perhaps the most admirable of Stojan's skills was to harmonize fully his national, social and political concerns with his high standards of spirituality—a task certainly not easy. As an admirer of Father F. Sušil, Stojan could not remain indifferent to one of the worst sore-spots in the Austria of his time; that is, the government's inability to deal with the non-German and non-Hungarian nationalities with justice. The elements of the Josephinian system that survived, that is the centralized Austrian monarchy controlled by Germans and the awakened nationalistic passion among the Viennese Germans, were not able to reconcile themselves with the just demands of the Slavic nationalities, even though, numerically, the Slavs were in the majority.

Consciously Czech, Stojan stepped forward, both in the interest of justice and in pursuit of the Sušil Cyrilomethodian ideology with its slogan: "Only a patriot can be a good Christian!" — a slogan which was pronounced even from the pulpit in Velehrad in the year 1869. He always defended the just interests of different nationalities in the exercise of the ministry, in meetings of organizations, and particularly in sessions of the Parliament in Vienna, where he used to begin his speeches in the Czech language and then continue them in German, so that everyone would be able to understand.

No one ever doubted the ardent patriotic sentiments of Stojan as a priest, a deputy or as an archbishop. He was a nationalist of the Sušil school, but a nationalist without prejudice or ill-will against Germans. He would say: "We do not want the Germans over us, but next to us." It is particularly significant that he did not wish to exclude Catholic Germans from supporting his principal life-work, the *Apostolate of Sts. Cyril and Methodius.* He always addressed his announcements to them as well as to the Czechs. The response, however, was very small so Stojan ceased to count on their support.

It was again the Cyrilomethodian ideal that helped him to resolve the problem of nationalism without prejudice, in a spirit of justice and tolerance—a problem on which much energy was expended in Austria,[5] where all the energy could have been more profitably applied to social, ecnomic, and cultural problems. After all, Sts. Cyril and Methodius came to Moravia only because they placed their ethnicity second to higher interests and goals. They bequeathed this spirit as a duty imposed on those who venerated and followed them, expecially in the priestly state. Stojan was keenly aware of this and acted accordingly.

Old Austria not only lacked an understanding of justice to nationalities, but was also faced with pressing social questions. Among those who took a social justice viewpoint (without comprehension, if not negatively) of the socio-political movement of young Catholics, were also the aristocratic bishops. The pope who issued the encyclical *Rerum Novarum* (1891) was the one who, in reply to a question, told Cardinal Schönborn of Prague that it was absolutely necessary to understand the efforts of Christians who worked for social justice and to support them. Nothing could have been more encouraging for Stojan, then pastor of Dražovice, who was acquiring a reputation as an unusually self-sacrificing priest with a great love for the people. His social origins and his compassionate goodness of heart predestined him for impartial social politics, and this phase of his activities has produced the greatest number of anecdotes about him. Despite numerous entertaining accounts, the essence of his personality is grave and perceptive. There are many humorous stories about his generosity and charity. This quality made him capable of pulling money out of his own pocket as well as from the pockets of others. Stojan begged and borrowed from almost anyone to provide help for believers as well as unbelievers, for friends as well as foes, for the worthy as well as the unworthy. To take the coat off his back, even the shoes off his own feet, was nothing unusual for him. Love of neighbor formed Stojan's character in times of peace, but even more so during the First World War. He provided support for families and households which the War left fatherless.

It was no wonder then, that after the exhortation in Leo XIII's encyclical on labor, Stojan deliberately took his place in the ranks of the new generation of priests working for social emancipation, whose slogan was: "Out of the sacristy, into the marketplace of public life!" As a practical man he well knew that if any good idea was to produce fruit, it had to be exposed and fought for in a public forum. Hence he harmonized political activity with his spiritual principles when acting as a public servant. Together with Jan Šrámek, Stojan founded a political party, the *Křěstǎnsko-Sociální Strana Moravských Katolíků* (The Christian-Social Party of Moravian Catholics, founded in 1899). The ideological foundations for this party were formulated by the *Jednota Katolických Tovaryšů* (Union of Catholic Workmen, already founded in 1849). The party held its conventions in Velehrad.

In Stojan as a politician and delegate of his party, one of his youthful visions was brought to fruition—to be a leader and to be active among those who control the destiny of the people and their nation. Stojan understood well the challenge of the times. He perceived it as a new and adequate opportunity to assert himself in public life and to promote Catholic interests. Since his days as a young priest, he was a member and vice chairman of the local Catholic Political Union. Later he was elected district chairman. Stojan then became a candidate for office, and in the local elections of 1897 was elected as the single delegate for the two Catholic parties, which formed a coalition for this election. In subsequent elections he was elected to Parliament in 1901, in 1907, and in 1911. In the years 1900, 1902, and 1907, he was sent as representative of his voters to the Land Diet of Moravia.

The position of a priest as politician and deputy was not an enviable one in Austria at that time. The German ecclesiastical circles showed an unfavorable attitude toward him; political democracy was not favored. Too much trust had been placed in having a Catholic emperor and in having a Catholic numerical majority in positions of power. Rome, however, would not let itself be deceived by this type of complacency, and it indicated—just as in matters of socio-political questions—that development in the direction of political democracy was a healthy one. The suspicious attitude of some ecclesiastical aristocrats flowed from too much regard for the imperial government, which was afraid that opposition would grow among Czech Catholics. Stojan's political program as a deputy, however, was not at all chauvinistic. His youthful ambitions had left him. There remained only the will to serve out of love of neighbor, for country and for the Church. Actually, only an ardent desire to help everyone through his political influence could keep Stojan, the parish priest and provost, in the Austrian Parliament. For a person of an active and practical disposition, it was tedious to listen to the unending verbal battles; for a priest it was downright torture to hear attacks against the Church and blasphemous remarks, which were not spared even in comments on Stojan's speeches. But even his enemies acknowledged Stojan as the most conscientious, most effective, and most self-sacrificing member of the parliament. He was in truth "a national deputy from the people and for the people."

Looking back on all aspects of Stojan's public life, one can see that his spiritual profile increased in intensity and magnitude because he was loved by everyone, even his political adversaries. It was really amazing that political activity did not affect his human and spiritual outlook in any way. On the contrary, having been exposed to it seemed to reinforce his moral principles and become a constant challenge to him in the public forum. This in itself is a testimonial of his saintly personality, firmly rooted in virtue and manifested by brave and heroic actions that benefitted not only individuals but the church, society and the country. If one's sole survival in secular society is principally due to one's spiritual strength, then one must be a spiritual giant able to dominate the national scene. Stojan was such a spiritual giant and Pope John XXIII extolled his name in his apostolic letter, *"Magnifici eventus"* (1963).[6] He singled out his zealous endeavors for Church unity which were extended by the Council of Vatican II (1962-65) to an all-inclusive ecumenism. As a matter of fact,[7] some have contended the saintly Archbishop Stojan had similar ideas and the same charism as Pope John XXIII, the pope of Ecumenism. John XXIII was undeniably a man who accomplished more than was expected of him. His greatest accomplishment is that he released and activated new forces in the Church. This he did by his spirit of dialogue, warmth, and by allowing his own person to remain in the background—as was noted by his enthusiastic critics immediately after his death on June 3, 1963.[8]

Though separated by time, these two figures are close to each other in temperament, spirit, and goals. They lend to each other a helping hand in the generous, selfless service of a great idea, which both of them conceived. The idea and the service made both of them great— the yearning for reconciliation; for the unity of Christians and peoples. One of the critics of the deceased Pope John XXIII posed the question of the sanctity of the pope of peace and of the Council; he pointed out qualities which were quite evident. He wrote: ". . . I think that he had what it takes to be a saint. . . In principle, a saint can be defined, or at least described, as one who lives in complete harmony with the divine will, demonstrating in an outstanding way all virtues, in particular humility, charity, and heroic suffering."[9] The same can be said of Stojan and that in its full sense, judging by Stojan's favorite and frequently repeated motto: "Give me souls, take the rest, O Lord."[10] Spiritual concerns dominated so much of his personality that his sanctity was evident in everything he did in life and in the legacy he left.

Stojan's continuous concern for the integral holiness of the priest-hood in general and that of Czech and Moravian priests in particular is perhaps not only the most important part of his own spiritual personality but also the most revealing symptom of the key for the reform of the Church and society, namely the need for good priests. That this was Stojan's major priority in his spiritual endeavors is clearly evident from the account of František Cardinal Tomášek, the present archbishop of Prague who was himself ordained by Stojan in 1922 and who detailed Stojan's solicitude for priestly perfection in the following testimonial:[11]

"From the earliest years of his priesthood until the very end of his life, Father Stojan dedicated himself to the welfare and problems of candidates for the priesthood. With untiring devotion and vigilance he dedicated his entire life to this mission."

Stojan's concern increased when he was appointed archbishop of Olomouc. It was an extremely painful ordeal for him when in the first year of his episcopate in 1921 he was able to ordain only three seminarians who were in poor health. Because of their ailing health, they were exempt from the draft and able to pursue their studies. Stojan was also very much aware that candidates for the priesthood were really nurtured in upright Christian families. Therefore he constantly insisted upon good Christian behavior and Christian living within families. In all seriousness he exhorted these families not to cause their sons any obstacles when after mature consideration they decided to enter the seminary. On the other hand he always reminded the parents that they must never force a son to enter the priesthood if he himself was not so inclined. He always favored a complete freedom of choice.

In support of this view is a document presented to us by one of Stojan's former altar boys in Dražovice. The latter's mother wanted him to be a priest and turned for advice to her spiritual mentor, Stojan. But the sympathy of the latter was with the young man. He supported the student's decision to become a teacher and patiently explained that as a teacher, her son could do a great deal of good and told her not to force her son into something he himself did not want. This particular young man eventually became an excellent teacher and subsequently a supervisor who was grateful to Stojan his entire life.

It happened more than once that a priest had a nervous breakdown because he didn't have the right attitude or relationship to his calling. As far as the Church and its followers are concerned it is a matter of lesser importance to have a great number of priests.The sanctity and dedication of priests are of much greater importance. Consequently the following saying is quite correct: "A saintly priest educates people in devotion; a pious priest instructs people in decency, and a decent priest leaves his people without devotion."

Despite his strong desire to have more young men entering the seminary he was uncompromising in his regard for the required qualities and capabilities of aspirants. If the candidate did not have the requisite aptitudes or sentiments, Stojan disregarded human concerns. His main concern was dedication to God. He knew that false charity was an affront to the individual to be served as well as to God. He refused to ordain such individuals. Stojan not only lectured about the magnitude, importance and merits of the priesthood, but also wrote about it in pastoral letters and in the press. He also explained to parents that they could not look upon the priesthood from a monetary viewpoint. He reminded them that it is a call to spiritual heroism and to a life-consuming sacrifice for others. Some young people do have the understanding and courage to devote themselves to this unselfish way of Christ to follow in his footsteps.

He kept stressing to the seminarians that only within the realm of priesthood can they accomplish such good. This he said with deep conviction based on his own experiences. Although Stojan untiringly emphasized the importance of the priesthood he looked upon the individual's choice of vocation with great moderation. He was quite open-minded about celibacy. At the end of World War I, during the revolution in 1918, some segments of the clergy started a movement against celibacy. That subsequently led to a schism. Some dedicated and serious-minded priests were often charged with conduct unbecoming their priestly profession. Therefore they asked Archbishop Stojan to petition Benedict XV about the question of optional celibacy. Stojan listened to this petition requested by a group of theologians and presented it to Rome. Upon his return from Rome, he reported his conversation with the Holy Father who declared he could not grant the request.

All Benedict's successors, including John XXIII, voiced the same opinion. No one could accuse John XXIII of narrowmindedness and harshness. Even those who are not followers of the Church honored him for his deep human concerns and his goodness which is hard to match. At the time of the Ecumenical Council, the same request was presented to the Holy Father. He became quite serious and said: "I am aware that the question of celibacy leads sometimes to personal tragedies. No one knows how even I, myself, often suffer under it. I could take a pen in my hand and by the stroke of my signature make the required change of church practice. But I cannot take upon myself such a great responsibility. The welfare of the souls and the welfare of the Church are more important."

Apropos celibacy in his talks to the seminarians after his interview with Benedict XV Stojan used to say: "I present you the reality of this condition as it is. If anyone of you think that he cannot conduct himself accordingly, and obey the teachings of the Church and fulfill the requirements of celibacy, he should right now decide to leave the seminary. We will support him in his studies so that in time he can choose another profession." On that particular occasion, not one of the seminarians left the seminary.

Stojan, while still a priest, experienced whipping, thorn-crowning and even stoning from his own people. At various meetings they harassed him or expelled him as a speaker. Often he had to defend himself with bitter humor against the harshness of his audience. Such was the climate after World War I when the current saying was: "We settled our account with Vienna and thus will we settle with Rome also." In one town, someone approached him and said: "It's easy for you as a deputy to travel around the world. You have no wife and no children. I have eight children and can't travel around the world as you do." Stojan replied: "You have children? Be thankful to God that they are healthy and capable. It's a good sign that you and your wife love each other." Then Stojan turned to all present and added wittily: "Be glad that we do not marry; we would choose the best looking girls and what then would be left for you?" He turned again to the father and added: "Honor your family and don't complain. God doesn't abandon his faithful servants."

Once a seminarian was experiencing an interior crisis, just at the time that Stojan was to perform the tonsure, initiating the candidate into the first spiritual step of a seminarian's journey to the priesthood. He remembers in what an emotionally distressed state he entered the chapel where the ailing Archbishop waited. The liturgical ceremony started thus: "When I see you all here before me, I think to myself: Dear God, should I admit these young people into the spiritual state in these difficult times? But when I recall the words of Jesus Christ: 'Not even a sparrow falls from the roof without God's willing it,' I am convinced that you haven't come here without a determined purpose and therefore I will with great joy perform the tonsure." These words about divine providence had such a deep effect upon the seminarian as the Archbishop cut his hair that he courageously voiced his conviction as it is written in the book of Psalms: "The Lord is my fate. You dear God will compensate me for all I am renouncing through my love for You."

One of the last messages of Archbishop Stojan before his death August 3, 1923 was addressed to seminarians before their annual congress in Velehrad. The one who was the heart and soul of these congresses from 1891 to 1922 was lying on his deathbed. On his way to the congress Father Francis Cinek visited the Archbishop. In a room with drawn curtains, and in an oppressive summer heat, lay the ill and helpless Archbishop on his bed. When he recognized his visitor,

Stojan's face lit up. Father Cinek said: "Your excellency, I am on my way to Velehrad for the Congress of Seminarians. Is there any message you would like to relay?" The archbishop's eyes filled with tears and he started to sob uncontrollably. Father Cinek wanted to leave because he thought his presence had unduly upset the patient. But the suffering Archbishop held him back. In emotional spasmodic words, interrupted by tears, he said: "I will never see Velehrad again. . . Tell the seminarians that the only thing I ask of them is the same as the words of the dying St. Cyril, spoken by him to his brother: 'Don't abandon my good people.' "

This message of God's servant, Antonín Cyril Stojan, and the example of his entire life serves not only as a constant reminder to all of us but is also the most eloquent testimony of his own sanctity as well. This holy man could produce such an earnest longing for the idealistic concept of the spiritual formation and personaltiy of a priest in which he was successful. Confirmation of this is reflected in the period after his death when an ever greater number of similar testimonials, some of which were incorporated in this book. Perhaps the most expressive tribute was that of Abbot Method Zavoral of Strahov in his eulogy over Stojan's bier in Olomouc (1923): "In vain we torture ourselves with the bitter question: Why, dear God, why so soon and why just now, when we need so many more Stojans? . . .Hostyn . . .Velehrad. . . To what exalted heights he yearned to raise this see of St. Methodius, and what many things for a long number of years he brought as a sacrifice, that he might continue the work of St. Methodius, and as far as was humanly possible, complete it. At Velehrad, his plans went immeasurably further than at Mount Hostyn. There he had in mind not only to bring the Czech nation close to God, to shake it loose from religious indifference and to raise it to a higher moral level—there, in the spirit of St. Methodius, he, a second Methodius, looked at all the other Slavic nations, wished to risk everything and to dare all things to bring them closer to the same divine love and unite them in that love. . . ."[12]

No wonder that soon after Stojan's death (1923) the process of gathering information for the purpose of eventual beatification was begun immediately by the Archbishop of Olomouc, Josef Karel Matocha, as soon as he became Metropolitan of the see of St. Methodius (1848-61).[13] Unfortunately due to subsequent sad events, a cruel persecution of religion, of Church and bishops, including Archbishop

Matocha,[14] occurred. The archdiocesan process could not be completed and a petition[15] could not be forwarded to the Holy See. However, the saintly profile of Stojan was not silenced by the ongoing persecution of the Church in Czechoslovakia. Requests for a continuation of the process in Rome were organized by Czechoslovak exiles and by Father Josef Olšr, S.J.[16] who took the initiative in the process in Rome. Very helpful and effective in promoting Stojan's cause was an appeal[17] of the late Abbot Ambroze Leo Ondrak, O.S.B. of St. Procopius Abbey in Lisle, for the prayers for the beatification of Archbishop Stojan, which were published in all Czech journals abroad, after the Czech Catholics of Chicago celebrated in 1951 the centennial of the birth of Stojan[18] in St. Procopius Church. Perhaps this helped to restore interest for Stojan's cause also in Communistic Czechoslovakia, because Father Josef Vrana who, since 1971 had been president of the Czech national unit of the government-sponsored association of priests, *Pacem in Terris* and the vicar capitular of the archdiocese of Olomouc, in the middle of February 1972 had come to Rome to deliver documents for the beatification procedure for Stojan.[19] Later, in February of 1973, he was named, and on March 4 consecrated, as titular bishop and administrator of Olomouc—the last with the restriction "ad nutum santae Sedis" (which, according to Church law, could facilitate a possible future removal from office). The Prague government had agreed that Vrána should give up his office with the *Pacem in Terris* organization. Evidently this agreement was not kept and the Vatican Congregation for the Clergy by decree of March 8, 1982, indirectly pressed for its fulfillment by prohibiting priests to associate with such organizations and publishing the decree coincidentally with the occasion of the arrival of five bishops[20] from Czechoslovakia for their "ad limina"[21] to Rome. This was, evidently, to embarrass especially Bishop Vrána as administrator of Olomouc, for his defiant behavior, which ironically appeared rather to be in sharp contrast to the so well-known *semper fidelis* loyalty of a saintly Stojan to the Holy See. Yet, nobody ever doubted a great benefit for the nation would result from the speedy promotion of the beatification of this faithful servant of God, Stojan, whose significance was everywhere increasingly felt more strongly, especially in Moravia as ever and in these sad times of Communist oppression of Czechoslovakia.

From the past history of this nation it would seem to be clearly evident that the prelate, Pietro Ciriaci, a Papal Nuncio who negotiated the *modus vivendi*[22] between the Holy See and the Republic of Czechoslovakia February 2, 1928 in Prague, was right when he stressed his view of Czechoslovakia as a bridge between the East and West. He claimed that from this flows its obligation in the ecclesiastical and political sphere. He saw an ideological foundation for this role in the Cyrilomethodian idea when he stated: "As the representative of the Holy See in this Republic, I have seen, even from the beginning, the immeasurable significance of this state, in which the East meets with the West, for the exalted work of unionism; and it is precisely in the *Apostolate of Sts. Cyril and Methodius* that these noble efforts are centered. The Velehrad Unionistic Congresses have earned a very good reputation in the Catholic world and especially in the Slavic world, so that the Holy See itself has distinguished them in a special manner and recently has adorned the place itself, blessed by the activities of the saintly Apostles to the Slavs,[23] the shrine of Velehrad, and granted it the title of Minor Basilica."[24] This high appraisal of the unionistic endeavors together with the important mission of the nation, in the center of Europe is implicitly a public tribute not only to Stojan's work but a posthumous approval of his rich legacy as well. There is full documentation available for its substantiation with three monuments as evidence, namely, one living, that is, the veneration and love in the hearts of the Moravian people. Then, two of stone, that is, Hostyn and Velehrad. The latter contains the dark-red marble tombstone in the Royal Chapel of the Velehrad Basilica, close to the tomb of the first Moravian Metropolitan of all the Slavs, Archbishop St. Methodius[25] of Thessalonica.

Stojan's tomb is decorated and frequently visited by those who venerate him. On his tombstone are the biblical words: "A great priest, who in his time renovated the house of God and in his days reinforced the temple. Like a fire shining, and incense burning in the fire (Sirach, 50: 1, 9). In all things I have shown you that by so toiling you ought to help the weak and remember the word of the Lord Jesus, that he himself said, 'It is more blessed to give than to receive.' " (Acts, 20:35.) And should *vox populi vox Dei* (voice of people, voice of God) as memorialized on Stojan's tomb, be true, then this servant of God, of such a noble calibre, is certainly a worthy candidate to be extolled on the altar for public veneration in recognition that he was always a faithful witness to God's truth and also for his zealous sharing in the Son of God's salvific mission as a dedicated priest in the Lord's vineyard with as much decisive commitment as one can feel from his beloved motto: "Give me souls, take the rest, O Lord." His whole life was selflessly dedicated to the glory of God. With God's reward in Stojan taking an honored place in *Czech Heaven*[26] with all the other Czech saints and beati, the faithful of Moravia, of all Czechoslovakia and all Slavic nations certainly not only proudly acclaim him as one of their own but pray that his legacy of the Cyrilomethodian heritage may again be restored and fully realized to the benefit of all.

NOTES

1. František Cinek, *Arcibiskup Dr. A.C. Stojan, Život a dílo* (Olomouc, 1933), 1.179.
2. Dr. Mořic Hruban, *Z Časů nedlouho zašlých* (From times of recent past). Memoirs of Dr. Maurice Hruban, ed. by Jan Drábek (Rome-Los Angeles, 1967), 95-97.
3. S. Scheicher, *Erlebnisse und Erinnerungen*, 4 vols. (Vienna, 1906-1912); K. Eder, *Der Liberalismus in Alt-Osterreich* (Vienna, 1963); F. Maase, *Der Josephinismus*, 5 vols. (Vienna, 1951-1902).
4. J.R. Aherne, "St. Clement Mary Hofbauer," *Encyclopedic Dictionary of Religion*, (Philadelphia, 1978) II, 1630; Butler, I, 601-604; John Hofer, C.SS.R., *St. Clement Maria Hofbauer, a Biography* (transl. from German by Rev. John B. Haas, C.SS.R. (New York, 1926.
5. F.W. Foerster, *Europe und die Deutsche Frage* (Luzern, 1937; Czech transl. Prague, 1938) has demonstrated Austria's guilt in dealing with Slavic nationalities, particularly in his two chapters, "Nationalization of Nationalistic Austria" and "Serious Offenses of the Austro-Hungarian Policy against the Slavs."
6. *Magnifici eventus* of May 11, 1963, see in *A.A.S.* (1963).
7. Bohumil Zlámal, *Antonín Cyril Stojan* (Rome, 1973), 151-2.
8. E.E.Y. Hales, *Pope John and His Revolution* (New York, 1965), passim.
9. Raymond Etteldorf, *America* of June 22, 1963, p. 885.
10. This motto is to be sttributed to St. John Bosco (1815-1888). See note 10 in Chapter I. František Cinek, *Arcibiskup Dr. Antonin Cyril Stojan* (Olomouc, 1933), 58 insists that "this was a motto of many saints, as it was the beloved motto of priest and bishop Stojan."
11. František Cardinal Tomášek, "arcibiskup Stojan a knežský dorost" with its English trans. as "Archbishop Stojan and the Candidates for priesthood," by the author. The Cardinal originally sent this item to the author to show how Stojan's concern for priestly spirituality was vital, and the author incorporated it into the text. The article appeared in the journal *Hlasatel* (Chicago)

of Sept. 17, 1982, pp. 5-7, and in the Catholic weekly *Hlas Národa* (Voice of the Nation) (Chicago) of Sept. 29, 1982.

12. Bohumil Zlámal, *op.cit.*, 122-123.
13. *A.A.S.* 40 (1948), 358; *Lidová demokracie* of March 24, 1948, p. 1.
14. Ludvik Nemec, *Episcopal and Vatican Reaction to the Persecution of the Catholic Church in Czechoslovakia* (Washington, DC, 1953), passim.
15. Canon 1999; see John A. Abbo and Jerome D. Hannan, *The Sacred Canons*, 2 vols., (St. Louis, 1951-52) II, 773.
16. Professor of the Oriental Institute in Rome. See his book: Josef Olšr, *Služebník Boží, Antonín Cyril Stojan, Olomoucký Arcibiskup* (Servant of God, Archbishop of Olomouc) (Rome, 1966).
17. Kalendar *Katolík* (Chicago, 1953), 143,145.
18. Kalendar *Katolík* (Chicago, 1953), 158: "České Katolické Chicago důstojně slavilo 100. výročí narozenin arcibiskupa Stojana" (Czech Catholic Chicago celebrated the 100th anniversary of the birth of archbishop Stojan. Pontifical Mass was celebrated in St. Procopius Church and all the festivities were transmitted by the *Voice of America* to Czechoslovakia.
19. Hansjacob Stehle, *Eastern Politics of the Vatican, 1917-1979* (transl. by Sandra Smith) (Athens, Ohio, London, 1981), 337.
20. Cardinal Tomášek of Prague, Bishop Julius Gabriš of Trnava, Bishop Jan Pastor of Nitra, Bishop Josef Ferance of Baňská Bystrica and Bishop Vrána of Olomouc.
21. *La Republica* of March 11, 1982: "E tempo di togliere la parola ai preti che fanno politica" di Domenico Del Rio, see also *Our Sunday Visitor* of March 21, 1982; Vatican's *Congregation for the Clergy* issued on March 8, 1982, a document on government-sponsored associations of priests, prohibiting priests from forming organizations in support of a particular political ideology, or to be members of military organizations; see another article: Vescovi di Praga in difficoltà—a Roma fanno presto a dire", ibid. *L'Osservatore Romano* of March 13, 1982 has the Pope's whole speech to bishops of Czechoslovakia. *Declaration* of the Sacred Congregation for the clergy, in *A.A.S.* LXXIV (1982), 642-645.
22. *A.A.S.* XX (1928) 65-66, see Eduard Beneš, "Exposé Ministra Beneše *o modu vivendi mezi Československem a Vatikánem" Zahraniční politka* VII (1928) 200-203. Text speech of February 1, 1928.
23. Encyclical *Rerum Orientalium* of September 7, 1928; see *A.A.S.* XX (1928), 277-288, stressing importance of the work of Sts. Cyril and Methodius for Church unity.
24. Letter to Archbishop Leopold Prečan in 1928, see Bohumil Zlámal, *op.cit.*, 118.
25. Peter Ratkoš "K otázce sídla panonsko-moravského metropolity" *Verbum* II (1948); F. Robenek, "Morava, nejstarší metropole slovanská", *Hlídka* (Brno, 1930); J. Poulík, "Nález kostela z doby velko-moravské v trati "Špitálky" ve Starém Městě" *Památky archeologické* 46 (1955) 307-351; V. Hrubý, *Staré Město Velkomoravské Pohřebiště Na valách"* (Prague

1955); Josef Cibulka, "První tři velkomoravské kostely objevené na hradišti u Mikulčic, jejich význam a otázka Metodějova hrobu" in *Soluňsti Bratři* (Prague, 1963) 85-157, see especially p. 156-7.

26. Paul Claudel, *Carona Benegnitatis Annis Dei* 6th ed. (Paris, 1915), see "Images Saints de Bohéme." Gerge Bertold Pontan, *Spirituale Regni Bohemiae* (Prague, 1599); Václav Kašpar, *České nebe* (Czech Heaven) (Prague, 1939, passim.

Illustrations briefly portray the principal apostolate of Antonín Cyril Stojan. On the center is a painting of Stojan encircled by wheat and grapes that become the Holy Eucharist, the center of his life. On the left is an image of Our Lady, gloriously standing above the basilica built to revere her. Below him is a representation of the jeweled crown so generously provided by him and his faithful followers who wished to express their ardent devotion. Beside the crown is an illustration of the Book of Statutes of the Apostolate of SS. Cyril and Methodius apropos Church Unity.

On the right is depicted in Velehrad the great apostles of the Slavs, SS. Cyril and Methodius, in whose footsteps Stojan followed. Below them is a sketch of the basilica of Velehrad, the focus of all devotional endeavors for Church Unity.

BIBLIOGRAPHY

Abbo, John A., and Hannan, Jerome D., *The Sacred Canons*; a concise presentation of the current disciplinary norms of the Church, 2 vols., St. Louis: 1952.

Abbott, Walter M., SJ, ed. *The Documents of Vatican II*, New York, 1966.

Acta I Conventus Velehradensis, Theologorum commercil studiorum inter occidentem et orientem cupidorum, Prague, 1908; Review by J. Tampach *ČKD/* 1908/264.

Acta II Conventus Velehradensis, Prague, Bohemorum, 1910.

Acta III Conventus Velehradensis, Prague, 1912.

Acta IV Conventus Velehradensis, Anno 1924, Olomouc, 1925.

Acta VII Conventus Velehradensis, Olomouc, 1937.

Agnew, Hugh LeCaine, *Czech National Consciousness between Enlightenment and Romanticism, 1780-1815*, Standord, 1981.

Allen, Joseph J., ed., *Orthodox Synthesis: The Unity of Theological Thought*, Crestwood-Tuckahoe, NY; 1981.

Ammann, A., *Abriss der ostslavischen Kirchengeschichte*, Vienna, 1950.

Anastos, Milton V., "Political theory in the lives of the Slavic Saints Constantine and Methodius," *Harvard Slavic Studies II*, 1964, 11-38.

Anonymous, "Antonín Podlaha, 1865-1932. Půl století od smrti Antonína Podlahy a Čeňka Zíbrta," *Hlas Národa* of February 27, 1982.

—— "Muž modlitby a práce" /The man of prayer and work/, *Nový život* 3, /Rome, 1951/, 3-5.

—— *Průvodce posvátným Velehradem a okolím* /Guide through the memorial Velehrad and neighborhood/, Velehrad, 1936.

—— "Pozdrav z Moravského Velehradu všem svobodomilovným krajanům žijícím v zahraničí, všem exultantům, věřícím, i nevěřícím, kteří na nás nezapomínají," *Hlas Národa* VI, no. 31-32 /August 15, 1981/, 1-2.

Antonovych, V., "Studies in the National Movements in Ukraine" /in Ukrainian/, *Ukrainian Historical Library* XIV, Lvov 1897.

Atwater, Donald, "Facts that make reunion with the Orthodox Church difficult," the *Catholic Mind* XLII, October, 1944.

Baran, Ludvík and Staňková, Jitka, *Lidové kroje Slovácka* /The national costumes of the region "Slovacko"/, Prague, 1982.

Bartoli, D., and Maffei, J., *The Life of St. Francis Xavier*, New York, 1882.

Battifol, Pierre Henri, "Pope Benedict XV and the Restoration of Unity", *The Constructive Quaterly* VI, 1918, 209-225.

Bea, Card. A., "L` Eucaristia e 1` unione dei cristiani," *La Civiltà Cattolica* 116 /Sept. 4, 1965/ vol. 2765, 401-413.

Bea, Augustin Cardinal and Visser` t Hovft, Willem A., *Peace among Christians* /transl. by Judith Moses/, New York, 1967.

Bednarik, M. Eileen, Ss.C.M., "Slovak Music," *Slovak Studies* XV, /Cleveland, Rome, 1975/, 177-194.

Bednář, F., *Sbírka zákonů a nařízení ve věcech náboženských a církevních v Republice Československé, normy platné v celém území republiky, zvláštní předpisy týkající se církve zemí českých*, Prague, 1929.

Beisner, T. Ryan, *The Vatican Council and the American Secular Newspapers, 1869-70*, Washington, D.C. 1941.

Beneš, Eduard, Exposé Ministra Dra. Beneše o modu vivendi mezi Československem a Vatikánem," *Zahraniční Politika* VII, Prague, 1928 /text of speech of Feb. 1, 1928/.

— — *Le Problème autrichien et la question tchèque*, Paris, 1908.

Berg, L., Andreas Szeptickyj, Russkij Katoliceskij ekzarchat v Russii," *Ex Oriente*, /Mains, 1927/, 66-77.

Berkeley, G.F.H., *Italy in the Making*, Cambridge, 1936.

Bezdíček, Josef, "Antonín Stojan, God´s Faithful Servant," *Katolík* 61 /Chicago, 1954/, in follow-up of several articles.

Bidlo, Jaroslav and others, *Slovanstvo: Obraz jeho minulosti a přítomnosti* /Slavs: Picture of their past and present/, Prague, 1912.

Bitnar, Vilém, "O Stojanovi, českém chudáčku Božím," /about Stojan, the Czech God`s pauper/, *Lidové listy*, /Olomouc/, May 22, 1931.

Blet, Pierre and others, ed., "Le Saint Siège et la situation religieuse en Pologue et dans les Pays Baltes," *Actes et Documents du Saint Siège relatifs à la seconde guerre mondiale* III, Vatican, 1967, part 1.

Blet, Pierre, Graham Robers, Martini Angelo and Schneider Burkhard, eds., *Records and Documents of the Holy See Relating to the Second World War*, 9 vols., Vatican City, 1965-75.

Bloomfield, John, *Passive Revolution: Politics and the Czechoslovak Working Class, 1945-1948*, New York, 1979.

Boček, B., Podzemní Velehrad, vykopávky roku 1937 /Subterranean Velehrad; excavations in the year 1937/, Velehrad, 1938.

Bociurkiw, Bohdan R., The Uniate Church in the Soviet Ukraine: A case Study in Soviet Church Policy," *Canadian Slavonic Papers* VII, /1965/, 112-130.

Bourdeaux, Michael, "Eastern Catholics in the Ukraine," *America* 116 no. 3/11/67, 344-345.

Boyle, Leonard, O.P., "Osud ostatků svatého Cyrila" /The Fate of the relics of St. Cyril,/ *Se znamením Kříže*, /Rome, 1967, 45-60.

Boyer, Louis, *Roman Socrates* /tr. by M. Day/, New York, 1958.

Boysak, Basil, *The Fate of the Holy Union in Carpatho-Ukraine*, Toronto-New York, 1963.

Bozesky, Theodosia, *Life of St. Josafat*, Cornet Press, 1955.

Brock, Peter, *The Slovak National Awakening: an essay in the intellectual history of East Central Europe*, Toronto, 1976.

Broderick, James J., SJ., *St. Francis Xavier* /1506-1552/, New York, 1952.

Brown, Robert McAffee, *The Frontiers of the Church Today*, Oxford, 1973.

Brown, William A., *Toward a United Church*, New York, 1946.

Browne-Olf, Lillian, *Their Name is Pius*, Milwaukee, 1941.

Brož, Luděk, "Phänomen Wojtyla," *Communio Viatorum* 24 no. 1-2 /Prague, 1981/, 21-28.

Brtáň, Rudo, *Barokový slavizmus* /the baroque Slavism/, Lipt. Mikuláš, 1939.

Brueckner, Alex., *Der Eintritt der Slaven in die Weltgeschichte*, Berlin, 1909.

—— *Die Wahrheit über die Slavenapostles*, Tübingen, 1913.

Bunetta, Sr. M., O.S.F., *Give Me Souls* /A biography of Raphael Cardinal Merry del Val/, Westminster, Md., 1958.

Bušek, Vratislav, Hendrych, Jaroslav, Laštovka, Karel, Muller, Václav, *Československé církevní zákony* /Czechoslovak Church laws/, Prague, 1931.

Butvin, Jozef, "The Great Moravian Cyril and Methodius tradition in the Slovak national revival," *Studia historica slovaca* VII, /Bratislava, 1973/, 96-118.

Čada, Josef, "American Pan-Slavism," *Hlas Národa*, /Chicago/, August 12-19, 1978, 20.

Casaroli, Cardinal, "Uchovejte si dědictví Otců," *Nový život* XXXIII No. 10, October, 1981, 150-152.

Český kancionál svatováclavský /The Czech Cancional of St. Wenceslaus/, Prague, 1947.

Chada, Joseph, *The Czechs in the United States* /New York, 1981/.

Chmelar, Josef, *Political Parties in Czechoslovakia*, Prague, 1926.

Cibulka, Josef, *Grossmährische Kirchenbauten*, Sancti Cyrillus et Methodius, Leben und Wirken, Prague, 1963.

—— "Velkomoravský kostel v Modré u Velehradu a začátky křesťanství na Moravě," *Monumenta Archeologica* VII, Prague, 1958.

Cinek, František, *Arcibiskup Dr. Antonín Cyril Stojan, Život a dílo*. Pokus o nárys duchovní fysiognomie /Arch. Ant. C. Stojan: Life and Work. Attempt for an autline of spiritual physiognomy/, Olomouc, 1933.

—— *K náboženské otázce v prvních letech samostatnosti* /Concerning religious question in the first years of independence/, Olomouc, 1926.

—— *Velehrad víry; duchovní dějiny Velehradu* /Velehrad of the Faith; spiritual history of the Velehrad/, Olomouc, 1936.

—— *Velehrad víry* /Velehrad of Faith/, 1936.

—— *Basilika velehradská po obnově 1935-1938.* /The Basilica of Velehrad after its renovation 1935-38/, Brno, 1939.

Codex Juris Canonici /CJC/, Pii X. Pontificis Maximi iussu digestus, Benedicti Papae XV auctoritate promulgatus, Romae, 1919.

Congar, Yves, *After Nine Hundred Years*, New York, 1959.

Connolly, J.C., *John Gerson, Reformer and Mystic*, New York, 1928.

Corriden, James A., ed., *The Once and Future Church*, Staten Island, NY, 1971.

Corrigan, Raymond, *The Church and the Nineteenth Century*, Milwaukee, 1938.

Daim, Wilfred, *The Vatican and Eastern Europe*, London, 1970.

Daněk, Ant., "Dr. Ant. Cyril Stojan, vzpomínka z let studentských," *Moravská Orlice* of October 1, 1923.

Daniélou, Jean Cardinal, *Christian Faith and Today's Man*, Huntington, Ind., 1970.

David, L., *Werdegung del Los von Rom Bewegung bis 1899*, Wien, 1906.
Dawson, Christofer H., *The Making of Europe*, London, 1945.
—— *Understanding Europe*, New York, 1952.
—— *The Dividing of Christendom*, New York, 1965.
Dekan, Jan, *Velká Morava, Doba umenie* /Great Moravia: Time and Arts/, Bratislava, 1979.
De Lubac, Henri, *The Church: Paradox and Mystery*, Staten Island, NY, 1969.
De Rossi, G.B., "Del sepolcro di S. Cirillo nella basilica di S. Clemente," *Bolletino di Archeologia Cristiana*, ser. 1. 1, /1863/, 9-13.
Dirscherl, Denis, "The Soviet Destruction of the Greek Catholic Church," *Journal of Church and State* XII, /1970/, 428-440.
Dobrovský, Josef, *Cyril a Metod, Apoštolové slovanští* /s poznámkami Josefa Vajsa/ /Cyril and Methodius, Apostles of Slavs /with the notes of Josef Vajs/, Prague, 1948.
Doležal, Dr. Josef, *Český kněz* /Czech Priest/, Olomouc, 1931.
Doležil, Humbert, "Česká píseň reformační a vývoj protestantského chorálu" /Czech Reform Song and development of Protestant hymn/ in Vilém Mathesius, ed., *Co daly naše země Evropě a lidstvu*, /Prague, 1940/ 96-101.
Domanski, Francis, *The Great Apostle of Russia, Servant of God, Archbishop Cieplak*, Chicago, 1954.
Doroshenko, D., "The Uniate Church in Galicia, 1914-1917," *Slavonic Review* XII, 1934, 622-627.
—— *History of Ukraine from 1917 to 1923*, 2 vols., /Užhorod, 1930-1932/.
Dostál, Hynek, "Apoštol Moravy," *Hlas*, St. Louis, of February 8, 1921.
Drábek, Jan, ed., *Z časů nedlouho zašlých*, /From the recent past/. Memoirs of Doctor Maurice Hruban, Rome-Los Angeles, 1967.
Drozd, Josef, "Andreas Szeptyckyj, metropolita leopoliensis, praeses academiae Velehradensis 1910-1939", *Acta Academiae Velehradensis* XVIII, /Olomous, 1947/, pp. 92-102.
Dudík, Beda, *Dějiny Moravy* /History of Moravia/, Brno, 1890.
Dunn, Dennis J., "Stanlinism and the Catholic Church during the era of World War II," *The Catholic Historical Review* LIX No. 3, 1973, 404-528.
Durych, Jaroslav, "Odpověď Rusům," /Answer to Russians/, *Rozmach* 2 /Prague, 1924/, 266-73.
Dvorník, Francis, *Les Légendes de Constantin et de Méthode vues de Byzance*, Prague, 1933.
—— *National Churches and the Church Universal*, Westminster, Md., 1944.
—— "The Study of Church History and Christian Reunion," *The Eastern Churches Quarterly* 6, 1945, 1-20.
—— *The Making of Central and Eastern Europe*, London, 1949.
—— *The Ecumenical Councils*, New York, 1961.
—— *Czech Contributions to the Growth of the United States*, Chicago, 1961.
—— "The History of the Velehrad Unionistic Congresses," *Proceedings of the First Unionistic Congress, Sept. 28-30, 1956 at St. Procopius Abbey, Lisle, Ill.*, /Lisle, Ill., 1956/, 37-39.
—— *The Slavs in European History and Civilization*, New Brunswick, NJ, 1962.

—— *The Slavs: Their Early History and Civilization*, Boston, 1956.
—— "Practical Results of Research in Orientalia toward the Unity of Christendom," *Proceedings of the Second and Third Unionistic Congresses, St. Procopius Abbey*, /Lisle, 1960/, 40-50.
—— "The Significance of the Missions of Cyril and Methodius," *Slavic Review* XXIII, No. 2, July, 1944, 195-238.
—— "*Moravská Ríše a její apoštolové*," Se Znamením Kříže, /Rome, 1967, 9-19.
—— "*Svatí Cyril a Metoděj v Římě*," Se Znamením Kříže, /Rome, 1967/, 23-29.
—— *The Photian Schism: History and Legend*, Cambridge, 1948.
—— *Byzantium and the Roman Primacy*, New York, 1966.
—— *Byzantine Missions among the Slavs*, New Brunswick, NJ, 1970.
—— *Byzantské Misie u Slovanů*, Prague, 1970.
Dýmal, L., Velehrad; soubor 15 fotografií R. Šmahela /Velehrad; collection of 15 photographs of R. Šmahel/, Lipník nad Bečvou, 1969.
Eder, K., *Der Liberalismus in Alt-Österreich*, Vienna, 1963.
Edlinskii, G., "Uniia s Rímom i metropolit graf Sheptitskii," *Revolutsica i tserkov*, No. 1-3, /1924/, 108-109.
"Egregiae virtutis," apostolic letter of Dec. 31, 1980 by Pope John Paul II in *L'Osservatore Romano* of Dec. 31, 1980. Czech trans. as *Ochránci Evropy*, Rome, 1981.
Ehler, Sidney Z. and Morrall, John B., eds., *Church and State through the Centuries*, a collection of historic documents with commentaries, Westminster, Md., 1954.
Erni, Raymund, *Die Kirche in Orthodoxer Schau: Ein Beitrag zum ökumenischen Gesprach*, Freiburg, Schweiz, 1980.
Esterka, Peter, "Toward Union: The Congresses at Velehrad," *Journal of Ecumenical Studies*, 8 No. 1, /Spring, 1971/, 10-51.
Falconi, Carlo, *The Popes in the Twentieth Century—from Pius X to John XXIII*, /transl. by Muriel Grindrod/, Boston, 1967.
—— *The Silence of Pius XII*, Transl. by Bernard Wall, Boston, 1970.
Flajšhans, Václav, *Písemnictví české* /Czech Writings/, 2 vols., Prague, 1900-1901.
Flannery, Austin, O.P., *Vatican Council II*: The Conciliar and Post-Conciliar Documents, Northport, NY, 1975.
Florinsky, H.T., *Russia, A History and an Interpretation*, New York, 1953.
Florovsky, G., "The Orthodox Churches and the Ecumenical Movement Prior to 1910," in R. Rouse and S. Neill, *A History of the Ecumenical Movement, 1517-1948*, /Philadelphia, Pa., 1954/, 171-217.
Foerster, F.W., *Europa und die deutsche Frage* /Luzern, 1937/; Czech transl. 1938.
Fueilleu, Mercenier P., "Le Métropolite André Szeptyckyj," *Irénikon* 19, /1946/, 49-65.
Funk, F., *Kirchengeschichtliche Abhandlungen*, Paderborn, 1897-1907.
Garver, Bruce M., *The Young Czech Party, 1874-1901* and the *Emergence of a multi-party System*, New Haven, 1978.
Giannini, Amedeo, *Il "Modus Vivendi" fra la S. Sede e la Cecoslovacchia*, Rome, 1928.

Gibbons, H.A., "Ukraine and the Balance of Power," *Century Magazine*, 102, /1921/, 463-471.

Giordano, Igino, *Le Encicliche sociali dei papi /da Pio IX a Pio XII, 1864-1946/*, Rome, 1946.

Gogolák, Lajos, *Panszlavizmus*, Budapest, 1940.

Goldmann, Karel, "K výročí Jana Středovského," *Národ*, /Chicago/, Jan. 5, 1974, 3.

Gordillo, M., "Velehrad e i suoi congressi unionistici," *La Civiltà Cattolica*, 1951, 569-583.

Graham, Robert A., *Vatican Diplomacy: A Study of Church and State on the International Plane*, Princeton, NJ, 1960.

Grivec, Francis, *Konstantin und Method, Lehrer der Slaven*, Wisbaden, 1962.

— — *Pravoslaví* /transl. by M. Chudoba/, Velehrad, 1921.

Grivec Franciscus–Tomšič Franciscus, *Constantinus et Metodius Thessalonicenses: Fontes*, Zagreb, 1960.

Gsovski, Vladimír, *Church and State behind the Iron Curtain*, New York, 1955.

Habenicht, J., *Dějiny Čechův Amerických* /History of American Czechs/, St. Louis, 1904.

Halecki, Oscar, *Sacrum Poloniae millenium*, Rome, 1958.

— — *From Florence to Brest*, Rome, 1958.

— — *A History of Poland*, New York, 1943.

Hanahoe, Edward F., *Catholic Ecumenism*, Washington, D.C., 1953.

Hanák, J., Slovaks and Czechs in the early 19th century," *Slavonic and East European Review* X, No. 30, /London, 1932/, 588-601.

Hantsch, H., "Pan-Slavism, Austro-Slavism, Neo-Slavism: The All-Slav Congresses and the Nationality Problems of Austria-Hungary," *Austrian History Yearbook*, 1, /1965/, 23-37.

Hardon, John A., *Christianity in the Twentieth Century*, Garden City, NY, 1971.

Havlík, L., *Velká Morava a středoevropští Slované* /Great Moravia and the Central European Slavs/, Prague, 1944.

Hebblethwaite, Peter, *The Year of Three Popes*, Cleveland, 1979.

Hefele, Carl Joseph, *Conciliengeschichte*, 6 vols., Freiburg im Breiszau, 1890.

Heidler, Alexander, "Ekumenický pohled na české duchovní dějiny," *Studie* I, No. 29, /Rome, 1972/, 620-630.

Heidler, Friedrich, *Urkirche und Ostkirche*, 2 vols., München, 1937.

Helfert, Vladimír, *"Průkopnický význam české hudby v 18. století,"* /Pioneering significance of Czech Music in XVIII Century/ in V. Mathesuis, *Co daly naše země Evropě a lidstvu*, /Prague, 1940/, 216-221.

Hellmann, R. Olesch, B. Stasiewski, F. Zagiba, eds., *Cyrillo-Methodiana, zur frühgeschichte des Christentums bei den Slaven, 863-1963*, Köln Graz, 1964.

Henry, John St., *Essays in Christian Unity*, Westminster, Md., 1955.

Hergenroether, Joseph, *Handbuch der allgemeinen Kirchengeschichte*, 2 vols., /Freiburg im Breisgan, 1870-1881/.

Hitler, Adolf, *Mein Kampf* /transl. by Ralph Manheim/, Boston, 1943.

Hlinka, Anton, "Vztahy medzi vitakánom a česko-slovenskou vládou," *Jodnota* of 4-21-82, 9-12.

Hnik, Frant. M., Za Lepší Církví /For the Better Church/, Prague, 1930.

— — *Duchovní Ideály Československé Církve* /Spiritual Ideals of Czechoslovak Church/, Prague, 1939.

Hofer, John, C.Ss.R., *St. Clement Maria Hofbauer: a Biography* /transl. from German by Rev. John B. Haas, C.Ss. R./, New York, 1926.

Hoffman, Gerhard, *"Die Ökumene ist des Herrn," Ökumenische Rundschau*, 30 No. 4, /Frankfurt M., 1981/, 381-394.

Hollý, Jan, *Básně* /Poems/, 4 vols., Buda, 1841-42.

Holmes, Derek, *The triumph of the Holy See*, A short history of the Papacy in the nineteenth century, Shepherdstown, W. VA., 1982.

Hooft, W.A., Visser`t, *The Meaning of Ecumenical*, London, 1954.

Hronek, Josef, *Přehled katolické theologie české* /Perspective of Czech Catholic Theology/, Prague, 1939.

Hruban, Mořic, *Z času nedlouho zašlých* /From the Recent Past/, ed. by Jan Drábek, Rome-Los Angeles, 1967.

Hrubý, V., "Staré Město, velkomoravské pohřebiště na Valách," *Monumenta Archeologica* III, Prague, 1959.

— — "Staré Město-Velehrad; ústředí z doby Velkomoravské říše" /Stare Mesto-Velehrad; the center from the period of Great Moravian Empire/, *Monumenta Archeologica*, Prague,.1964.

Hrynioch, Ivan, "The Destruction of the Ukrainian Catholic Church in the Soviet Union," *Prologue*, IV, /1960/, 5-10.

Hucke, Helmut /transl. by Eileen O`Gorman/, "Musical requirements of Liturgical Reform," *The Church Worships, Concilium* vol. 12 /New York, 1966/, 45-75.

— — "Jazz and Folk Music in the Liturgy," *The Crisis of Liturgical Reform, Concilium* vol. 42, /New York, 1969/, 138-172.

Hughes, Philip, *A popular History of the Catholic Church*, /New York, 1947/.

Hurt, R., *Dějiny cisterciáckéhokého kláštera na Velehradě* /History of the Cistercian Monastery at Velehrad/, 2 vols., /Olomouc, 1934-1938/.

J., F., "Křížová cesta apoštolátních stanov," /The Crossroad of the Statutes of the Apostolate/, *Apoštolát sv. Cyrila a Metoda*, No. 2, /1931/, 42-43.

Jacobson, Roman, *Nejstarší Duchovní Písně české* /Oldest Czech Religious Hymns/, Prague, 1929.

Janda, Antonín, *Papežská korunovace Matky Boží svatohostýnské* /Papal Coronation of Our Lady of Hostyn/, Brno, 1913.

Jašek, Adolf, *Výklad idee cyrillomethodějské* /Interpretation of the Cyrilomethodian idea/, Velehrad, 1909.

— — "Třetí unionistický sjezd na Velehradě," /The Third Unionistic Congress at Velehrad/, *Apostolate of Sts. Cyril and Methodius*, 1911.

— — *Msgr. Dr. A.C. Stojan*, Olomouc, 1915.

— — *Was is die Cyrillo-Methodeische Idee?* Velehrad, 1911.

Jeřabek, Esther, *Czechs and Slovaks in North America*, A Bibliography, New York and Chicago, 1976.

John XXIII, Pope, *Journal of a Soul* /transl. by Dorothy White/, New York, 1965.

"John Paul I, Pope /1912-1978/," *The Pope Speaks,* Washington, DC, special Winter issue of 1978.

── *The Message of John Paul* I, ed. Daughters of St. Paul, Boston, 1978.

Jouandeau, M., *St. Philip Neri* /tr. G. Lamb/, New York, 1960.

Juza, Vilém, *Kroměříž,* /Prague, 1963/.

Kalista, Zdeněk, *České baroko,* /Czech Baroque/, Prague, 1941.

Kallis, Anastasios, ed., *Dialog der Wahrheit: Perspectives für die Einherit zwischen der Katholischen und der orthodoxen kirche,* Freiburg, Basel, Vienna, 1981.

Kalvoda, Josef, *Czechoslovak`s role in Soviet Strategy* /Washington, D.C., 1980/.

Kann, Robert A., *The Multinational Empire—Nationalism and National Reforms in the Habsburg Monarchy 1848-1918,* New Brunswick, NJ, 1950.

Kaplan, Robert D., "Ghosts in Prague. The Church, like the Dissidents, faces repression," *Commonweal* of May 7, 1982, /New York:, pp. 267-269.

Kasalaj, Anton, "Das Cyrillo-Methodianische Velehrad and Seine Unionskongresse," *Slovak Studies* XII, /Rome-Cleveland, 1972/, 153-191.

Kašpar, Václav, *České nebe* /Czech Heaven/, Prague, 1939.

Kasper, Walter, "The Dialogue with Protestant Theology," *Concilium: The Church and Ecumenism,* 4, /New York, 1965/, 150-173.

Kazbuda, Karel, *Pouť Čechů do Moskvy 1867 a Rakouská diplomacie,* Prague, 1924.

Kimball, Stanley B., *The Austro-Slav Revival: A Study of Nineteenth Century Literary Foundations,* Philadelphia, 1973.

Kirch, Johann P. and Veit, Ludwig Andreas, *Kirchengeschichte,* 4 vols., Freiburg im Breisgau, 1930.

Kirschbaum, J.M., *Pan-Slavism in Slovak Literature: Jan Kollar—Slovak Poet of Panslavism /1793-1852/,* Winnipeg and Toronto, 1966.

Klatovský, Karel, "Co se Slovanstvím?" /What with the Slavism?/, *Studie* 29, /Rome 1-1972/, 643-647.

Klopp, Wiard, *Leben and Wirken des Socialpolitkers Karl Freiher von Vogelsang,* Vienna, 1930.

Klostermann, R.A., *Probleme der Ostkirche: Undersuchungen zum Wesen und zur Geschichte der Griekirsch-Ortho-doten Kirche,* Göbeborg, 1955.

Kohn, Hans, *Pan-Slavism: Its History and Ideology,* Notre Dame, 1953.

── "The Impact of Pan-Slavism on Central Europe," *The Review of Politics,* XXIII, /1961/, 321-333.

Kolejka, Josef, "Cyrilometodějská tradice v druhé polovině 19. století," (Cyrilomethodian Tradition in the second half of XIX century/, *Velká Morava,* ed. Jan Böhm, /1963/, 97-112.

Kolejka, Josef—Šťastný, Vladislav, "Die Cyrillomethodische and Gross-Mährische tradition im tschechischen Politschen Geshehen im 19 and 20 jahrhundert," *Magna Moravia,* ed. by Joseph Macůrek, /Prague, 1965/, 587-609.

Kolísek, Alois, *Cyrillo-Methodějství u Čechů a Slováků* /Cyrillo-methodian heritage of the Czechs and the Slovaks,/, Brno, 1935.

Kollár, Jan, *Rozpravy o slovanské vzájemnosti* /Dissertations about Slavic solidarity/, ed. by Miloš Weingart, Prague, 1929.

Komárek, Fr., "Frant. Cyrill Kampelík," *Hlídka,* 1900, 353 ff.

Konečný, F., "Moravskopanonský metropolitní problém," *Studie* II-III, No. 18-19, /Rome, 1969/, 336 ff.

Konstantinidis, Chrysostomos, "Autorität in der Ortho-doxen Kirche," *Ökumenische Rundschau,* 31 no. 1, /Frankfurt/M, 1982/, 31-47.

Kopal, Pavel, *Das Slaventum und der Deutsche Geist. Problem Einer Weltkultur auf Grundlage der religiosen Idealismus,* Jena, 1914.

Kopecký, Milan, "Cyrilometodějská Tradice v starší České Literatuře," /Cyrilo-methodian tradition in older Czech literature/, *Magna Moravia,* ed. by Josef Macůrek, /Prague, 1965/, 567-586.

Kořalka, Jiří, *Všeněmecký svaz a česká otázka koncem 19. století,* Prague, 1963.

Korolevsky, Cyrille, *Métropolite André Szeptyckji, 1885-1944,* Rome, 1964.

Kosmák, Václav, *Kukátkář,* 2 vols., Brno, 1905.

Kozák, J.B.,–Žilka-Maxa-Hajn, *Naše pokrokovost a Řím* /Our Progressiveness and Rome/, Prague, 1925.

Kozák, Jan Blahoslav, *V boji o duchovní hodnoty* /In struggle for spiritual values/, Prague, 1930.

Krajcar, J., *Bohuslav Balbín, S.J., als Geschichtsschreiber,* Rome, 1956.

Kramář, Karel, *Na obranu Slovanské politiky* /In Defense of the Slavic Policy/, Prague, 1926.

–– *Pět přednášek o zahraniční politice* /Five Lectures on Foreign Policy/, Prague, 1922.

Kratochvíl, Antonín, "Problémy a otázky současného katolicismu v ČSSR," /Problems and questions of contemporary Catholicism in Czechoslovakia/, *Nové obzory,* vol. 1, No. 2-3, /St. Gallen, 1982/, 53-62.

Krofta, Kamil, *Stará Ústava česká a Uherská* /Old Czech and Hungarian Constitution/, Prague, 1931.

–– *Dějiny československé* /Czechoslovak History/, Prague, 1947.

Kubalík, J., "Náboženská společnost českomoravská církví Husovou?" /A Religious Czech-Moravian Society a Huss'Church?/, *ČKD* 81, 106 /1941/, 217-223.

–– "Nepravdivá mystika v boji o duši českého člověka," /False mystique in a struggle for the soul of Czech man/, *ČKD* 85, 110 /1945/, 142-150.

–– "Věrouka náboženské společnosti českomoravské," /Doctrine of Czechomoravian religious associations/, *ČKD* 82, 107 /1945/, 292-298.

Kudrnovský, Alois, Congrua katol. duchovenstva," /Congrua of Catholic clergy/, *ČKD* 80, 105 /1940/, 161-191, 233-270, 313-361, 393-400.

Kung, Hans, *The Council, Reform and Reunion,* New York, 1961.

Kútník, Josef, "Jana Hollého Katolický zpěvník I. a II. /The Catholic Cancional I and II of John Holly/, *Most* 28 Nos. 3-4 /1981/, 26-65.

Lacko, Michael, SJ, "East Meets West in Sts. Cyril and Methodius," American Ecclesiastical Review CXLI, /Washington, 1959/, 241-245.
—— "Hrob a pozostatky Sv. Cyrila v Ríme," /Grave and the relics of St. Cyril in Rome/, *Most* X No. 1-4, /Cleveland, 1963/, 230-235.
Lambert, Bernard, *Ecumenism: Theology and History* /transl. by Lancelot C. Sheppard/New York, 1967.
Lauterbach, R.E., *These are the Russians,* New York, 1945.
Lawler, Justus G. and Moody, Joseph N., eds., *The Challenge of Mater et Magistra,* New York, 1963.
Ledit, Joseph, *Archbishop John Cieplak,* Montreal, 1964.
Lemoyne, J.B., S.C., *A Character Sketch of the Venerable Don Bosco* /New Rochelle, NY, 1927/.
Leonis XIII, Pontificis Maximi Acta, 23 vols. /Rome, typo-graphia Vaticana, 1881-1905/.
Liscová, Míla, *The Religious Situation in Czechoslovakia,* Prague, 1925.
Lossky, Nicholas, "Orthodoxy and Ecumenism," *One in Christ* 17 No. 2 /Survey 1981/, 143-148.
Ludwig, Emil, *Bismarck*/transl. by Eden and Ledar Paul/, New York, 1926.
Maase, F., *Der Josephinismus,* 5 vols., Vienna, 1951-1962.
Macůrek, Joseph, "La Mission Byzantine en Moravie au cours des annes 863-885 et la Portée de son Héritage dans 1` Historie de nos days et de 1`Europe," *Magna Moravia,* /Prague, 1965/, 17-70.
Maguire, J.F., *Rome, Its Ruler and Its Institutions,* London, 1859.
Mamatey, Victor S. and Luža, Radomír, eds., *A History of the Czechoslovak Republic 1914-1948,* Princeton, NJ, 1973.
Manhattan, Avro, *The Vatican in World Politics,* New York, 1949.
Mareš, Frant., *Pravda o Rukopisech* /The Truth about the Manuscripts/, Prague, 1931.
Marshall, Romey and Taylor, Michael, *Liturgy and Christian Unity,* Englewood Cliffs, NJ, 1965.
Masák, Emanuel, *Dějiny Dědictví sv. Cyrila a Metoděje 1850-1930.* /History of the Heritage of Sts. Cyril and Methodius 1850-1930/, Brno, 1932.
Masaryk, Jan, *Ani opona ani most* /Neither Curtain nor Bridge/, Prague, 1947.
Masaryk, T.G., *Los von Rom,* Boston, 1902.
—— *Modern Man and Religion,* London, 1930.
Mastylak, Joannes, *Fuitne Vladmirus Soloviev Catholicus?* Rome, 1942.
Mathesius, Vilém, ed., *Co daly naše země Evropě a lidstvu* /What our lands have given to Europe and humanity/, Prague, 1940.
Matt, Leonard von and Vian, Nello, *St. Pius X,* Chicago, 1955.
Matt, Leonard von and Henri Bosco, *Don Bosco* /New York, 1930/.
Maynard, Theodore, *The Odyssey of Francis Xavier,* London-New York, 1936.
McBrien, Richard P., *The Church: the Continuing Quest,* New York, 1970.
McGratty, Arthur R., SJ, *The Fire of Francis Xavier, the story of an apostle,* Milwaukee, 1952.

Medek, Václav, *Osudy Moravské církve do konce 14tého věku* /Events of a Moravian Church till the end of the 14th century/, Prague, 1971.

Mercati, Angelo, ed., *Raccolta di Concordati su Materie Ecclesiastiche de la Santa Sede e le Autoritá Civili* /Collection of Concordats on Ecclesiastical Matters between the Holy See and civil authorities/, 2 vols., Vatican City, 1954.

Mercier, Cardinal Desire /transl. by M. Lindsay/, *Modernism*, London, 1910.

Meyendorff, John, *The Orthodox Church*, Crestwood-Tuckahoe, NY, 1981.

— — *The Byzantine Legacy in the Orthodox Church*, Crestwood, NY, 1982.

Mikula, Felix, "Unionistické kongresy" /Unionistic Congresses/, *Nový Svět* /New World/, Cleveland, Oct. 25, 1956, 3.

— — "O původci Velehradské písně," *Národ* XXXII No. 22, July 5, 1978, pp. 1-6.

Milcent, Ernest, *"A l`est du Vatican: La papautè et les démocraties populaires,* Series "Rencountres International" 16, /Paris, 1980/, pp. 145-146.

Miller, J. Michael, *The Divine Right of the Papacy in Recent Ecumenical Theology*, Rome, 1980.

Moede, Gerald F., *Oneness in Christ: The Quest and the Questions*, Princeton, NJ, 1982.

Molnar, A., et al, *Český Ekumenismus*, Theologické kořeny a současná tvář církví /Prague, 1976/.

Montguere, Jean-Marc, *St. Francis Xavier*, Garden City, NY, 1963.

Morley, John F., *Vatican Diplomacy and the Jews during the Holocaust, 1939-1943*, New York, 1980.

Mydlowsky, Leo, *Bolshevist Persecution of Religion and Church in Ukraine in 1917-1957*, London, 1958.

Nahayewsky, I., *History of the Modern Ukrainian State, 1917-1923*, Munich, 1966.

Navrátil, B., *Biskupství Olomoucké 1576-1579* /Prague, 1909/.

Nejedlý, Zdeněk, *Počátky husitského zpěvu* /Origins of the Hussite Song/, Prague, 1907.

— — *Dějiny předhusitského zpěvu v Čechách* /History of the pre-Hussite Song in Bohemia/, Prague, 1904.

— — *Dějiny husitského zpěvu za válek husitských* /History of the Hussite singing during the Hussite wars/, Prague, 1913.

Nemec, Ludvik, *The State and Church in Czechoslovakia*, New York, 1955.

— — "Father Dvornik`s views on the Reunion of Churches," *Perspectives* 6 No. 2, 1961, 15-19.

— — "American Velehrad," *The Byzantine Catholic World* 7 Nos. 14-15, 1962, 8-14.

— — "Unionistic Endeavors in Velehrad," The *BCW* 7 No. 10-12, /Pittsburgh, 1962/, 6-19.

— — "The Ruthenian Uniate Church in its historical perspective, *Church History* 37 No. 4, 1968, 1-25.

— — "The Recent re-investigation of Cyrillomethodian Sources and their basic problems," *Czechoslovakia Past and Present*, ed. by M. Rechígl Jr., /Hague, 1964/, II pp. 1151-1174.

— — "Photius—Saint or Schismatic?" *Journal of Ecumenical Studies* 3 No. 2, 1966, 277-313.

— — "The Czech Jednota, the Avant-garde of modern clerical progressivism and unionism," *Proceedings of the American Philosophical Society* 112 No. 4, Jan. 1, 1968, 76-100.

— — "The Festive Profile of Francis Dvornik, the scholar, the historian, and the Ecumenist," *The Catholic Historical Review*, LIX No. 2, July,1973, 185-224.

— — , ed., "80 František Dvorník," *Proměny* 3 No. 10, New York, July, 1973, 1-103. /a multilingual Festschrift on 80th anniversary of Dvornik/.

— — *The Czechoslovak Heresy and Schism.* The Emergence of a national Czechoslovak Church, Philadelphia, 1975.

— — , ed., *Czech Catholics at the 41st International Eucharistic Congress, held August 1-8, 1976 in Philadelphia, U.S.A.* /Philadelphia, 1977/.

— — *Pope John Paul II: A Festive Profile,* New York, 1979.

— — *Our Lady of Hostyn, Queen of the Marian Garden of the Czech, Moravian, Silesian and Slovak Madonnas,* New York, 1981.

Neumann, Aug., *Katolictví a naše osvobození* /Catholicism and our independence/, Olomouc, 1922.

— — *Pravda o Sv. Hostýně* /The truth about the Holy Hostyn/, Olomouc, 1933.

Nolan, L., O.P., *The Basilica of San Clemente in Rome,* Rome, 1911.

Novotný, Josef, SJ, "Trnitá cesta moderního ekumenismu," /Difficult way of modern ecumenism/, *Hlas Národa* /Voice of the Nation/ of March 27, 1982, p. 5.

Novotný, Václav, *Náboženské hnutí české ve 14. a 15. století* /Religious Czech movement in 14 and 15 centuries/, Prague, 1915.

Odložilík, Otakar, *The Way of Light. The Glory and Martyrdom of Czechoslovak Schools,* Chicago, 1942.

— — "Components of the Czechoslovak Tradition," *The Slavonic and East European Review,* XXIII, /1945/, 97-106.

— — "T.G. Masaryk in the Past and Present," Symposium: *Tributes to T.G. Masaryk,* London, 1950.

— — "From Velehrad to Olomouc," Harvard Slavic Studies, 2, 1954, 75-90.

Olšr, Joseph, Moscow—"The Third Rome," *Proceedings of the Second and Third Unionistic Congress,* /Lisle, St. Procopius, 1960/, 14-23.

— — *Služebník Boží, Antonín Cyril Stojan, Olomoucký Arcibiskup* /Servant of God, Antonin Cyril Stojan, Archbishop of Olomouc/, Rome, 1966.

— — "Dr. Antoní Cyril Stojan, Olomoucký Arcibiskup I, Stojan Lidumil, *Nový život* 12, /Rome, 1060, 189-190; idem, "Stojan-Kněz," ib. 13 /1961/ 8-9; idem, "Může býti arcibiskup Stojan kanonizován?" Nový život 13 /1961/, 104-106.

Orel, D., *"Hudební prvky svatováclavské,"* /Musical materials connected with S. Wenceslaus/, *Svatováclavský Slovník* II, Prague, 1937.

L'Osservatore Romano 99 No. 194/July 18, 1959/3: "Il c. Congreso Unionistico in America." Ottaviani, Alaphridus, *Institutiones juris Publici Ecclesiastici:* 2 vols., /3rd ed., Rome, 1947/.

Palacký, František, *Dějiny národu českého*, Prague, 1850-76.

Palmieri, O.S., "United Ruthenian Church of Glaicia under Russian Rule," *Catholic World* 103, 1916, 349-359.

Paneyko, B., Glaicia and the Polish-Ukrainian Problem," *Slavonic Review* IX, /1931/, 567-587.

Paredi, A., *Saint Ambrose: His Life and Times* /New York, 1964/.

Parente, Pascal P., *The Ascetical Life*, St. Louis, 1944.

Pastrněk, F., *Dějiny slovanských apoštolů Cyrilla a Methoda* /History of Slavic Apostles Cyril and Methodius/, Prague, 1902.

Paulová, M., "L' idée cyrillo-methodienne dans la politique de Charles IV et la fondation du monastére slave de Prague," *Byzantinoslavica* II /1950/ 174 ff.

Pecháček, Jaroslav, "Politický Katolicismus v parlamentní Demokracii" /Political Catholicism in the parlamentarian Democracy/, *Studie* I, II, /Rome, 1976/, 1-18.

Pekař, Josef, *Smysl českých dějin* /Meaning of Czech History/, Prague, 1929.

— — "O poloze starého Velehradu," Velehradský Sborník 9 /1938/ 5-9.

Pelesz, J., *Geschichte der Union der Ruthenischen Kirche mit Rome*, 2 vols. /Vienna, 1881/.

Pelikán, J., *Balbínovy pomůcky a prameny* /Prague, 1936/.

Peters, Walter H., *The Life of Benedict XV*, Milwaukee, 1959.

Petřík, Emil, "Opatství Svatoprokopské mohutným středem apoštolské práce," /St. Procopius Abbey, an influential center of apostolic work/, *Národ Calendar* 1961, /Chicago, 1961/, 127-131.

— — "Opat Ondrák a hledání ostatků svatého Cyrila" /Abbot Ondrak and search for the relics of St. Cyril/, *Se znamením kříže*, /Rome, 1967/, 41-44.

— — "Májová pobožnost u Mariánského sloupu v Lisle," /The May devotion at the Marian Pillar in Lisle," *Hlasatel* /Chicago: of June 6, 1981, pp. 8-9.

Petrovich, M.B., *The Emergence of Russian Panslavism 1856-1870*, New York, 1950.

Pfülf, O., *Bishop von Ketteler /1811-77/ Eine geschichtliche Darstellung*, 3 vols. /Mainz, 1899.

Pichon, Charles, *The Vatican and Its Role in World Affairs*, New York, 1950.

Pierling, P., *La Russie et le Saint-Siège*, 3 vols., Paris, 1901.

Pius IX, Pontificis Maximi Acta, 9 vols. 1846-1857; Roma: tipografia delle Belle Arti, 1857.

Plicka, Karel, *Prague en images*, Prague, 1950.

Podlaha, Antonín, *Posvátná místa království českého* /Sacred Places of the Czech Kingdom/, 7 vols., Prague, 1907-1913.

Polach, Otto, "Metropolitní sídlo sv. Metoda a Nitra," *Historický Sborník Matice Slovenské* 4 /1946/, 274-297.

Polakovič, Štefan, *Začiatky slovenskej národnej Filosofie*, Bratislava, 1944.

Polc, Jaroslav V., ed., *Otec Vlasti 1316-1378* /Father of Homeland 1316-1378/, Rome, 1980.

Pokorný, Ferdinand, *Vlastivěda moravská. Příborský okres*, Brno, 1917.

Polak, George, "Slovak Greek Catholics in America," *Slovak Studies* V /Cleveland Slovak Institute, 1965/, 295-365.

Ponnelle, L., and Bordet, L., St. *Philip Neri and the Roman Society of His Times* /Tr. R.T. Ken, New York, 1933./

Pospíšil, J., *Mše Svatá podle obřadu církve Východní* /Holy Mass according to the Rite of the Eastern Church/, Olomouc, 1910.

Pospishil, Victor, *Orientalium Ecclesiarum: The Decree on the Eastern Catholic Churches of the II Council of Vatican*, New York, 1965.

Poulík, Josef, *Staří Moravané budují svůj Stát* /Ancient Moravians build their State/, Gottwaldov, 1960.

— — *Mikulčice. Sídlo a pevnost knížat velkomoravských.* /Mikulčice: Seat and Fortress of the Great Moravian Princes/, Prague, 1975.

Preisner, Río, *Kultura bez konce* /The Culture without the end/, Munich, 1981.

Premoli, Orazio M., *Contemporary Church History 1900-1925*, London, 1932.

Proceedings of the First Unionistic Congress, September 28-30, 1956 /Lisle: St. Procopius Abbey, 1956/.

Proceedings of the Second and Third Unionistic Congress /Lisle, St. Procopius, 1960/.

První Unionistický sjezd ve Spojených Státech /First Unionistic Congress in the United States/, Chicago, 1956.

Ráček, Blažej, SJ, *Československé Dějiny* /Czechoslovak History/, 2nd ed., Prague, 1933.

Rahner, Karl, *Gefahren im heutigen Katholicismus*, Einsiedeln, 1955.

— — "What is heresy? *Theological Investigations* 5 /Baltimore, 1966/ 468-512.

— — *Concern for the Church*, Theological Investigations XX /transl. by Edward Quinn/, New York, 1981.

Reshetar, John S., "Ukrainian Nationalism and the Orthodox Church," *The American Slavic and East European Review X* /1951/, 38-49.

— — *The Ukrainian Revolution, 1917-1920: A Study in Nationalism* /Princeton, NJ, 1952/.

Rezek, Antonín, *Bohuslav Balbín*, Prague, 1908.

Riasonowski, N., *Russia and the West in the teaching of the Slavophiles: A Study in Romantic Ideology*, Cambridge, MA, 1953.

Richards, Jeffrey, *The Popes and the Papacy in the Early Middle Ages, 476-752*, Boston, 1979.

Richter, Vladimír, "Na věčnou paměť cyrilometodějského apoštola Antonína C. Stojana," *Národ*, /Chicago/, Sept. 29, 1973, 5.

Robenek, F., *Moravská Metropole. K dějinám její lokalisace* /Moravian Metropolis: Concerning history of its location/, Kroměříž, 1934.

Rozkošný, Rudolf, S.J., "Z činnosti Ant. C. Stojana, kaplana příborského," *Hlasy svatohostýnské* /1925/ No. 13, p. 13.

— — "Matice svatohostýnská, 25 letá činnost její," /Foundation of Holy Hostyn, 25 years of its activity/, *Hlasy svatohostýnské* XIX, pp. 30-32.

Rouse, R. and Neill, S.C., *A History of the Ecumenical Movement* /London, 1954/.

Runciman, Steven, *The Eastern Schism*, Oxford, 1935.

— — The Orthodox *Churches and the Secular State* /London, 1971/.

Rutkowski, Francis, *Arcybiskup Jan Cieplak 1857-1926* /Warsaw, 1934/.

Sadovská, M. "U Tatíčka Stojana byla: Hrdinská láska k Bohu a k bližnímu," *Calendar Národ,* vol. 78, /Chicago, 1973/, 79-84.

Salaville, S. and Barton, J., *An Introduction to the Study of Eastern Liturgies,* London, 1938.

Sbírka zákonů a nařízení státu československého /Collection of laws and proclamations of the Czechoslovak State/, Prague: annual.

Scheicher, J., *Erlebnisse und Erinnerungen,* 4 vols., Munich, 1933-1935.

Schmidlin, Josef, *Päpstgeschichte der neuesten Zeit,* 3 vols., Munich, 1933-1935.

Schmidt, Josef Hermann, *Der Kulturkampf,* Padeborn, 1926.

Schulz, Hans-Joachim, "The Dialogue with Orthodox," *Concilium: The Church and Ecumenism* 4, /New York, 1965/, 131-149.

Schwab, J.B., *Johannes Gerson, Professeur de theologie und Kanzler de Universität Paris,* 2 vols., Paris, 1958.

Sedlák, Jan, *M. Jan Hus,* Brno, 1915.

Sehnal, J., "Práce brněnského varhanáře Ant. Richtra na Velehradě, 1745-1714." *Vlastivědný věstník moravský XX,* /Brno, 1968/.

Shereghy, Basil, *The Divine Liturgy of St. John Chrysostom,* Pittsburgh, 1965.

Šída, B., "Kult cyrilometodějský a česká Vídeň," *Apoštolát sv. Cyrila a Metoda,* 1932, 163 ff.

Sis, Vladimír, ed. *Dr. Karek Kramář, Život–Dílo–Práce, Vůdce národa* /Prague, 1936/.

Skalický, Karel, "Katolicka filosofie a teologie zvláště tomistická v české společnosti XIX a XX století," *Studie IV* No. 40 /Rome, 1974/ 258 ff.

Škutil, Josef, *Z pravěku Hostýna* /From the antiquity of Hostyn/, Olomouc, 1940.

Šmahel, Rudolf, *Olomouc ve Fotografii,* Ostrave, 1965.

Smiciklas, J., *Strossmayer,* Agram, 1906.

Smržík, Š SJ., Stephen, *The Glagolitic or Roman-slavonic Liturgy,* Rome-Cleveland, 1959.

Snopek, Frant., *Konstantin–Cyril a Methoděj Slovanští Apoštolové,* Prague, 1913. *Die Slavenapostel Kritische Studien,* Kroměříž, 1918.

Solle, Zdeněk, and Gajanová, Alena, *Po stopě dějin: Češi a Slováci v letech 1848-1938,* /On the Trail of History: Czechs and Slovaks from 1848 to 1938/, Prague, 1969.

Solovay, Meletius, "De objectionibus contra Unionem Ecclesiarum ex parte Orthodoxorum dissidentium" *Proceedings of the Second and Third Unionistic Congresses,* /Lisle: St. Procopius, 1960/, 146-149.

—— *Ze života nového arcibiskupa; Slavnost svěcení a nastolení arcibiskupa Stojana,* /From the life of a new archbishop. Festivities of consecration and installation of the archbishop Stojan/, Olomouc, 1921.

Součková, Milada, *Baroque in Bohemia,* Ann Arbor, 1980.

Šorm, Antonín, *Ve jménu demokracie* /In the name of democracy/, Prague, 1922.

Špidlík, Tomáš, "Palčivá otázka českého ekumenismu," /Delicate problem of Czech ecumenism/, Nový život XXXIV, Nos. 1-2, /Rome, 1982/, 2-4.

Spivak, Jonathan, "In Stalinist Prague There Is No Sign of Spring," *The Wall Street Journal* /New York of April 30, 1982, p. 31.

Srb, Adolf, *Politické dějiny národa českého od počátku doby konstituční* /Political history of the Czech nation from the beginnings of the Constitutional Times/, 2 vols. /Prague, 1926/.

Staar, Richard F., *Communist Regimes in Eastern Europe*, 4th ed., Stanford, CA, 1981.

Stauracz, Franz, *Los von Rom*, 2nd ed. /Hamm i. Westf., 1901/.

—— *Dr. Karl Lueger, zehn jahre Buergermeister*, Wien, 1907.

Stefani, Gino, "Does the liturgy still need music? In the *Crisis of Liturgical Reform, Concilium*, vol. 42. /New York, 1969/, 71-86.

Stehle, Hansjakob, *Eastern Politics of the Vatican 1917-1979*, transl. from German by Sandra Smith, Athens, Ohio-London, 1981.

Stojan, Antonín Cyril, *Památka ze Sv. Hostýna* /Souvenir of Mount Hostyn/, Příbor, 1881.

—— *O sjednocení národů slovanských u víře s církví římskokatolickou podle úmyslu sv. Otce Lva XIII.* /Concerning the unity of the Slavic nations in faith with the Roman Catholic Church according to the intentions of the Holy Father Leo XIII/, Olomouc, 1896.

—— "Pouť do Říma /Pilgrimage to Rome/," *Škola Bož. Srdce Páně* /1881, 182-184.

—— "Zpráva o pouti svatohostýnské," *Hlasy svatohostýnské* /1921/ 130 and passim.

—— *Apoštolát sv. Cyrila a Methoda*, Velehrad, 1901.

Středovský, Jan Jiří, *Sacra Moraviae Historia sine Ss. Cyrilli et Methudii*, Salzbach, 1710.

—— *Rubinus Moraviae*, 1712.

Štúr, Ludovít, *Das Slaventhum und die Walt der Zukunft* /Bratislava, 1931/.

Sukienniski, "Stalin and Byelo-Russia`s Independence," Polish Review 10 No. 4, /1965/, 84-107.

Šuránek, Antonín, Šilperský panáček, *Našinec*, Olomouc, Jan. 1, 1929.

—— "Drobty k životu Stojanovu" /Details toward Stojan`s Life/, *Museum* 57 /1925-26/, 16-25.

Sušil, František, *Moravské písně s nápěvy do textu vřaděnými* /Moravian songs with melodies inserted into text/, Brno, 1860.

Šuvarský, Jaroslav, *Biskup Gorazd*, Prague, 1978.

Swanberg, David, "Deficiencies of Eastern Orthodoxy," *New Oxford Review* XLIX No. 3, /Oakland, 1982/, 4-6.

Swidler, Leonard, *Dialogue for Reunion*, New York, 1962.

—— *Ecumenical Vanguard: The History of the Una Sancta Movement*, Philadelphia, 1966.

Taborský, Eduard, *President Eduard Beneš between East and West, 1938-1948*, Stanford, 1981.

Tachiaos, A.E., ed., *Cyrillomethodianum*, Thessalonica, 1981.

Tenora, J. and Foltynovský, J., *Blah. Jan Sarkander: jeho doba, život, blahoslavení* /Blessed John Sarkander: His Times, Life and Beatification/, Olomouc, 1920.

Thomson, S. Harrison, *Czechoslovakia in European History*, Princeton, NJ, 1943.

—— "A century of a phantom: Pan-Slavism and the Western Slavs," *Journal of Central European Affairs* XI /1951/, 57-77.

Tibenský, Jan., "The function of the Cyril and Methodius and the Great Moravian Traditions in the ideology of the Slovak Feudal nationality," *Studia historica Slovaca* VII /1972/, 69-95.

Tittel, L., *Historia archdiocesis Olomucensis ejusque praesulum* /Olomouc, 1889/.

Tomášek, Kardinál František, "Arcibiskup Stojan a kněžský dorost" *Hlasatel* /Chicago of Sept. 17, 1982/, pp. 5-7.

Tracy, David, *The Analogical Imagination: Christian Theology and the Culture of Pluralism*, New York, 1981.

Trapl, Miloš, *Politika českého katolicismu na Moravě 1918-1938* /The Policy of Czech Catholicism in Moravia 1918-1938/, Prague, 1968.

Turek, Rudolf, *Čechy na úsvitě dějin* /Bohemia in the twilight of history/, Prague, 1963.

Uhrová-Vávrová, Olga. ed., *Listář Olomoucké University, 1566-1938* /Documents of the University of Olomouc/, Olomouc, 1946.

Urban, Rudolf, *Die Slavischnational Kirchlichen Bestiebungen in der Tschechoslovakei* /Leipzig, 1938/.

Valášek, Emil, "Ketteler jako sociální politik a myslitel," *Nové Obzory* 1 No. 2-3, /St. Gallen, 1981-82/, 41-43.

Vajs, Josef, *Cyril a Metod*, Prague, 1948.

Vašica, Josef, *České literární baroko* /Czech literary Baroque/, Prague, 1938.

Vavřínek, Vladimír, "Die Christianizierung und Kirchen organization Grossmährens," *Historica* VII /Prague, 1963/, 5-56.

Vavrovič, Joseph, "Jean Palarik, Son ecuménisme et son panslavisme," *Slovak Studies* XIV, /Cleveland-Rome, 1974/, p. 278.

Viceník, A., "Ze života příborského panáčka," *Kalendář: Posel Apoštolátu na rok 1932*, Olomouc, 1932.

Victora, Claude G., "The Apostolate for Reunion at St. Procopius Abbey," *Proceedings of the First Unionistic Congress, Sept. 28-30, 1956* /Lisle: St. Procopius, 1956/, 19-25.

Vídeňský, SJ., Frant. B., *Sv. Hostýn ve svém původu a svých osudech* /Holy Hostyn in its origin and events/, Prague, 1913.

Vischer, Lukas, "The Holy See, the Vatican State, and the Churches Common Witness: A Neglected Ecumenical Problem," *Journal of Ecumenical Studies* /JES/ 11. No. 4, /Fall, 1974/, 617-635.

Vondráček, Felix John, *The Foreign Policy of Czechoslovakia, 1918-1935* /New York, 1937/.

Vrchovecký, Josef, *T.G. Masaryk a náboženství* /Masaryk and Religion/, Prague, 1937.

Vyšný, Paul, *Neo-Slavism and the Czechs, 1894-1914* /Cambridge, 1937/.

Wegman, Herman A.J., *Geschichte der Liturgie im Western und Osten*, Regensberg, 1979.

Weingart, M., "Vznik první české duchovní písně," /Origin of the first Czech Religious Song/, *Byzantinoslavica* II, Prague, 1930.

Welykyj, A., *Documenta Romana historiani ecclesiae in terris Ucrainae et Bielorussiae spectantia*, 35 vols. /Rome, 1953-1970/.

—— *From the Annals of Christian Ukraine*, 3 vols., Rome, 1968.

Williams, George Huntston, *The Mind of John Paul II*. Origins of his thought and action, New York, 1981.

Winter, Eduard, *Tausand Jahre Geisterkampf im Sudetenraum*, Salzburg-Leipzig, 1938.

—— "Der Kampf der ecclesia ruthena gegen den Rituswechsel." *Festschrift Eichman*, Paderborn, 1940.

—— *Byzanc und Rome im Kampf um die Ukraine*, Prague, 1944.

—— *Russland und die slavischen Völker in der Diplomatie des Vatikans, 1878-1903*, Berlin, 1950.

—— *Der Josefinismus und Seine Geschichte. Beiträge zur Geistesgeschichte Oesterreichs, 1740-1848*, Brünn-München-Wien, 1943.

Wiskemann, Elizabeth, *Czechs and Germans: A Study of the Struggle in the Historic Provinces of Bohemia and Moravia*, London-New York-Toronto, 1938, and ed. in 1967.

Wolf, SJ., Donald J. and Schall, SJ., James V., eds., *Current trends in Theology*, Garden City, NY, 1965.

Wolkan, Rud., *Das deutsche Kirchenlied der böhmischen Brüder im XVI jahrh* /Prague, 1891/.

Wolny, Dr. Gregor, *Kirchliche Topographie von Mähren II*. Abteilung Brünner Diozese III Band, Brünn, 1860.

Zagiba, Franz, "Neue Probleme in der Kyrillo-methodianischen Forschung, *Ostkirchliche Studien* XI /Würzburg, 1962/, 97-130.

Žampach, A., *Katolíci v zahraničních bojích za československou samostatnost*. /Catholics in foreign struggles for Czechoslovak independence/, Prague, 1928.

Zapletal, Florian, *Z Minulosti Hostýna a Bystřice* /From the Past of Hostyn and Bystrice/, Bystřice, 1939.

Žatko, James J., *Descent into Darkness. The Destruction of the Roman Catholic Church in Russia, 1917-1923*, Notre Dame, 1965.

Zeman, Zbynek A.B., *The Break-up of the Habburg Empire, 1914-1918*. A study in national and social revolution. London, 1961.

Zeme, M., - Bartůšek, A., *Dějiny Žďáru nad Sázavou* /History of the Zdar above Sazava/ 2 vols., /Havíičkův Brod, 1956-58/.

Zion, William P., "Only Eastern Orthodoxy remains," New Oxford Review XLIX, No. 1, /Oakland, 1982/, 6-8.

Žižka, E., *Czech Cultural Contributions*, Chicago, 1937.

Zizola, Giancarlo, *The Utopia of Pope John XXIII* /transl. by Helen Batolini/, Maryknoll, NY, 1979.

Zlámal, Bohumil, "Barokní chvála sv. Cyrila a Metoděje" /Baroque praise on Sts. Cyril and Methodius/, *Apoštolát sv. Cyrila a Metoda* /1938/ 193-197, 242-247 and 276-281.

—— "Cyrilometodějské baroko," *Apoštolát sv. Cyrila a Metoda* /1938/ 347-358.

—— "Co dovedl říci lidový kazatel 17. století o sv. Cyrilu a Metoději," *Apoštolát sv. Cyrila a Metoda* /1939/ 34-38.

—— "Cyrilometodějství Kristiana Bohumíra Hirschmenzla," *Slezský Sborník*, 48, /Opava, 1950/.

—— *Antonín Cyril Stojan: Apoštol křesťanské Jednoty* /Antonín Cyril Stojan, Apostle of Christian Unity/, Rome, 1973.

—— *Blahoslavený Jan Sarkander* /Blessed John Sarkander/, Rome, 1973.

—— "Co znamenal první český biskup v Brně," /What the first Czech bishop meant in Brno/, *Duchovní Pastýř*, No. 2 /1982/ passim.

Zlámal, Oldřich, *Povídka mého života* /The Story of my life/, Chicago, 1953.

INDEX

Bukowski, Al., 44, 48, 50
Bulgakov, S., 142, 145
Bušek, Vratislav, 208
Bystřice, 13, 118
Byzantine-Slavonic liturgy, 149
Bzenec, 28
Časopis katolického duchovenstva,
  64, 157
Catholic Moderna, 87, 139
Catholic mocernist movement, 160
Catholic National Party, 76
Cerularius, 101
Česká Beseda, 61
Charles IV, 102, 168
Chevětogne, 143
Chicago, 142
Church unionism, 150, 167
Cibulka, Jan, 13, 14, 32, 56
Cibulka, Josef, 42, 102
Cicognani, A.G., 174
Cinek, František, 3, 5, 34, 38, 41,
  42, 59, 77, 107, 198, passim
Clement IV, Pope, 102
Clement, St., 174
Clifford, Vincent Ferrer, SSJ., X
Club of the Reformist Clergy, 88
Concordat, 155, 156, 158
Congar, Y.M.J., 134
Congress of Seminarians, 48
Congress of Vienna, 190
Congrua, 68, 86, 93
Constantantinople, 174, passim
Constitution on the Sacred Liturgy,
  168, 171
Corporate reunion, 176
Corrigan, James, 41
Cyrilka, chapel, 54, 58, 137, 171
Cyril jednota, 32
Cyrilometodějské Dědictví V
  Velehrad, 171
Cyrilomethodian Faculty in
  Olomouc, 85, 86
Cyrilomethodian heritage, 20, 24,
  38, 39, 40, 41, 87, 88, 89,
  106, 136, 140

Cyrilomethodian idea, 37, 40, 102,
  168, 172
Cyrilomethodian legacy, 107,
  108, 181
Cyrilomethodian movement, 21,
  23, 44, 140
Cyrilomethodian Press Organiza-
  tion, 48
Cyrilomethodian tradition, 100
Cyrilomethodian unionism, 87,
  173, passim
Cyrilomethodian University, 65
Cyrilomethodianism, 65, 172
Czech Brethren, 168
Czech Heaven, 202
Czechoslovak National Assembly,
  84
Czechoslovak National Church, 88,
  89, 90, 133, 177, passim
Czechoslovak Republic, 99, 132,
  passim
Czechoslovak Peach Chapel on
  Mount Olivet, 176
Czechoslovak Society of Arts and
  Sciences, 2
Danielou, Jean, 208
Dawson, Christopher, 188
Decree on Eastern Catholic
  Churches, 176
Decree on Ecumenism, 172, passim
Dědictví sv. Cyrila a Metoděje, 41
d'Herbigny, Michael, 142
de Journel, Ronet, S.J., 148
de Lubac, Henri, 184
DeMaster, Pl., 53
Dimitrij of Rostov, 50
Dobravka, Princess, 180
Dobrovský,Josef, 209
Doellinger, Ignatz, 157
Dokoupil, Antonin, 74
Doležal, Josef, 80, 91
Domaželice, 138
Domobrana, 79
Dorozinsky, 54
Dositej, Orthodox bishop, 98

DATE DUE

HIGHSMITH   # 45220